BODY AND SOUL

BODY AND SOUL

THE BLACK PANTHER PARTY
AND THE FIGHT AGAINST
MEDICAL DISCRIMINATION

Alondra Nelson

University of Minnesota Press
Minneapolis
London

Published by the University of Minnesota Press
111 Third Avenue South, Suite 290
Minneapolis, MN 55401-2520
http://www.upress.umn.edu

Library of Congress Cataloging-in-Publication Data

Nelson, Alondra, author.
Body and soul : the Black Panther Party and the fight against medical discrimination / Alondra Nelson.
pages cm
Includes bibliographical references and index.
ISBN 978-0-8166-7648-4 (hc : alk. paper)—ISBN 978-0-8166-7649-1 (pb : alk. paper)
1. Minorities—Medical care—United States. 2. Discrimination in medical care—United States. 3. Race discrimination—United States. 4. Black Panther Party. I. Title.
RA448.5.N4N45 2011
362.1089'96073—dc23
2011040833

Printed in the United States of America on acid-free paper

The University of Minnesota is an equal-opportunity educator and employer.

25 24 23   11 10 9 8

For my parents

CONTENTS

PREFACE
Politics by Other Means

H ealth is politics by other means.[1]
  Milestones in health and medicine are conveyed as bearing on the broadest political and social ideals. The recent tenth anniversary of the decoding of the human genome, for example, brought with it cautious hope for the progression of genetic science from the lab bench to the bedside. This scientific landmark was notably accompanied by then president Bill Clinton's proclamation that this feat had established "our common humanity."[2]

Health is also deemed to embody conceptions of the good society. In 2010 the administration of President Barack Obama ushered in historic healthcare reform with the Patient Protection and Affordable Care Act. At the time of its passage, this legislation marked the most sweeping changes in U.S. health policy since the establishment of Medicaid and Medicare in 1965. The Affordable Care Act, which promised to extend medical benefits and coverage to tens of millions of previously uninsured and underinsured Americans, was passed despite heated partisan debates redolent of the political battles over health policy of the late 1960s. The controversy that preceded (and then followed) the implementation of the act concerned far more than bodily well-being. Underlying the impassioned back-and-forths that pitted accusations of "socialized medicine," "government takeovers," and "death panels" against assertions of "a right to health" and the ethics of "universal health care" were stark ideological distinctions—Republican versus Democrat, laissez-faire versus interventionist, libertarian versus progressive. In other words, healthcare reform was the dialect through which fundamental political disagreements about the proper function of the state and the appropriate parameters of business influence were articulated.

Also contested under the banner of health were the very terms of social inclusion in the United States. While the Obama administration and many on the left sought to expand the health polity to include those who lacked medical care, some on the right framed healthcare reform as centrally concerning the constriction of citizenship. The conservative pundit Glenn Beck, for example, suggested with a question to his radio audience that one's position on so-called Obamacare boiled down to an issue of national loyalty: "Are you an American or a European?"[3] Rush Limbaugh, for his part, craftily constructed the reforms that would draw the United States closer than ever before to universal healthcare coverage as benefiting the few over the many. It was African Americans who would be the beneficiaries of changes to national health policy, Limbaugh complained to his listeners, adding that proposed reforms amounted to "reparations" and a stealth "civil rights act."[4] Healthcare reform discourse was couched in competing claims about what constituencies mattered, which lives were valued, and what bodies were deserving of biomedical care.

As revelations of the last few years demonstrated, health and medicine can be vectors of power, political and otherwise, in further ways. Questionable scientific practices conducted with vulnerable communities that have recently come to light make evident this register of health politics. In 2010 the historian Susan Reverby uncovered the deliberate infection of Guatemalan men and women with syphilis in the late 1940s by a U.S. researcher who was also involved with a notorious study of the disease in Tuskegee, Alabama, that began in the 1930s.[5] As with the Tuskegee study, this Latin American syphilis experiment was undergirded by "racialized assumptions" that attributed the frequency of the disease among minority populations to their supposed moral inferiority and biological peculiarity.[6] In a somewhat similar vein, the journalist Rebecca Skloot recently and vividly depicted how a Johns Hopkins researcher surreptitiously appropriated the fatally prolific cervical cells of Henrietta Lacks, a black working-class woman who died of cancer in 1951. In the second half of the twentieth century, Henrietta's thriving cells became vital to modern science, even as the Lacks family was devastated, over the same decades, by the many consequences of her loss.

Reverby's and Skloot's revelations compounded an already bleak record of vexed, uneven encounters between agents and racialized subjects of biomedicine that the science writer Harriet Washington has characterized as "medical apartheid."[7] On top of the long history of dubious and often invidious research with black subjects delineated by Washington, racially discriminatory practices in medicine have included Jim Crow healthcare facilities; a formerly segregated medical profession; stubborn health disparities evidenced by many indices; and "unequal treatment" for blacks under medical treatment protocols for such conditions as cancer and heart disease.[8]

This cascade of medical discrimination has had far-reaching implications. Racial health disparities in the United States, for example, have been shown to persist partly because of African American communities' past and continued distrust of the medical system. Owing to this trepidation, developed over generations in response to abuse, neglect, and racialization, some blacks are reticent about or even resistant to seeking necessary healthcare or participating in research studies.[9] By way of a corrective to this shared apprehension—that is quite literally sickening in result—Washington has bravely proposed that shining a light on medical apartheid may effect a kind of social catharsis that will "remove barriers between African Americans and the bounty of the American health-care system."[10]

Yet in the years after the publication of Washington's acclaimed book, occurrences such as the strong resistance in some quarters to the H1N1 virus vaccine, reportedly grounded in fears of maltreatment, suggest that uncovering past abuse may not in and of itself inspire public confidence in biomedicine and the healthcare system.[11] More pointedly, at a time when the subjection of marginalized communities to biomedical authority is attracting renewed attention, the recuperation of moments during which members of these groups endeavored to shift the balance of power in medicine may be an effectual counterweight to enduring medical mistrust. *Body and Soul* uses one such case to illustrate circumstances in which African Americans confronted medical discrimination in the healthcare system, in biomedical theories, and in research design. In doing so, these communities did not assert a blanket rejection of medicine. Rather, they laid claim to a critical conception of healthfulness: a right to health equality and freedom from medical discrimination.

This book began more than a decade ago as a reflection on the intersections of science and race via the works of Lee D. Baker, Troy Duster, Stephen Jay Gould, Evelynn Hammonds, Sandra Harding, Dorothy Roberts, Audrey Smedley, William Stanton, Keith Wailoo, and others.[12] In response to this eclectic body of writing that, very generally speaking, considered the stakes of racial formation and racial subjugation in and through science, I became interested in exploring whether and how African Americans responded to these processes. Given that scientific practices have played (and continue to play) a key role in constructing ideas of race, were challenges to biomedical racialization an element of the African American protest tradition? If so, at what moments and through which tactics did black communities strive to tilt the balance of authority from researchers and physicians to subjects and patients?

It was with these questions in mind that I began to explore African American health advocacy in the twentieth century and, eventually, to carry out research into the Black Panther Party's health politics of the late 1960s and early 1970s. Although I had passing knowledge of the Party's health-related activities, delving deeper, I also discovered that the organization's endeavors were both more extensive and more multifaceted than I had imagined. In investigating Party health initiatives, I perceived that its activism both reflected and amplified the distinctiveness of a tradition of black health advocacy in which pragmatic matters of disease and healing (e.g., the founding of health institutions) were coextensive with broader political matters (e.g., challenges to racism).

In addition, I observed that the Party's health politics ranged from practical issues to ideational concerns. The organization's efforts included providing basic medical care to the poor, working with lay community members and trusted professional health workers in alternative facilities established by the activists. The Party furthermore engaged in public debates in which they disputed the racial biology of violence and research studies based on this assumption. And it also boldly advanced suggestions for how genetic studies of human groups could be refined to avoid justifying racism. The Party's health politics was therefore wide in scope and responded to a broad set of needs. The activists and the communities with which they worked confronted the paradox of profound healthcare neglect and disparate biomedical inclusion: poor blacks were not only medically underserved but also overexposed to the worst jeopardies of medical practice and bioscientific research. The resulting lack of comfort and familiarity with preventive medicine and attendant fear of biomedical abuse remain salient factors contributing to health inequality.

My exploration into the Party's health activism accordingly yielded insight into how a segment of African Americans endeavored to gain access to reliable, affordable healthcare services while placing a check on the authority and racial claims of biomedicine. This course of research, however, presented me with some unexpected challenges. Although the Party's activities were exhaustively documented in the mainstream and alternative media of the time, and continued to be accounted for in both memoirs and scholarship of subsequent years, little of this coverage treated health-related activities in any detail. This oversight was likely because of preoccupation with other, more sensational matters. For, as the communications studies scholar Jane Rhodes suggests, the Party's activities were "framed," for the most, by mainstream press representations that "focuse[d] attention on *selected* aspects" of the organization—most particularly its surveillance of local police and its armed militancy.[13] For these reasons, in the writing of this book, I encountered ample textual and visual resources about the more spectacular facets of the Party, but substantially less information about its health politics. Uncovering details about this element of the Party's activism consequently required bridging several fields of inquiry, including sociology, history, and African American studies, as well as using an ecumenical methodology that combined archival, hermeneutic, theoretical (and to some degree, ethnographic) approaches.

Specifically, *Body and Soul* draws on primary sources culled from government documents and official correspondence, state and library archives, ephemera and personal papers. A survey of the voluminous press coverage of the Party on broadcast television, documentaries, magazines, and in mainstream and alternative newspapers was consulted alongside close reading of the group's weekly newspaper, the *Black Panther*. Launched in 1967, the paper—even in its most propagandistic moments—provided the most complete record of the Party's health-related activities and of the broader political aspirations to which these were linked.[14] Some chapters of the Party occasionally published their own newsletters, and I made use of these as well.

Secondary literatures in post–World War II African American history, the long civil rights movement, the social studies of science and medicine, and social movement theory helped me conceptualize the Party's health politics. In addition, in crafting this account, I relied on medical journals and scientific papers from the 1960s and 1970s. Editorials and essays in these publications featured scientific and policy debates in biomedicine and also supplied a glimpse into medical professionals' perspectives on the emergence of health radicalism, including that of the Party.

The book draws on my encounters with many former Black Panthers and their collaborators. Interviews with Norma Armour, Elaine Brown, Arthur Harrison, Billy X Jennings, Cleo Silvers, Bernard Thompson, and other Party members contributed crucial details about the practical operation and political framing of the health-related aspects of the group's activism. I also relied on the published oral histories of Party members and consulted as well several Panther memoirs penned over the last four decades. In October 2006 I attended the Party's fortieth-anniversary gathering in Oakland, California, during which members narrated the organizational histories of their respective Party chapters. During the telling of these collective oral histories, the activists expounded on the breadth of the Party's health-based programming, among many other matters.

Health and medicine are unique among the bases of collective action for the degree to which political interventions in these domains may rely on deep engagement with expertise and, moreover, often necessitates that like-minded members of the professions aid the social movement (even in the case of those radical health movements in which a critique of expertise is a centerpiece of the activism). As a result, this book additionally reflects my interviews with members of the professions who worked in solidarity, and often shoulder to shoulder, with the Black Panthers. The remembrances of several Party collaborators—including the attorney Fred Hiestand, Dr. Marie Branch, Dr. William Bronston, Dr. William Davis, Dr. Terry Kupers, and Dr. Tolbert Small—elucidated the lay-expert network that undergirded and facilitated the Party's health initiatives.

Visiting former locations of Party chapters and clinics in Oakland, New York City, and Seattle was also instructive. I made trips to sites that remain as material manifestations of the Party's activism, such as the Harriet Tubman Medical Clinic in West Oakland, California, that was established by Small in the late 1970s and still today serves poor clients in the Bay Area. I also visited Seattle's sliding-scale Carolyn Downs Family Medical Center named for and inspired by the work of a late Black Panther, who in 1968 established the local Party chapter's clinic at a nearby location. A novel and more complex picture of the Black Panthers resulted from the amassing of these eclectic resources.

The progress of the Party's health activism—from the group's founding in 1966 to its reconsolidation in Oakland in the 1970s, after rapid organizational growth—occurred in the years immediately after the legal dismantling of Jim Crow, by way of the Civil Rights Act (1964) and the Voting Rights Act (1965). There were concomitant transformations to the social welfare system, especially the expansion of the United States as a healthcare state, exemplified by the passage of the Social Security Act (1965) that installed the Medicare and Medicaid programs. In this same period, there was an increase in state policies and programs related to healthcare that issued from President Lyndon B. Johnson's War on Poverty along with determined pushback from medical lobbies and the insurance industry. The antipoverty programs were swiftly followed by cries of a fiscal "health crisis" from the administration of President Richard M. Nixon that engaged in austerity politics and enacted severe budget cuts. This time also saw a "health crisis" of credibility in the early 1970s when revelations of the Tuskegee syphilis study and the forced sterilization of numerous black women, including most disgracefully the teen sisters Minnie and Mary Alice Relf, who were deceived into submitting to surgical sterilization, came to light.[15]

From the purview of the Party's health politics, it becomes possible to, in the words of the sociologist Charles Tilly, see "how people lived the big changes" or, put another way, to perceive how ordinary people experienced these and other pivotal societal transitions.[16] It was no coincidence then that the Party's health politics (and activism more generally) emanated from a constellation of consequential social-structural transformations, including the advent of a postindustrial economy, the slow diminution of the American welfare state, and the social and legal developments of the civil rights era that immediately preceded the Party's birth. At this critical juncture in the late 1960s and early 1970s, health offered new moral terrain for a struggle that was no longer typified by the Manichaean inscription of "whites only" signs and Jim Crow transportation, employment, accommodations, and schooling, but instead by the vacillation of social abandon and social control. Through their health politics, the Black Panthers laid claim to recent civil rights land-marks even as they stridently exposed the limits of those milestones under late capitalism.

An early instantiation of what might be described as postsegrega-tion politics, Party health activism also prefigured issues of relevance in the so-called postracial era, most particularly, the significance of race after the genomic turn and what integration into this "brave new world" proffers for African Americans given historic vulnerability to biomedical authority. Shaped by past tragedies, contemporaneous inequality, and future optimism, by the recognition that biomedicine is both rocky and curative terrain, the Black Panthers' politics of health and race exhibited twinned aspirations: defense against biomedical neglect with hope of attaining full civil, social, *and* human rights.

ABBREVIATIONS

AMA	American Medical Association
ANA	American Nurses Association
BCN	Black Cross Nurses
CCCJ	California Council for Criminal Justice
COFO	Council of Federated Organizations
COPAP	Committee Opposing Psychiatric Abuse of Prisoners
CPU	California Prisoners' Union
CRLA	California Rural Legal Assistance
Health/PAC	Health Policy Advisory Center
LEAA	Law Enforcement Assistance Administration
MAPA	Mexican-American Political Association
MCCR	Medical Committee for Civil Rights
MCHR	Medical Committee for Human Rights
NACGN	National Association of Colored Graduate Nurses
NIH	National Institutes of Health
NMA	National Medical Association
NOW	National Organization of Women
NSCDRF	National Sickle Cell Disease Research Foundation
NWRO	National Welfare Rights Organization
OEO	Office of Economic Opportunity
PFMC	People's Free Medical Clinic
PSCAF	People's Sickle Cell Anemia Foundation

SDS	Students for a Democratic Society
SHO	Student Health Organizations
SHPs	SHO's Summer Health Projects
SNCC	Student Nonviolent Coordinating Committee
UFOC	United Farm Workers Organizing Committee
UNIA	Universal Negro Improvement Association
USPHS	U.S. Public Health Service

INTRODUCTION

Serving the People Body and Soul

O ver three days in the spring of 1972, the Black Panther Party, the radical political organization that had emerged in Oakland, California, almost six years prior, held a Black Community Survival Conference—a gathering that combined elements of a rally, a street fair, and a block party—in that city's De Fremery Park.[1] On March 27, standing before a large banner carrying the slogan "Serve the People Body and Soul," the Party's chairman and cofounder Bobby Seale spoke on a public address system to the assembled mass of Panther loyalists, political allies, locals, police, and passers-by about the organization's slate of free community service programs. These "survival programs" were established partly to help poor blacks cope with the surveillance and harassment they experienced at the hands of agents of a mounting "law-and-order" state. These programs were also intended as a stopgap solution to the diminished provision of social services by a shrinking welfare state.

Against a backdrop of barbecuing; children's presentations on black and radical history; speeches by members of other activist groups, such as Johnnie Tillman of the National Welfare Rights Organization; a performance by the pioneering a cappella group the Persuasions, and other entertainment, Party cadre and volunteers distributed information about more than a dozen no-cost community service initiatives, including escorts for senior citizens to medical appointments, free elementary

Bobby Seale addresses attendees to the Community Survival Conference in Oakland at De Fremery Park in March 1972, at which the Black Panther Party featured its health programs. Courtesy of Steven Shames and Department of Special Collections and University Archives, Stanford University Libraries.

education at their school, and a bus service to prisons for visits with incarcerated friends and family.[2] Concurrently, Party rank and file showed Seale's words in action, handing out bags of free food and clothing to an appreciative crowd.[3]

On this same weekend, the Party also held a voter registration drive in anticipation of its May 1972 announcement of Seale's and Minister of Information Elaine Brown's respective candidacies for mayor and Sixth District city council seat—on a "Community Survival ticket"—in upcoming Oakland elections.[4] Accordingly, some scholars have interpreted this gathering and the subsequent survival conferences that occurred that year as marking the Party's "deradicalization"—a shift in the organization from revolutionist to reformist principles and from radical militarist tactics to mainstream electoral politics.[5] Less remarked on, however, is the fact that this episode was also a signpost of the Party's health politics.[6]

At this event, the breadth of the Party's health-focused activism was

Panther children make a presentation at the Community Survival Conference. Courtesy of Steven Shames and Department of Special Collections and University Archives, Stanford University Libraries.

Community Survival Conference at De Fremery Park: musical performers are onstage, and behind the stage are bags of free groceries to be dispensed at the event, an element of "serving the people body and soul." Courtesy of Steven Shames and Department of Special Collections and University Archives, Stanford University Libraries.

evident: Party members publicized the activities of the People's Free Medical Clinics. Party cadre touted grocery giveaways as ameliorating the malnutrition that often accompanied poverty and thus as contributing to community members' healthfulness. Working with their collaborators and also with volunteers, the activists reportedly screened thousands for sickle cell anemia—a genetic disease that predominates in persons of African descent. Moreover, in this same month, Party cofounder Huey P. Newton and Brown, the group's chairwoman, amended the organization's founding ten-point platform to include a revised point 6, a demand for "COMPLETELY FREE HEALTH CARE FOR ALL BLACK AND OPPRESSED PEOPLE." The extent of these activities confirms that the provision and politicization of medicine was a significantly developed feature of the Party's broader mission. By spring of 1972, Party health activism was full-fledged.[7]

This community survival conference illustrated in microcosm the scope and ambition of the Black Panthers' health politics. Given the extent of these efforts, it is surprising that the Party's health initiatives have received mostly passing mention in both scholarly analysis and popular recollection and have been overtaken in popular memory by the penumbra of debates about whether the Party's primary aim and lasting bequest was social disorder or social transformation. Indeed, the Party's community service programs have become ready ammunition in the so-called culture wars of recent decades. An unfortunate consequence of the tendency to either pillory or valorize the Party's activities in a zero-sum manner is that scant attention has been paid to its considerable engagement with medical and health concerns. Bellicose critics of the Party's survival programs dismiss them merely as attempts by the activists to downplay the organization's promotion of violence and shore up its credibility after run-ins with law enforcement decimated its membership and eroded its public support.[8] Equally pugnacious champions of the Party, including several former members turned memoirists, by contrast, invoke these programs as reflecting the activists' true mission and as counterpoints to claims that the organization comprised nothing more than an assortment of aimless youth with violent tendencies.[9] The historical truth, of course, lies somewhere between and also beyond these characterizations.

In the mid-1960s the eye of the civil rights storm set course for "freedom North."[10] To be sure, African American equality struggles had always been waged both below and above the Mason-Dixon Line. In this period, however, the spotlight of public attention that had since the 1950s shone brightest on civil rights activism centered on the South—exemplified by events like the Montgomery, Alabama, bus boycott and the Student Nonviolent Coordinating Committee's (SNCC) Freedom Summer project—shifted to urban centers in the West, Midwest, East, and North. In these latter settings, resistance to racial and economic oppression was often more stridently projected, as exemplified by the militant radicalism of the Black Panthers and the scores of urban rebellions that punctuated the "long hot summer" of 1967.[11] The moral authority that was accorded to opponents of antiblack southern racism derived in large measure from the Christian principles that undergirded their nonviolent tactics.[12] In the mid-1960s, when black radicals employed "un-civil" tactics such as armed confrontation with state authorities *and* denunciations of state-sanctioned institutional racism, the issue of health imparted another moral mantle to their efforts.[13]

Health was a powerful and elastic political lexicon that could signify many ideals simultaneously. In settings where racial oppression was more commonly advanced through social abandon (e.g., nonexistent or insufficient social welfare programs) and social control (e.g., police harassment, medical mistreatment) than through staunch Jim Crow practices, health was a site where the stakes of injustice could be exposed and a prism through which struggles for equality could be refracted. Health could also connote inalienable human attributes and freedoms. Martin Luther King Jr., for example, invoked the idea of health as both a fundamental and a paramount property of human life during an address before the Medical Committee for Human Rights (MCHR) in 1966. "Of all forms of inequality, injustice in healthcare is the most shocking and inhumane," King proclaimed.[14] The Black Panthers translated the polyvalence of "health" into practical social programs and political ideology. *Body and Soul* is an exploration of why and how health issues, broadly understood, came to be an indispensible element of the Party's politics. As is described here, ideological foundations, historical continuities, and tactical exigencies precipitated the Party's commitment to these concerns.

The Long Medical Civil Rights Movement

Seale and Newton established the Black Panther organization in October 1966 to afford protection for poor blacks from police brutality and to offer varied other services to these same communities. In ensuing years, as the Party's ranks quickly swelled in Oakland and beyond, Party headquarters instituted guidelines for new chapters and members that specified, among other procedures and practices, the establishment of no-cost community-based medical clinics (or PFMCs). Mandated by the Party leadership, but not funded by it, the operation of the clinics depended on the ingenuity of the Panther rank and file and members' abilities to mobilize local resources. At the PFMCs, Panther cadre worked with both lay and *trusted-expert* volunteers—including nurses, doctors, and students in the health professions—to administer basic preventive care, diagnostic testing for lead poisoning and hypertension and other conditions, and, in some instances, ambulance services, dentistry, and referrals to other facilities for more extensive treatment. At the free clinics, the Party also administered extramedical patient advocacy; Black Panthers and volunteers helped clinic clients to navigate housing, employment, social welfare programs, and similar matters. Party health politics also ranged beyond the physical site of the PFMCs in many ways: the activists conducted health services, outreach, and education in homes, parks, churches, and other venues. They used vans and ambulances to take healthcare services out into poor communities.[15] The Black Panther leadership also engaged in public debates about the significance of race for healthfulness and medical care via its newspaper, interactions with the mainstream media, and the legislative process.

A novel interpretation of the Black Panthers' mission, trajectory, and impact becomes available when we shift the focus to their broad health-focused activities. The fact of Party health politics contravenes accepted wisdom that neither black activists' express participation nor their particular perspectives contributed to the development of the health political landscape of the late 1960s and early 1970s. Suggestive of this tendency is a claim ventured by the sociologist Paul Starr in his monumental work, *The Social Transformation of American Medicine*. Starr writes that

> the civil rights struggle lost its momentum as a protest movement in the seventies, but it set the example for dozens of other movements of similar purpose. Instead of marching through the streets, they marched through the courts. And instead of a single movement centered on blacks, the new movements advocated the rights of women, children, prisoners, students, tenants, gays, Chicanos, Native Americans, and welfare clients. The catalogue of groups and rights

entitled to them was immensely expanded in both variety and detail. Medical care figured prominently in this generalization of rights, particularly as a concern of the women's movement and in the new movements specifically for patient's rights and for the rights of the handicapped, the mentally ill, the retarded, and the subjects of medical research.[16]

Here Starr suggests that the civil rights and health rights activism of this period were effectively detached from each other.

Yet African American activism of import did not fade from the political scene in the 1970s, and black activists of this decade did not precipitate the degeneration of civil rights struggles. A recent significant wave of research pioneered by the historian Jacqueline Dowd Hall and taken up by numerous others has generated a fuller accounting of African Americans' battles for equality and has recast standard narratives that draw hard distinctions between the civil rights and black power movements. This school of thinking highlights the "long civil rights movement" by recalibrating the temporality, geography, and scale of the twentieth-century black protest tradition.[17] The civil rights movement did not first emerge after World War II; it was inaugurated *at least* several decades earlier through the actions of not only large social movement organizations like the National Association for the Advancement of Colored People but also local communities' specific political struggles in both the southern and the northern United States.[18] While the regional, thematic, and tactical focuses of the black freedom struggle may have evolved over its *longue durée*, the movement continued through the 1970s and endures today.

Moreover, "race" was not the wholesale political "metalanguage" of late twentieth-century civil rights activism, to rework the historian Evelyn Brooks Higginbotham's important observation about the hierarchization of social categories.[19] Civil rights activists' bailiwick included, to varied degrees, class inequality, fair employment, gender equality, health rights, and opposition to the Vietnam War. Ella Baker, A. Phillip Randolph, and the Black Panthers, to name but a few examples, fervently articulated that economic oppression and racism *together* placed limited horizons on blacks' life chances.[20] Similarly attuned to overlapping vectors of inequality, King Jr., in his capacity as a leader of the Southern Christian Leadership Conference, in 1967 began planning the Poor People's Campaign, an innovative "interracial alliance" aimed at declaring "'final victory over racism and poverty.'"[21] Fannie Lou Hamer, the iconic vice chair of the Mississippi Freedom Democratic Party's efforts to unseat that state's exclusively white, pro–Jim Crow delegation to the 1964 Democratic National Convention, was drawn into activism as a way to overturn the intersecting system of racial, gender, class, and health inequality that characterized her experience in the South. She famously used the phrase "Mississippi appendectomy" to describe the medical oppression of poor black women who, like her, were surreptitiously sterilized while seeking treatment for other matters by abusive physicians.[22] Activists from Randolph to Hamer to the Black Panther Party addressed the many sources of racial injustice. Health politics therefore must be understood as an important feature of a broader conceptualization of the civil rights movement.[23]

Pace Starr, the battle against Jim Crow was not merely a faded object lesson for the Party and its health activist contemporaries. Rather, the struggles for health access and for just distribution of both the benefits and the harms of biomedicine were a protraction of civil rights struggles in at least two ways. First, the Black Panthers' health activism was a signpost in the long civil rights movement as well as a manifestation of an established tradition of African American health politics. This legacy was evident in the Party's own *tactical repertoire* that drew on the example of black communities' prior responses to health inequality and medical mistreatment. Health activism was (and remains) a prominent facet of black political culture. The Party was firmly rooted in a tradition that had developed during slavery in interface with how bondage, racism, and segregation affected the well-being of black communities. During the twentieth century, black health activists fought for access to humane and equitable medical treatment, from the Progressive Era during which black leaders endeavored to dispense healthcare services for their communities in the face of institutionalized Jim Crow by establishing hospitals that, like disease, did not abide a "color line," to the 1950s and 1960s during which reformers staged a "medical civil rights movement" to desegregate medical schools and workplaces.[24] The Party drew practically on the influence of these prior health activists. For example, although the Panthers' establishment of independent health clinics was in keeping with the community control and self-determinist ethics of 1970s black nationalism (and New Left health activists), this alternative institution building harked back as well to early-twentieth-century endeavors, such as the "black hospital movement."[25] In these ways, the Black Panthers employed tactics that were demonstrably derived from a line of African American health advocacy that had developed in response to racially segregated medical institutions and health professions.

Black Panther health politics represented a continuation of civil rights struggles in a second significant way. Actors and organizations involved in Party health politics bridged civil rights and health rights endeavors. This is particularly apparent in the cross-fertilization between the Panthers, SNCC, and the MCHR. The MCHR, a group of doctors, nurses, students of the health professions, and others, first came together as medical support for SNCC's 1964 Freedom Summer campaign. At this time, the SNCC leadership included H. Rap Brown, Stokely Carmichael, and Kathleen Cleaver, who would be among the earliest members of the Panther organization. As described in chapter 1, the Party's health work extended directly from the efforts of the SNCC organization. Moreover, members of the MCHR worked closely with the Party on its health projects in Los Angeles, Chicago, and other locations to establish and run community-based health clinics not unlike ones started by SNCC. From an organizational perspective as well then, the founding of the Party did not mark the conclusion of the civil rights era but rather its extension. As Elaine Brown described, the Party did not discriminate between phases of the black freedom struggle and, indeed, appreciated its continuity: "We never called it the 'civil rights movement.' It was just 'the movement.' . . . Everybody called it 'the movement.' Everybody would tell you that. . . . We never really distinguished ourselves from Martin Luther King; we thought he was a great hero as we did with Malcolm X, of course."[26]

Civil Rights, Health Rights

"A poor man has no medical or legal rights," a member of the Party lamented in an issue of the group's newspaper: "He is a colonized man."[27] As this quote suggests, while Black Panther health activism did not indicate the twilight of civil rights struggles, it was certainly a referendum on contemporary social issues. Indeed, the organization's emergence responded to the profound dissatisfaction still felt by many African Americans despite the fact that their civic membership in the United States had been fortified anew in the Civil Rights Act of 1964 and the Voting Rights Act of 1965. For the Party, the reality of urban poverty and structural racism showed recent civil rights strides *at their limits*. Moreover, the persistence of health inequality despite recent improvements only highlighted the indefatigableness of the systematic social and economic exclusion of blacks.

The Panther activists apprehended that the provenance of birth was no guarantee of citizenship, especially for the poor. Despite dramatic legislative transformation and changes in social mores, citizenship could remain tenuous for members of marginalized groups. Some recent observations by theorists of citizenship are instructive for understanding the dynamics that conditioned this exclusion. For example, the historian Alice Kessler-Harris and the sociologist Margaret Somers, drawing on the works of T. H. Marshall and Hannah Arendt, have underscored the fact that holding civil rights neither guarantees social rights nor precludes economic oppression, despite legislation or expectation.[28] In the twentieth-century United States, social rights typically emanated from civil rights, so that individuals could, for example, expect to receive health benefits through their place of employment. Yet this course of social inclusion has been unreliable for individuals who are more likely to be under- or unemployed or whose labor has not traditionally been remunerated (e.g., stay-at-home mothers and caregivers, "surplus" labor). Kessler-Harris explains that the provision of rights has "rested on sometimes hidden, normative assumptions about who 'cares' and who 'works'; who deserves what sorts of rights; and who required protection from the market," or, to use Somers's words, on ideas about who has the "right to have rights."[29] This gap between civil rights and social benefits, or this *citizenship contradiction,* as I call it, has been especially acute for women and African Americans, who consequently may be relegated to incomplete and "problematic form[s]" of citizenship.[30] In such instances, individuals are dependent on powerful institutions, organizations, and others to secure their rights. Alternately, members of these groups may possess an emaciated citizenship that may be "conditional on political whim" or the vagaries of the market.[31] Returning to the Black Panthers with Kessler-Harris's and Somers's analyses in mind, we can understand the organization's health politics as an effort to provide resources to poor blacks who formally held civil rights, but who by virtue of their degraded social status and social value lacked social and economic citizenship and thus the privileges that accrue to these, including access to medical care. Through its activism, the Black Panthers intended to fulfill a most basic human need (i.e., medical treatment) while insisting on a full measure of social inclusion for the black urban poor.

In the late 1960s, with social citizenship decoupled from civil rights, despite recent changes in U.S. political culture, the Party exposed the citizenship contradiction facing poor black communities and demanded rights on their behalf. The Panthers regarded healthcare as "a right and not a privilege," as did many other health radicals of this period and as had prior reformers and activists.[32] More proximate to the Black Panthers was the capacious idea of a right to health elaborated in the 1948 constitution of the World Health Organization, underlain by the United Nations Universal Declaration of Rights formalized in the same year, which affirmed the "inherent dignity" and "inalienable rights" of all human beings.[33] The WHO, the UN entity tasked with coordinating global health issues, advanced a robust definition of health as both a basic and a universal right: "Health is a state of complete physical, mental and social well-being and not merely the absence of disease or infirmity . . . health is one of the fundamental rights of every human being without distinction of race, religion, political belief, economic or social condition."[34]

In developing its health politics, the Party borrowed liberally from the WHO charter. Given that in the Party's original ten-point platform of 1966, the activists requested assistance from the UN to create an autonomous political community, or "plebiscite," it is perhaps unsurprising that the Party's expansive definition of health would be appreciably indebted to that of the WHO. In an article in its newspaper touting the group's free medical services, for example, the Panthers declared that it is "the government's responsibility to provide its people with this right [to health] and other basic human rights."[35] Also following the UN body, the activists defined health as "a state of physical, social and mental well-being" and "one of the most basic human rights of all human beings."[36] Holding a conception of health that included many registers of well-being, the Black Panthers were understandably disaffected by recent narrow civil rights gains.

Building on the WHO's assertion of health as a universal right as well as traditions in both African American culture and leftist thinking that drew together iatric and social well-being, the Party developed a distinctive perspective and approach that I term "social health."[37] With the phrase "social health" I mean to characterize the activists' efforts on the terrain of health and biomedicine as being oriented by an outlook on well-being that scaled from the individual, corporeal body to the body politic in such a way that therapeutic matters were inextricably articulated to social justice ones.[38] The Party's social health position reflected its particular understanding of the history of racial subjugation and its commitment to social equality combined with a Marxist-Leninist critique of the "medical–industrial complex"—health radicals' term for the confluence of business interests, the medical profession, the insurance industry, and pharmaceutical companies that drove the commodification of healthcare.[39]

The Party's social health "frame" was also distinctly elastic.[40] In addition to allowing the fashioning of metonymy between individual illness and social dis-ease, the elasticity of the social health perspective allowed the Party to advance alternatives to mainstream explanations for why certain diseases, like sickle cell anemia, persisted among black populations and to suggest why these communities were disproportionately depicted by biomedical researchers as the loci of disease and pathology. As a praxis, social health linked medical services to a program of societal transformation. The Panthers' clinics, for example, were imagined as sites of social change where preventive medicine was dispensed alongside both extramedical services (e.g., food banks and employment assistance) and ideology via the Party's political education (PE) classes. Reflecting many influences, social health was the frame for the Panthers' engagements with biomedical knowledge and a guiding principle for the group's health initiatives. It was an articulation of the Party's unique critical discourse of citizenship and health rights.

Health Crisis

The Party's focus on health and medicine was impelled by several factors, described in the chapters to follow, including its founding political ideology, the influence of prior African American health activism, internal organization dynamics, and state repression. The Party's activism was also notably au courant. Its health politics intensified at a time when healthcare was at the forefront of political and policy debates in the United States (alongside desegregation and the implementation of recently passed civil rights legislation, President Lyndon B. Johnson's War on Poverty, and the failing Vietnam War). In the late 1960s and early 1970s, there was general agreement in the United States that the country was in the midst of a healthcare "crisis."[41] During this time, crisis discourse was taken up by austerity hawks who complained that state-sponsored healthcare coverage strained the federal government's resources to the limit, and by welfare statists on the left, who pointed to the exigencies of a profit-driven medical system as the culprits. The Party also took up this health crisis rhetoric. For the Panther organization, and other health radicals, the emergency lay at the nexus of rising health inequality, deficient medical care, and waning confidence in a medical profession that was unaccountable to its patients. Moreover, for the Panthers, the crisis was also due to the fact that blacks disproportionately suffered ill health and poor medical treatment. These realities, the activists insisted, were corporeal manifestations of the vicissitudes of urban poverty in the United States.

As I detail below, varied political camps—including two presidential administrations, professional associations, and health activists—advanced diverse diagnoses of and remedies for the crisis. In 1965 President Johnson established Medicare and Medicaid—government health insurance for the elderly and the disabled and the poor, respectively—when he signed into law the Social Security Act of 1965, as a cornerstone of his Great Society model, which enlarged the federal government's role in healthcare and other social welfare programs. In this same year, partly following the example of Freedom Summer—SNCC's and the Council of Federated Organizations' two-month campaign to register and empower black voters, during which "Freedom Schools" and "Freedom Clinics" were also established in Jim Crow Mississippi—the Johnson administration began a community clinic program in an effort to provide healthcare to the poor.[42] This initiative, funded by the Office of Economic Opportunity, mandated the "maximum feasible participation" of local communities in administering the clinics.[43]

Within a few years of the passage of the Social Security Act, there were pitched battles over proposals to federally fund universal healthcare coverage that pitted the conservative President Richard Nixon, the American Medical Association, and other medical industry lobbyists against the health reformer and Democratic senator Edward M. Kennedy, labor unions, and health activists of mixed political provenance. Healthcare for workers was fundamentally transformed when Nixon signed into law the Health Maintenance Organization Act of 1973. A centerpiece of his administration's national health strategy, this legislation required businesses with more than twenty-five employees to supply both indemnity and healthcare insurance coverage to their workers and primed the pump of the managed care system by supplying government-backed grants and loans to qualified health maintenance organizations.[44] Moreover, with this plan the Nixon administration could appear to respond to calls for medical care in the United States to be made more affordable and accessible, without acceding to demands for state-sponsored universal healthcare that surpassed the coverage provided by Medicaid and Medicare.

Activists, too, were conversant in the political rhetoric of the health crisis.[45] In diametric contrast with the Nixon administration and healthcare lobbyists who were committed to the continued commodification of medical care, health radicals—a coterie that included the Black Panther Party, health workers such as the MCHR and the Student Health Organization (SHO), and the New Left–oriented Health Policy Advisory Center (or Health/PAC)—understood the most acute aspect of the crisis to be the proliferation of a capitalist medical system that produced and exacerbated inequality. The Chicago Black Panther Party minister of health Ronald "Doc" Satchel's complaint in the pages of the *Black Panther* that "the medical profession within this capitalist society . . . is composed generally of people working for their own benefit and advancement rather than the humane aspects of medical care" typified this activist argument.[46] The health Left often parted ways with liberal reformers, such as Senator Kennedy, who believed that mainstream medicine could be made more equitable. For these radicals, a for-profit healthcare system was fundamentally and inherently flawed. Accordingly, they took no succor in the proliferation of the medical–industrial complex—even in a liberal guise.

Health activists, moreover, pointed to the *consequences* of the skewed health status quo as further evidence of the crisis: legions of people suffered medical neglect, they declaimed. Healthcare options available to the poor were often either deficient or too expensive and thus inaccessible. The elderly and impoverished people who received federal healthcare assistance in the form of Medicare and Medicaid, activists protested, were too frequently subject to substandard care. What is more, persons without any insurance coverage whatsoever might receive slipshod treatment in the emergency rooms of large, often dilapidated, public medical facilities. Writing on behalf of the Party, Elaine Brown voiced this objection in a 1974 dossier describing the organization's service programs. "Private hospitals and doctors charge fees more expensive than poor people can afford," Brown declared, "while public hospitals and clinics are so overcrowded and understaffed that their services are almost totally inadequate."[47]

Those with access to healthcare often experienced the medical encounter as coercive and authoritarian, especially if they were poor, female, institutionalized, or members of minority groups. Disproportionately incarcerated blacks and Latinos were subject to medical abuse and experimentation, perhaps most notoriously at Pennsylvania's Holmesburg Prison from the early 1950s to the early 1970s.[48] Further, the circulation of prisoners' and patients' accounts of "being 'treated like animals'"[49] at these "butcher shops"[50] and "butcher houses"[51]—some actual, many apocryphal—eroded public faith in mainstream medicine.[52] As a June 1970 newsletter published by the Los Angeles–based, Southern California chapter of the Black Panther Party put it, "Poor people in general and black people in particular are not given the best care available. Our people are treated like animals, experimented on and made to wait long hours in waiting rooms."[53] That this accusation was warranted was confirmed for many skeptics after the *New York Times*'s disclosure in 1972 of the four-decades-long Tuskegee syphilis study in which close to four hundred African American men were left untreated for the disease so researchers could observe its ravages on the human body.[54] This controversy generated considerable public outrage and distrust on the part of poor and minority communities as well as the larger population.[55] From politicians, to the Party, to the general public, there was acute awareness of the health crisis of the late 1960s and early 1970s.

The Chapters Ahead

The Panthers were heirs to a mostly uncharted tradition of African American health politics. In chapter 1 I draw out this tradition from the long civil rights movement. I demonstrate and argue that health advocacy, variously conceived, has been a deep-rooted concern of black political culture, across the range of institutions, community organizations, and social movements that constitute this protest tradition. Spanning the period from 1880 to 1965, the chapter links up the Party's efforts with a line of health advocacy that was the necessary response of black communities to the myriad forms of health inequality to which they were subject for generations, including lack of access to healthcare resources; exclusion from whites-only hospitals; refusal of admission to professional schools, associations, and organizations; subpar medical care; and, in some instances, deliberate neglect and medical abuse. The Party's social health approach was indebted to an earlier

THE BLACK PANTHER

INTERCOMMUNAL NEWS SERVICE 25 cents

VOL. VIII NO. 20 Copyright © 1971 by Huey P. Newton SATURDAY, AUGUST 5, 1972

PUBLISHED WEEKLY **THE BLACK PANTHER PARTY** MINISTRY OF INFORMATION BOX 2967, CUSTOM HOUSE SAN FRANCISCO, CA 94126

GERM WARFARE DECLARED AGAINST BLACKS!

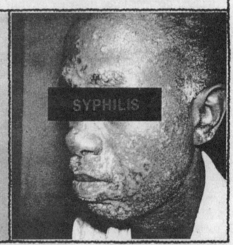

HUNDREDS OF BLACK MEN DISCOVERED MASSACRED IN SYPHILIS "EXPERIMENT".

SYPHILIS

SEE ARTICLE INSIDE PAGE 2

ALSO: SEE "OAKLAND - A BASE OF OPERATION"
SUPPLEMENT, PART II (PAGES A, B, C, D, IN CENTER)

SURVIVAL TICKET
VOTE FOR
SURVIVAL

**BOBBY SEALE FOR MAYOR OF OAKLAND
ELAINE BROWN FOR COUNCILWOMAN**

Front cover of the August 1972 issue of the Black Panther, *declaiming the Tuskegee syphilis study. The Black Panthers' health activism unfolded against the backdrop of African American fears of medical mistreatment. Courtesy of It's About Time Black Panther Party Archive/Billy X Jennings.*

"relationist" paradigm through which "clinical and socioeconomic factors . . . explain[ed] . . . sickness in the individual black [person] as well as the black community generally."[56] In addition to this relative definition of well-being that went beyond strictly biological concerns, Panther health activism shared with prior efforts a critical engagement with the construction of race in medicine, or what the historian David McBride terms "sociomedical racialism."[57] The Panthers were also bequeathed a legacy of tactical responses to racialized health inequality, including *institution building, integrationism* (or antisegregationism), and the *"politics of knowledge."*[58]

Party health activism was, at the same time, characteristic of the milieu of the late 1960s and early 1970s; it was an outgrowth of contemporary political currents and of its own organizational evolution. How and why the survival or "serve the people" programs came to play a central role in the Panther organization is explored in chapter 2, focusing in particular on a confluence of factors that precipitated the evolution of its health politics. Attention to community service was an expression of Party founders' initial commitment to the dual deployment of theory and practice in response to their frustration with what they deemed black cultural nationalists' preoccupation with rhetoric and the limitations of War on Poverty programs. The Party's community service orientation was thus forged between and in reaction to what the activists regarded as ineffective rhetoric, on the one hand, and paternalistic social initiatives, on the other.

Serving the people was also a pragmatic matter for the Party by 1968. Between January 1968 and December 1969, at least twenty-eight Panthers were murdered in confrontations with police.[59] Within the first few years of the Party's emergence, it became subject to repressive police power that decimated its membership with fatalities and incarceration and jeopardized its popular support.[60] The ideas of Ernesto "Che" Guevara, Mao Zedong, and Frantz Fanon provided a conceptual bridge between the Party's political philosophy, its community service ethos, and its health politics. These theorists' influence could be seen in how the Party afforded an integral role to medicine in its imagination of a "robust" social body: in its valorization of lay expertise, in its critique of "bourgeois" healthcare and medical power, and in its aim to foster medicine for and by "the people."[61]

The administration of the Party's locally controlled, alternative health clinics, including how they were staffed, supplied, and operated, is the focus of the third chapter. "Serve the people body and soul" was a familiar Black Panther aphorism, one that lyrically signaled the group's total dedication to its constituencies. This saying took on a decidedly literal meaning after the Party leadership's 1970 mandate that all current and future chapters institute health clinics.[62] Although concern for the health of poor and black communities was intrinsic to the Party's founding principles, and several chapters, including those in Chicago, Seattle, and Los Angeles, had already established PFMCs, this directive marked the beginning of a more coordinated effort.

The Party was not only a standard-bearer of the black power movement. It was also a significant "health social movement"—that is, an organization that challenged health inequality, in this case, by supplying access to medical services, contesting biomedical authority, and asserting healthcare as a right.[63] The Panthers were indeed a significant faction in the radical health movement of its era. As health activists in the late 1960s and early 1970s, Party members labored alongside feminist groups; hippie counterculturalists; leftists such as Students for a Democratic Society and Health/PAC; politicized medical professionals and students, including the SHO and the MCHR; and the Party's allies in the "rainbow coalition," most notably the Young Lords Party.[64] This multifaceted community—the radical health movement—was a decentralized aggregate of groups, collectives, and organizations with distinct missions that sought to transform medicine, institutionally and interpersonally.

These collaborations were critical to the functioning of the Party's clinics. In keeping with the era's DIY spirit, the activists enacted the better world they imagined by establishing their own independent healthcare initiatives and institutions. The radical health movement modeled practices that, in the words of some Bay Area radicals, valued "Health Care for People Not Profit."[65] This mission was frequently manifested in activist-run no-cost or low-cost clinics, such as the PFMCs established by the Panthers. Consistent with the period's antiauthoritarian zeitgeist, at these alternative institutions the activists empowered patients to have a voice in the medical encounter and encouraged laypeople to claim the mantle of expertise by taking a hand in their healthcare—and, sometimes, in producing medical knowledge as well. The democratization of both medical practice and knowledge in the clinic setting was a tactical cornerstone of the Party's health politics.

In addition to being brick-and-mortar embodiments of the Party's health politics, these clinics were sites where the Party's political ideals were translated into social practice by providing free basic care and advocating on behalf of patients. The Party provided healthcare services to populations who lacked them. The clinics addressed local needs, reflected local priorities, and drew on and mobilized local resources. The work of these chapter-based institutions did not end with providing health services. The clinics were exemplars of the Party's commitment to the *total* well-being of its constituents. A person entering a Party clinic might also receive help from a "patient advocate" with paying bills or dealing with a problematic landlord; this individual might also be encouraged to attend a political education class in which writings by Fanon and other theorists were discussed. In this way, the PFMCs were sites for social change.[66]

The Panthers' health clinics were also bases of operation for its sickle cell anemia campaign. Chapter 4 details the Party's efforts to highlight the problem of this disease, an incurable genetic condition. Its campaign, launched in 1971, was both practical and ideological. In response to what they perceived as deliberate and pernicious neglect of African American citizens by the healthcare state, the Panthers established their own genetic screening programs. The Party also initiated health education outreach and disseminated information about the disease to black communities via the *Black Panther* and other media outlets, pamphlets, and public events. In this process, medical jargon about sickling was translated into terms comprehensible to a general audience. It was also translated into political analysis. Framed in a social health perspective, the Party explanation for the disease's persistence emphasized the history of racial slavery, contemporary racism, and the inadequacies of profit-driven healthcare.

With its clinic network and the sickle cell anemia initiative, the Party worked to ensure the health of black communities by providing needed services. In another initiative, described in chapter 5, Newton led the Party and a coalition of activists to shield the impoverished, the incarcerated, and otherwise vulnerable populations from becoming biomedical research subjects. In 1972 and 1973 Newton, working with the progressive attorney Fred J. Hiestand and allied activists drawn from the civil rights, women's, and labor movements, successfully challenged the establishment of the proposed Center for the Study and Reduction of Violence at the University of California at Los Angeles. The center was planned with a multidisciplinary slate of research programs that were variously dedicated to investigating the origins of violent behavior, including a highly controversial project that hypothesized individual diseased brains as the source of violence and proposed invasive surgery as a method of behavior modification. This chapter describes the Party's manifold arguments against the center, particularly its opposition to the biologization of violence that it believed would inevitably result from research linking behavior with race and disease. In keeping with its social health perspective, the Panthers articulated an alternative etiology of violence that privileged social causation (e.g., racial oppression, poverty, reaction to state aggression) and defined violence as a social phenomenon rather than a biomedical one.

In the conclusion, I summarize the scope of the Party's activism and consider its implications for how we historicize and theorize health inequality. The Party attended to how poor black communities were both underserved by and overexposed to the medical system. Accordingly, its health politics displayed two interrelated emphases: demands for healthcare access and for emancipation from "medical apartheid."[67] The Panthers and their allies endeavored to remedy the lack of access to medical services for members of marginalized groups by supplying basic preventive care at its free clinics. The Party additionally sought to shield these same communities from the excesses of biomedical power, such as the clinical research and medical experimentation described in recent poignant books by Rebecca Skloot and Harriet Washington.[68] With its initiatives and interventions, the Party endeavored to provide a check on the healthcare state, protecting poor and black communities from neglect owing to a lack of access to healthcare services and from potential abuse from exposure to biomedical power. Importantly, vocal as they were in bringing attention to the potential for discrimination and abuse in medicine, the Panthers' own foray into providing healthcare and health advocacy reveals that the group, while skeptical of mainstream medicine, was not *anti*medicine. The activists appreciated that biomedicine was necessary and could be put to useful purposes if it was loosed from market imperatives and carried out by trusted experts.

The Party enacted a calculated *politics of health and race* in which theories of human difference were strategically jettisoned *and* espoused toward select ideological ends. In some instances, the Panthers strategically deployed scientific claims about African Americans and black bodies to support their larger ideological aims. For example, with its sickle cell anemia campaign, the Party repurposed evolutionary theory to argue that this genetic disease was an embodied vestige of slavery and colonialism. At other times, the activists rejected biological theories about race and the "nature" of communities of color as they did in their campaign to put down UCLA's planned "violence center." Thus squarely at the center of the Panthers' health politics were claims about the scientific, medical, and political significance of blackness and racism, about how and when the concept of race could be legitimately deployed.

In this way, the Party's activities offer some possibilities for thinking anew about contemporary debates over issues of health inequality. This account of the Party offers insight into how black communities sought health rights and attempted to challenge invidious forms of biomedical racialization; it also foreshadows contemporary debates about racial health disparities and links between genetics and disease identity.

The Black Panthers' health politics suggests why today some African Americans hold a complex and critical perspective that recognizes the particular vulnerability of blacks as patients and research subjects yet still demand participation in the healthcare system. We can see the beginnings of what the sociologist Steven Epstein describes as the "inclusion-and-difference paradigm" emerging in the 1970s.[69] For Epstein, this paradigm partly reflects the outcome of women's and minorities' successful campaigns for access to biomedicine's beneficial possibilities at the expense of acquiescence to categorical (read: racial) claims about human difference. Epstein demonstrates that civil rights discourse and affirmative action rhetoric were important to this transition. The Party story detailed here, in highlighting how health rights claims of the late 1960s and early 1970s were an extension of proximate black freedom struggles, suggests how civil rights discourse (if not civil rights themselves) would and could be an essential avenue through which many African Americans were incorporated into mainstream medicine.

At the same time, by illuminating the interdependency between civil rights activism and health social movements, this book deepens our understanding of collective action more generally. The account of the Party's activism detailed here is of consequence for how we understand "health social movements" and their burgeoning in the last three decades of the twentieth century. Black health activism in this period did not necessarily augur the emergence of "new social movements" or mark the decline of more recent antiracist activism. To the contrary, it represented an evolution of the civil rights movement. Consistent with sociological scholarship on "social movement spillover," the Party's influences and collaborations suggest how civil rights and health rights claims were mutually constituted (and how health activism proliferated with a civil rights frame).[70] More particularly, health rights activism of the 1960s and 1970s was an extension of the push for equal liberties and an effort to bridge the stubborn gap that separated civil and social citizenship.

Between its founding in 1966 and its formal end in 1980 (on the occasion of the closing of its Oakland elementary school), the Party blazed a distinctive trail in U.S. political culture, linking health to its vision of the good society. Its lasting significance is perhaps most robustly manifest in Panther iconography—in the symbol of the black panther borrowed from civil rights activists in Lowndes County, Alabama; in Minister of Culture Emory Douglas's idiosyncratic political art; in the graphic identity the organization established with its newspaper; and the many photographs that captured the countenance and posture of its fresh-faced yet knowing leaders. Although the Panthers' politics of health and race is a seemingly more ephemeral legacy, it endures in the commitment of health activists today, both former Party members and those inspired by them; in the persistence of community-based health-care in the face of medical inequality; and the idealism that a right to health might be assured.

AFRICAN AMERICAN RESPONSES
TO MEDICAL DISCRIMINATION BEFORE 1966

I n 1962 the National Association for the Advancement of Colored
People, the leading and largest civil rights organization of the twentieth century, filed suit on behalf of a group of African American
medical professionals and their patients in opposition to "separate but
equal" medical facilities, in hopes of toppling the edifice of racism,
improving healthcare for blacks, and according a modicum of dignity
to those most likely to treat them. A centerpiece of the "medical civil
rights movement,"[1] this initiative was spearheaded by the NAACP
Legal Defense and Education Fund and two members of the faculty of
the Howard University Medical School, the physicians Paul Cornely
and W. Montague Cobb. Cobb was, at this time, head of the NAACP's
National Health Committee and a member of its board of directors.
Editor as well of the *Journal of the National Medical Association (JNMA)*,
the periodical of the professional organization for African American
physicians, Cobb used that publication as his bully pulpit, driving
home his argument that black doctors should not acquiesce to medical Jim Crow.[2] Encouraged by Cobb's intrepid editorials, and the recent
Brown v. Board of Education of Topeka, Kansas Supreme Court decision
that outlawed separate-but-equal public schools, the plaintiffs, a group
of black doctors, dentists, and patients in Greensboro, North Carolina,
launched a successful challenge to segregation in state-funded medical
institutions.[3] The resulting *Simkins v. Moses H. Cone Memorial Hospital*

decision handed down in 1963 by the U.S. Court of Appeals for the Fourth Circuit (and later upheld by the U.S. Supreme Court), outlawed the practice of segregating hospital staff and wards by race in all facilities receiving public monies.[4] Although the *Simkins* medical desegregation case is less well-known than *Brown v. Board*, it is a reminder that health activism was intrinsic to the long civil rights movement, despite the fact that the topic is often marginal to histories of the black freedom struggle.[5]

In this chapter, I mine some of this little-known yet extensive history of African American health-focused activism as necessary context for understanding the Black Panthers' health politics.[6] While the battles in which the Party was engaged were specific to its time and ideological commitments, they were also in keeping with how black Americans had, for generations, responded to the life-or-death stakes of racialized health inequality. This chapter surveys signal moments of the long civil rights movement and excavates from within this arc of protest what might be termed the "long medical civil rights movement," a parallel tradition that took health as its focus. Mobilized in response to the distinctly hazardous risks posed by segregated medical facilities, professions, societies, and schools; deficient or nonexistent healthcare services; medical maltreatment; and scientific racism, activism challenges to medical discrimination have been an important focal point for African American protest efforts and organizations. The Panthers were heirs to health activism that directly reflected tactics drawn from this tradition. Its health politics, which combined attention to practical needs with a reframing of the definition and stakes of black well-being, were deep-rooted in African Americans' prior responses to health inequality, including principally the following: *institution building, integrationism* (or inclusion), and the *"politics of knowledge."*[7]

Institution building refers to the establishment of parallel facilities, alternative health initiatives, and autonomous organizations to compensate for a paucity of accessible healthcare options. As the historian of medicine David McBride describes, the black experience in the United States has been punctuated by epidemics, including tuberculosis and cholera owing not only to disease agents but also to poverty, healthcare inequality, and racial segregation.[8] In each case, the human, scientific, and capital resources allocated by public health agencies to curb these epidemics were often insufficient. In the early twentieth century, philanthropic organizations such as the Julius Rosenwald Fund helped fill this void—if only to protect white communities from the supposed scourge of black contagion. These efforts notwithstanding, adequate healthcare accommodations and services for blacks remained severely lacking throughout the twentieth century.[9] African Americans founded hospitals in underserved black communities, inaugurated public health initiatives, and established schools to train black medical professionals.[10] Given the long shadow of and neglect cast for decades over African American well-being, reformers and activists unsurprisingly worked to establish alternative avenues for delivering healthcare services and health education to black communities.

The desegregation of the healthcare system and the medical profession was a central aim of African American health activism. Integrationism was the organizing principle of black health advocates for much of the twentieth century and a second important tactic. This position was ardently endorsed in the writings and speeches of W. E. B. Du Bois and other leading black thinkers who insisted on blacks' right to full inclusion and participation in U.S. society—including its healthcare institutions. Health integrationists aimed to desegregate medical institutions, including professional associations, hospitals and clinics, and schools and training programs. They pushed for comparable and shared facilities and services for black and white medical practitioners and patients. They believed that African Americans' full inclusion in the healthcare state offered the best hope for reducing rates of mortality and morbidity in black communities. These health activists used the legal system to force open the doors of hospitals to black patients and challenged the medical establishment gatekeepers who placed a "color line" on the possibility of professional development for black doctors, nurses, and other medical workers. More idealistically, this tactic pushed U.S. society to live up to its egalitarian claims in the domain of health.

A third tack taken by black health activists was "the politics of knowledge."[11] Understanding that the creation of knowledge about black bodies in medicine was often an ideologically charged process, health advocates also deployed the politics of knowledge, the pursuit of intellectual projects, and conceptual interventions that in varying degrees challenged medical authority and disrupted biomedical racialization. Activists reinterpreted scientific findings, conducted independent research programs, and employed social scientific analysis to demonstrate that racism, not rationality, was at the root of scientific claims about the alleged inherent inferiority of African Americans.[12] Those using a politics

of knowledge approach often worked to forge connections between biological, social, and political spheres of life in response to the scientific
determinism of some biomedical theories.[13] This tactic opened the way
for black well-being to be assessed in the context of issues of social justice and racial equality—a course that was reflected in the Party's health
politics and its social health perspective.[14]

The use and significance of the tactics of institution building, integrationism, and the politics of knowledge in the African American
health activism tradition are elaborated below. To some degree, the Black
Panthers made use of all of them. They created alternative spaces for the
healing and medical training of blacks. They demanded inclusion and
racial equality in medicine. And they posed epistemological challenges
to biomedical claims about race.

Institution Building

African American activists' responses to the dynamics of racism in the
health professions and in medical institutions took many forms partly
because the health needs of black communities were often so great.
McBride notes that the abominable health status of blacks underwent
"scant change" in the many decades from "the late slavery era to the
start of the Great Depression."[15] "Excess black mortality and morbidity" remained constant even in "periods when medical care technology
and political integration, or both, [were] advancing," McBride continues.[16] Thus, even as social conditions gradually improved for African
Americans, their health status remained excessively compromised compared with whites.

In the face of epidemics and other health crises that disproportionately affected them, black communities had little choice but to
provide their own solutions to what ailed them. Grassroots efforts to
develop healthcare facilities, public health education, and educational
institutions—frequently collaborations between communities and medical professionals—were one solution. Institution building also entailed
disseminating health education to black communities, many of which,
owing to both tradition and racial exclusion, had little experience with,
or faith in, mainstream public health systems. Because of the wide impact that forms of medical segregation had on African American populations, their response was similarly extensive; health activists not only
aimed to increase black communities' access to healthcare services but,

in some instances, also provided otherwise scarce training and employment opportunities for black health professionals.

Black communities played crucial roles in institution building: although physicians and race leaders often served as figureheads and visionaries, efforts to provide healthcare services were often funded and administered by dedicated laypeople working to improve the welfare of their communities. In addition, activists established public health campaigns to provide instruction on such issues as sanitation and hygiene and to disseminate information central to eradicating diseases that disproportionately plagued black communities.

Some alternative institutions were established through the collaborative efforts of black doctors and nurses. Yet for the most part, this institution building could not depend on black professionals solely because, for much of the twentieth century, there were too few of them. Accordingly, laypeople—including club women, community organizers, and churchgoers—played a crucial role in devising ways to stretch their communities' professional resources and in confronting health inequality. Through donations of time and labor, black health activists established healthcare institutions and educational campaigns. In particular, these efforts were often organized by women working through both sacred and secular institutions such as social clubs.[17] Just as in the black protest tradition in the American South in which the "men led but women organized,"[18] these institution-building activities often had a gendered division of labor.[19] This was especially true of Progressive Era black health activism, during which the caring burden landed on black middle-class women committed to improving community health, and who filtered this concern through the prevailing imperatives to nurture and uplift the race, alleviate poverty, and promote high moral standards.[20]

Progressive Era Institution Building:
Provident Hospital and Booker T. Washington

The labors of black women health activists, for example, were foundational to the creation of Provident Hospital and Nurses' Training School in Chicago at the initiative of Daniel Hale Williams. Williams, a cofounder of the National Medical Association (NMA)—the African American physician's association formed partly in reaction to the segregated practices of the American Medical Association—was committed to improving the health of black communities and the working conditions of black medical professionals. Fueled partly by his aspiration to develop a nursing program for black women, Williams opened Provident in 1881 in a modest, converted two-story home that accommodated a dozen beds.[21]

The establishment of Provident owed in some measure to financial support from both black donors and white philanthropists.[22] Although some African Americans who contributed were wealthy, most donated small monetary contributions and labor. Provident's women's auxiliary board volunteers organized social events, the proceeds of which went to the hospital's efforts. The board expanded the women's existing fundraising programs and launched a public health campaign to reduce black infant mortality and improve the health of black children. The women's auxiliary provided monies to purchase much-needed supplies and equipment. Members of the surrounding community donated provisions and furnishings from their homes, including food, furniture, and linens.[23] The collective effort required to establish Provident as an institutional alternative to medical Jim Crow exemplified how black communities—professionals and laypersons, men and women, rich and poor—together responded to the dearth of medical care providers and adequate health facilities in their communities and otherwise negotiated the discriminatory practices of the mainstream health establishment.

In March 1915, two decades after the founding of Provident Hospital, Tuskegee Institute's founder and principal Booker T. Washington initiated National Negro Health Week.[24] Although by this time Tuskegee had already constructed its own icon of black health self-help by establishing Tuskegee Hospital and Nurses' Training School in 1892, National Negro Health Week was a more ambitious endeavor. With this initiative, Washington and those who took up the health activist mantle after his death in the fall of 1915 inspired health consciousness in black Americans, built a national infrastructure of health education, and coordinated local initiatives into a large-scale, nationwide campaign.

Washington, who founded Tuskegee Institute in 1881 and by the turn of the century had established it as the center of black American life, had long been concerned with (and had long connected) issues of health and hygiene. Washington developed a preoccupation with these issues as a young man working for the wife of the local coal mine owner. He described the training in cleanliness and orderliness he received as being as "valuable" to him as his later scholarly education.[25] Perhaps as a result, he secured a place as a student at the Hampton Institute—with no tuition because he was unable to pay—by impressing a college administrator with his ability to wash and tidy a room.[26] Washington's distinct passion for hygiene was later articulated in the ground rules and institutional culture at Tuskegee Institute and in the eventual founding of Tuskegee Hospital. Prospective Tuskegee students were well versed in the "gospel of the toothbrush," as the dissertation in Washington's autobiography about the importance of oral hygiene was known.[27] Some of his attention to hygiene no doubt stemmed from the fact that such matters were a characteristic concern of the Progressive Era, as reflected in the parallel development and expansion of the public health sector at this time. However, Washington also linked these issues to the project of black uplift more generally.[28]

The seed for National Negro Health Week was planted after Washington observed the thriving programs of the Negro Organization Society of Virginia, whose motto "Better Schools, Better Health, Better Homes, Better Farms" reflected a commitment to health-related uplift.[29] The organization had launched a successful sanitation and cleanup campaign among black Virginians as a bulwark against disease. In a 1914 address before the organization, Washington praised its members for "emphasizing the matter of health, the matter of cleanliness, the matter of better sanitary conditions throughout Virginia."[30] The example of the Negro Organization Society and the limited success of the health campaign persuaded Washington to take the campaign to the national level. Washington embarked on the planning of National Negro Health Week through which he hoped both to coordinate and to extend existing health activities in black communities.[31]

This visit to Virginia was also the occasion for the airing of Washington's convictions about the larger importance of health in southern racial politics. In his speech, he argued that segregation was the cause of much black disease and illness: "Wherever the Negro is segregated, it usually means that he will have poor streets, poor lighting, poor sidewalks, poor sewage, and poor sanitary conditions generally." He continued, "Segregation is not only unnecessary, but, in most cases, it is unjust."[32] Washington is most often remembered as an accommodationist for his less-than-radical approach to segregation, particularly for his famous Atlanta Compromise speech of 1895 during which he proclaimed that "in all things purely social we can be as separate as the fingers, yet one as the hand in all things essential to mutual progress."[33] However, Washington the health activist was, if not an integrationist, certainly an antisegregationist.

Perhaps more predictably, given his emphasis on vocational and industrial training, Washington contended that illness impeded the ability of blacks to be effective workers: "A weak body, a sickly body, is costly to the whole community and to the whole state [Virginia], from an economic point of view."[34] Washington also stressed (and cautioned whites about) the interdependence of black and white lives in the South. He maintained that if the health needs of blacks remained unmet, segregation could not save white communities from exposure; he cautioned that "disease draws no color line."[35]

With five hundred dollars from the white philanthropist Anson Phelps Stokes and the support of the Negro Business League, the National Urban League, and others, Washington held the inaugural National Negro Health Week in March 1915.[36] The campaign stressed the "organization of clean-up committees, special health sermons by colored ministers, health lectures by physicians and other competent persons, the thorough cleaning of premises, including dwellings, yards, outbuildings, and making sanitary springs and wells."[37] At local sites, black community leaders in education, health, and church affairs organized programs to increase public awareness of health problems and self-improvement measures for the school and home. Health week activities—including public jeremiads proclaiming the importance of health and public health exhibits—took place in sixteen states and in many major cities. The National Negro Health Week campaign gained increasing public support throughout the 1920s and 1930s, including assistance from the U.S. Public Health Service (USPHS). Indeed, one of the original health week backers at Tuskegee Institute concluded in 1929 that the health week movement had grown so much that "'it can be regarded as an institution.'"[38] In 1932 USPHS took over administering National Negro Health Week—now called the National Negro Health Movement—by establishing the Office of Negro Health Work with the encouragement and blessings of those at Tuskegee.[39] By 1950 Washington's idea had become the basis of a nationwide state-sponsored black health program.[40]

Marcus Garvey and the Black Cross Nurses of the UNIA
Institution building as a mode of health activism was also evident within the ranks of the largest African American social movement in U.S. his-

tory, the Universal Negro Improvement Association (UNIA). In this case, institution building comprised healthcare facilities and services and also an alternative corps of health professionals. Founded in 1914 in Kingston, Jamaica, the UNIA's ideological bedrock of African redemption, racial pride, and self-determination was brought to New York City by Marcus Garvey in 1916.[41] In 1918 Garvey officially incorporated the U.S. division of the UNIA in New York State. Within a year, the UNIA had become hugely popular in the United States and, at its apex in the early 1920s, claimed an international membership of several million.[42] The UNIA was envisioned as a black nation-state-in-waiting, as the infrastructure necessary to support the reassembly of the far-flung members of the African diaspora on the African continent. As such, the organization developed many symbols of nationhood, including a flag, national anthem, and a government.[43] Garvey also established a battery of paramedicals, the Black Cross Nurses (BCN), charged with caring for "the race." The establishment of the BCNs was a pragmatic necessity of Garvey's nation-building plans, as the successful relocation of the African diaspora to the Old World depended on the survival and proliferation of black people in the New World.[44]

In August 1920 Garvey assembled a historical, month-long gathering of over twenty-five thousand national and international members of the UNIA, the First International Conference of the Negro Peoples of the World, which culminated in the formulation of the "Declaration of Rights of the Negro Peoples of the World." This bold document began with a preamble that detailed the shared protestations of people of African descent and concluded with a bill of rights—a pronouncement of their demands. According to the preamble:

> The physicians of our race are denied the right to attend their patients while in the public hospitals of the cities and states where they reside in certain parts of the United States. . . . it is an injustice to our people and a serious impediment to the health of the race to deny competent licensed Negro physicians the right to practice in the public hospitals of the communities in which they reside, for no other reason than their race and color.[45]

Notably, and consistent with the necessary breadth of black health activism, this statement joined the problem of racial discrimination in the medical professions to the issue of racism as an "impediment" to black health to a more general concern with social justice. Members of the

UNIA agreed that the myriad causes of the lack of adequate healthcare for blacks required an urgent solution. The UNIA accordingly sought "complete control of our social institutions" through the BCNs and other endeavors.[46]

The BCN was one of several UNIA auxiliaries and the only one composed exclusively of female members.[47] The first BCN unit was formed in Philadelphia in the spring of 1920. As BCN units expanded throughout the many divisions and chapters of the UNIA, Garvey formalized their leadership structure and mandated that they be led at the national level by a nurse with at least three years of training.[48]

Although the BCNs were imagined as principle healthcare providers for the UNIA organization, they also were represented as a constructive answer to black women's limited career horizons in nursing.[49] The UNIA nursing corps was modeled after the nurses of the American Red Cross, who had served at home and abroad after national disasters and during epidemics since the late nineteenth century and who tended soldiers injured in combat in World War I.[50] Black women volunteered for service duty in the Red Cross during the Great War, but owing to Jim Crow few were called up.[51] Given the UNIA's avowed pessimism about equality for blacks in the medical professions and its leader's belief that "the only hope of eventual solution to the problem of race prejudice" would come from "independent endeavor," it was unsurprising that the organization fashioned an alternative to the Red Cross.[52] Thus the formation of an alternative health cadre, the BCNs, was an example of institution building that embodied a critique of medical Jim Crow.

Members of the BCN, like their Red Cross peers, were expected to tend to the armed forces—in this case the UNIA's own militia and the African Legion—should conflict come to pass.[53] Some BCNs had formal training as nurses or midwives; however, most "worked with practical training in first aid and nutrition."[54] (The small number of practical and registered nurses in the BCN was, of course, a function of discrimination in nursing schools, such as the practices that motivated the founding of Provident Hospital.) According to the UNIA bylaws, the BCNs were primarily charged "to attend to the sick of the Division" with which they were affiliated. In addition, the nurses were expected to "carry on a system of relief" in the face of "pestilence" or natural disasters, produce materials to "educate the public to the use of safety devices and prevention of accidents," and "instruct in sanitation for the prevention of epidemics."[55] BCNs were also responsible for "caring" duties, including tending to the homebound sick and instructing the women of the UNIA in first aid, infant care, "hygiene and domestic science," and proper nutrition and eating habits.[56] Additionally, this nurse auxiliary was at least symbolically responsible for the health of the frequently ailing Garvey and "indicated the readiness of the UNIA to come to the aid of . . . stricken [African diasporic] peoples all over the world."[57] In keeping with what the historian Tony Martin describes as Garvey's "dual tendency to score the white race for its injustice while simultaneously utilizing the language of condemnation to spur the black race on to greater self-reliance," UNIA health activism condemned the racist practices of the mainstream medical system and constructed alternatives to it.[58]

Scholars emphasize the importance of Garvey's experiment in nation building as a source of inspiration for black power politics.[59] For example, Malcolm X's parents were members of the UNIA.[60] Given that the Black Panthers were avid readers and followers of the ideas of Malcolm X, it is probable that Garvey's examples of institution building influenced the organization. More definitively, Panther health politics of the late 1960s and early 1970s was influenced by a more historically proximate model of a health activism tactic of institution building: the clinics and medical services sponsored by the Student Nonviolent Coordinating Committee (SNCC) and its close collaborator, the Medical Committee for Human Rights (MCHR).

Model Clinics: SNCC and the MCHR

Some of the most shocking photography and television footage of the civil rights revolution of the 1950s and 1960s depicted activists being hosed down, shot, attacked by dogs, and otherwise abused. Although these images brought into the open the terrible recalcitrance of the southern white power structure, they also begged the question of who would care for those wounded on the frontlines of the battle for civil rights. Could activists who risked life and limb by merely attempting to sit at the lunch counters and in the bus depots of the deep South realistically rely on local white health professionals for emergency healthcare? Would the limited number of black doctors practicing in the South, owing to decades of discrimination in the medical profession, be sufficient to heal activists taken ill during the normal course of their organizing labors or critically injured on the frontlines of the black freedom struggle?

For the strategists behind the 1964 Freedom Summer project, a landmark event of the black protest struggle, the answer to these questions was decidedly negative. Accordingly, planners sought the participation of students and medical workers alike. Organized under the umbrella of a coalition of civil rights groups—the Council of Federated Organizations—and spearheaded by SNCC, one of its member groups, the project's aim was to bring national pressure to bear on the white power structure that remained entrenched in the South. In the spring of 1964 SNCC field secretary Robert Moses and others settled on a strategy they hoped would turn the attention of elites to the plight of disenfranchised blacks in Mississippi: they called on white middle-class college students from the North to work alongside veteran activists on the frontline of the civil rights struggle during the coming summer. Planners counted on members of the northeastern establishment taking an interest in the well-being of their activist children and relatives and, as a consequence, develop more interest in racial politics.[61]

Weeks before the start of Freedom Summer, which began in June and ended in August, organizers appealed for assistance from medical professionals to provide emergency medical aid for civil rights workers in Mississippi.[62] The call went out to an interracial group of physicians, dentists, nurses, medical students, and others with medical training in New York City who since 1963 had been agitating for racial integration of the American Medical Association under the banner of the Medical Committee for Civil Rights (MCCR). The organization, which altered its name slightly in 1964 to the Medical Committee for Human Rights, sent more than one hundred volunteers to Mississippi during Freedom Summer. These MCHR volunteers would establish a rudimentary healthcare system for civil rights workers in Mississippi.[63]

Although dispatched to support the summer volunteers, medical activists were unable to ignore the impoverished conditions in which many rural Mississippians were forced to live and were distressed by the paucity of adequate healthcare services. Summer project chronicler Len Holt captured the experiences of the MCHR workers: "As these persons served, they learned. They saw and felt the interlocking chain of exploitation, poverty, discrimination, disease and human neglect."[64] Dr. David French, a leader of the MCHR, also voiced the transformation that occurred among the ranks of the medical volunteers. After journeying to Mississippi to treat civil rights workers, medical workers "found themselves suddenly in direct contact with . . . the health conditions of the Negroes living in a state of peonage in the rural areas of Mississippi. As the summer wore on . . . they desired to work together in a concerted effort to do some lasting good, not only in Mississippi but also in other areas of the deep South."[65]

In response, the MCHR expanded its purview from medical care for volunteers to healthcare services for local populations. Toward this end, the MCHR established health clinics.[66] For example, Dr. Alvin Poussaint, an African American psychiatrist and the southern field director of the MCHR, stayed behind in Holmes County, Mississippi, after Freedom Summer ended, to establish and manage a clinic that would provide medical care for poor local residents and serve as "a focal point for the dissemination of health education" to neighboring counties.[67] Other MCHR members who remained in the South past August 1964 introduced health initiatives that included an ambitious concept for a group health plan, public health education, the empowerment of laypeople through basic training in medical techniques, agitation for more and better medical professional schools in the South, research into the health needs of local communities, and inquiries into the state provisions that were supposed to be allotted to them.[68]

Many Freedom Summer volunteers returned from the trenches of rural Mississippi politically radicalized.[69] This was also true of the medical workers. By 1965 the MCHR had expanded from the original New York City core group to chapters in Los Angeles; Pittsburgh; New Haven; Washington, D.C.; Boston; Detroit; Chicago; and other major cities.[70] Some members of the MCHR returned to the Midwest, West, and Northeast committed to making changes in the healthcare system in their home cities. Concomitantly, veteran civil rights activists encouraged their temporary cotravelers in the summer project to open their eyes to racial discrimination in their own communities and work to effect change in their own backyards.[71] For example, at the first national convention of the MCHR at Howard University in April 1965, SNCC executive secretary James Foreman entreated group members to turn their attention to the needs of cities.[72] A good number of health activists heeded Foreman's suggestion. In the mid-1960s the MCHR developed a national health activist platform the signal component of which was the establishment of low-cost and no-cost health clinics.[73] This extended institution building, greatly inspired by experiences accumulated during SNCC's Freedom Summer, occupied a major portion of the MCHR agenda. Health radicals who participated in the SNCC–MCHR collaboration, such as the physicians Quentin Young and Terry Kupers, went on to work on Black Panther health projects, including its free medical clinics.

Integrationism

The Medical Civil Rights Movement

The integrationist, or inclusion, approach of black health activists was exemplified by the medical civil rights movement, described by the historian Herbert Morais as centrally involving a collaboration between the NAACP and the National Medical Association—the foremost professional organization for black physicians and dentists.[74] The NAACP was founded in 1909 and was largely composed of black professionals, including physicians and dentists, at the local and national levels. The NMA was founded in 1895 to counter the exclusion of African Americans from medical societies and came to be regarded as the authority on matters relating to African American medical professionals and often on black healthcare in general. The NMA's founding purpose was described by one of its leaders as a response to racial inequality: "Conceived in no spirit of racial exclusiveness, fostering no ethnic antagonisms, but born of the exigencies of the American environment, the National Medical Association has for its object the banding together for mutual co-operation and helpfulness, the men and women of African descent who are legally and honorably engaged in the practice of the cognate professions of Medicine, Surgery, Pharmacy and Dentistry."[75]

The professional activists of the medical civil rights movement were, for the most part, opposed to any program in which racially distinct accommodations or treatment was sanctioned, either tacitly or explicitly, and insisted that black health be a perennial matter of national concern rather than a symbolic issue once a year. Others remained resigned to separate-but-equal healthcare until after World War II, at which time there was a groundswell of demand for integration in all aspects of the healthcare sector.[76] By the late 1940s many black leaders saw full medical integration as the only viable solution for racial advancement and began to call for the demise of Washington's National Negro Health movement.[77]

In large measure, the partnership between the NMA and the NAACP that resulted in the medical civil rights movement was embodied in the person and political thinking of W. Montague Cobb.[78] Cobb transformed an unwieldy professional association into a political weapon. He preached the gospel of medical equality in his regular column "The Integration Battlefront," which he instituted in the first year of his two-decade stint as editor. In this column Cobb famously asserted that separate medical programs "no matter how good do not compensate for [the] failure of integration. The ghetto no matter how beautiful is still a ghetto."[79] Also, in the late 1940s, Cobb became the chair of the National Health Committee of the NAACP and, in 1950, joined its board of directors.

The NAACP and NMA operationalized integrationism as a black health activist tactic in two principal ways: first, with pronouncements and gatherings aimed at garnering public support against segregation in medical employment and hospitalization, and second, with litigation, the modus operandi of the civil rights movement at this time. In June 1953 Cobb announced the beginning of the medical civil rights movement at an NAACP annual conference. He described the campaign, which the NMA had also approved, as being aimed at "eliminat[ing] hospital discrimination in the United States" and framed it as the next "logical step in [the NAACP's] program to make the benefits and responsibilities of full citizenship available to all Americans."[80] He explained that the primary focus of attack was the Hospital Survey and Construction Act of 1946—also known as the Hill-Burton Act—which included provisions for federal funding for new hospital construction, the rebuilding and modernizing of the U.S. hospital system, and a clause that sanctioned separate health facilities for blacks.[81] In the segregated South, the act effectively bankrolled a separate-but-far-from-equal health infrastructure. Cobb and his allies protested that federal government acquiescence to the codified discrimination of the Hill-Burton Act amounted to implicit federal approval of segregation.

While the NAACP and the NMA focused on desegregating health facilities, they also had their eyes on prizes bigger than hospital construction. The activists sought to change the very culture of medicine. Cobb argued that "the disruption of the sacred doctor–patient relationship effected when a Negro physician must leave his patient at a hospital door because he cannot be a member of the staff, must be prevented. The subtle economic exploitation of the Negro staff by white physicians and institutions through racial bars in hospitals must be brought to an end."[82] The struggle over the separate-but-equal clause in the Hill-Burton Act was therefore both juridical and symbolic; it was hoped that its defeat would have ripple effects in other segments of the health sector, including improved health outcome, considerate treatment of black patients and doctors alike, and fully integrated medical societies and hospitals.

Medical civil rights strategists also took a less conventional path toward complete desegregation in hospitalization and health with the Imhotep National Conference on Hospital Integration.[83] Imhotep was an organization formed by members of the NMA, the NAACP, and the Medico-Chirurgical Society of Washington, D.C.—a local medical society composed of African American physicians of which Cobb was a leading member—with the shared goals of "the enactment of laws to render segregated practices illegal; the filing of court suits to end the use of public funds for the construction and/or maintenance of segregated projects; and the use of persuasion on the administrative front to achieve the elimination of discriminatory patterns."[84] Over several years, the group organized chapters in other parts of the country, each charged with keeping the cause of hospital desegregation alive in their local media and with their local political representatives.[85]

In 1956 Cobb and Cornely, his colleague from the public health school at Howard University, planned the group's first national conference. The conveners hoped to gather a critical mass of professionals, activists, and public officials committed to working toward healthcare integration to bring their respective regional experiences to bear on the tactics of the desegregation campaign. The conference continued annually for seven years, though support for it declined steadily after the first gathering. However, as the historian David Barton Smith notes, the conference, despite its attendance, was not without influence on the "integration battlefront": for the duration of its existence, Smith argues, the Imhotep meeting kept the idea of hospital integration in national circulation. Furthermore, in its final years, it succeeded in attracting the support and attention of President John F. Kennedy, who sent a telegram to Cobb on the eve of the sixth annual conference to declare his support of its aims, as well as that of other politicians such as New York Senator Jacob Javits and Michigan Representative John Dingell, who introduced a bill to eliminate the discriminatory section of the Hill-Burton Act in this same year.[86] In 1964 President Lyndon B. Johnson renewed an amended Hill-Burton Act that included an antidiscrimination clause. Cobb, in his capacity as president of the NMA, was at the president's side when the modified act was signed.[87]

Simkins v. Cone

The change in the Hill-Burton Act was also the result of successful litigation by the medical civil rights movement. The NAACP Legal Defense Fund, which had already begun building a series of lower-court rulings that culminated in the *Brown v. Board* decision, served as counsel in medical civil rights movement lawsuits, arguing the separate-but-equal clause of the Hill-Burton Act was in conflict with the Fifth and Fourteenth Amendments and was thus unconstitutional. The most important of these cases, *Simkins v. Cone Memorial Hospital*, was brought before a lower court in Greensboro, North Carolina, by the dentist George Simkins, who had a patient with an abscessed tooth that required immediate medical attention.[88] Simkins was unable to get care for this patient at the filled-to-capacity local black hospital or at any of the hospitals primarily serving whites in Greensboro.

Frustrated by this encounter, he contacted the NAACP, which took the case; other local black physicians and dentists signed on as plaintiffs. The plaintiffs' attorney argued that because Cone Memorial and another local facility, Long Hospital, had been built or renovated with Hill-Burton funds, their policies were subject to the equal protection mandates of the U.S. Constitution. Despite the support of U.S. Attorney General Robert Kennedy, who filed an amicus brief on behalf of the plaintiffs, a lower court ruled against them in 1962. When the Fourth Circuit Court in Virginia heard the case on appeal, the lower court decision was reversed, and the separate-but-equal clause of Hill-Burton used to bolster discrimination at Walker and Long Hospitals was declared unconstitutional. In a final appeal, in March 1964, the U.S. Supreme Court refused to hear the case, leaving the circuit-court ruling in place.

A milestone in the integrationist health activist strategy, the *Simkins* case, which unfolded in parallel with political debate on Capitol Hill over federal civil rights legislation, served as a symbolic tool for legislators and government officials seeking public and political support for laws to aid the goal of integration. In testimony before a congressional subcommittee assigned to consider the matter, Secretary of Health, Education, and Welfare Anthony Celebrezze mentioned that the plaintiffs' cause had been supported by the Kennedy administration and that the case was soon to be heard on appeal. In later supporting materials, the attorney general's office noted that the lower-court decision in *Simkins* had been reversed and argued that this ruling gave support to national legislation to eliminate all separate-but-equal provisions in federally funded programs and institutions. In March 1964, on the Senate floor, Senator Javits opined that the U.S. Supreme Court decision to let the Fourth Circuit Court decision stand lent further credence to ending federally backed segregation embodied in Title VI of the Civil Rights Act of 1964, which was signed into law later that year. Therefore *Simkins* was as important to the cause of integration in the healthcare sector as *Brown v. Board* was for civil rights more generally and also a landmark contribution to U.S. health activism.

Whites-only professional associations, however, proved much more resistant to the course of medical inclusion. Through the 1960s, medical societies of physicians, dentists, and nurses were private entities that did not receive public funding and, therefore, could not be bound by the courts to integrate their memberships. Thus health activists utilized politicking and moral persuasion to integrate these professional organizations. To some degree, the benefit of these efforts flowed to minority health professionals who, in achieving integration, also improved their educational opportunities, professional prestige, and wages. However, this tactic also promised to potentially curb the mortality and morbidity rates of African Americans because these African American physicians, dentists, nurses, and others were often the first responders to the health needs of black communities.

Indicative of the racial discrimination embedded in professional practices and challenged by health activists were struggles to integrate two of the most important organizations for medical professionals, the American Medical Association (AMA) and the American Nurses Association (ANA).[89] Both the AMA and ANA prohibited individual membership for much of their early history. This requirement was exploited in the early twentieth century by feeder medical societies on the local level in the Jim Crow South that used this stipulation to justify excluding black health professionals.[90] That is, a health worker had to join a local society in order to be able to join the AMA; direct individual membership in the AMA was not permitted.[91] This professional discrimination had serious repercussions for black doctors and nurses, who were often required to be members of the national organizations in order to be granted hospital privileges and who needed these memberships for professional development opportunities.[92]

While the ANA gradually desegregated in the early twentieth century, it was not until the late 1960s that the AMA leadership began to work proactively with local chapters to move toward full integration of the organization. Immediately prior to this decision, the AMA had been subject to increased lobbying from the NMA, the NAACP, and the MCHR. Although the AMA leadership was willing to pass resolutions stating that the body did not discriminate, and did so well into the 1960s, it demurred when asked to take a hard line against segregation and refused to penalize or sanction local affiliates that excluded black doctors. In response, in early June 1963, the MCCR demanded that the AMA be more forthright in its opposition to its affiliate members' exclusionary practices and more active in intervening in other spheres of the healthcare field in which discrimination was still prevalent.[93] Finding the AMA response to their requests inadequate, MCCR members—including black and white physicians and other medical workers—picketed the AMA's 1963 annual meeting. They also protested at the AMA headquarters in Chicago some weeks after the convention, this time collaborating with the NAACP, which was holding its annual meeting in that city and was engaged in its own medical civil rights campaign begun years earlier.[94] In 1965 with the AMA still segregated, two hundred protestors from the MCHR turned out at the annual AMA meeting in New York City; twice as many MCCR members and their allies protested at the AMA 1966 meeting held in Chicago. In 1966 the AMA agreed to work more closely with its southern affiliates to ensure that constituent societies adhered to the antisegregation rules of the AMA charter. Over time, the social climate changed so that it was untenable for even the most recalcitrant local medical associations to bar black physicians and other doctors.[95]

The ANA took a less gradualist approach to integrating its ranks, and much of the motivation to do so more quickly than the AMA came from the leadership of black women at the helm of the National Association for Colored Graduate Nurses (NACGN). In the first decade of the twentieth century, leaders in the nursing profession attempted to standardize the training and licensing of nurses. As the historian of nursing Darlene Clark Hine argues, however, these admirable goals had differential results: "The professionalization process raised the overall status of nursing, but in so doing it created a number of problems for black practitioners. . . . [African American nurses] quickly discovered that the application of these new laws and requirements erected additional barriers to their own professional advance."[96]

In 1908 African American nurses formed an alternative professional organization, the NACGN, in response to their marginalization by the ANA.[97] Hine argues that NACGN members sought to "achieve a modicum of status as professionals" and to gain "authority for their own personal and professional advance."[98] From 1934 until the late 1940s, Mabel Staupers and Estelle Riddle (NACGN executive secretary and president, respectively) "invest[ed] themselves totally in the quest for . . . elusive professional integration,"[99] and in the process improved professional status and working conditions for black nurses.

Beginning in the early 1940s, the ANA and the NACGN worked toward removing the barriers in nursing that made distinct professional bodies organized along racial lines necessary. Their cause was aided somewhat by the ratification of the Bolton Bill, which included provisions for the federal funding of nurse training beginning in 1943 and included an antidiscrimination clause: no hospital or school receiving Bolton funding could refuse to admit black nurses.[100] In addition, the profession had taken small steps toward integration of the nursing corps employed in World War II. At its 1948 national convention, the ANA approved a plan to short-circuit the discriminatory practices of southern nursing societies.[101] By 1951, and more than a decade before the AMA took significant strides toward full integration, the NACGN voted to disband and publicly announced that American nursing was desegregated and that a separate organization was no longer necessary.[102] (In a reversal of sorts in 1971, however, African American members of the ANA established the National Black Nurses' Association to continue the work of securing the professional status of African American nurses in the postintegrationist era and in a new climate of racial and gender marginalization.)[103]

The Politics of Knowledge

The third tactic utilized by black health activists was the politics of knowledge. This approach had two emphases: the first is *internal to scientific knowledge* and concerns health activists' challenges to inaccurate or biased biomedical theories about black bodies. The second is *extrascientific* and involves activists' recognition that the knowledge claims of biomedicine are often related to discrimination outside the healthcare sector. Primarily—though not exclusively—intellectuals and scientists, these early-twentieth-century health advocates challenged theories of black biological inferiority in medicine. The politics of knowledge was a necessary complement to health activists' tactics of institution building and integrationism because it addressed some of the ideological under-pinnings of medical discrimination.

Historically, disease has been linked to racial hierarchization.[104] A predominant idea linking race (blackness) and disease was "socio-medical racialism."[105] A hybrid of social Darwinism and popular or "folk" understandings of race, supported by scientific authority, these theories held that blacks had a biological distinctiveness that made them more susceptible to disease.[106] Sociomedical racialism was reinforced by a "crescendo of statistics" collected by state agencies during the first two decades of the twentieth century and gave credence to the notion that "blacks posed a major public health menace."[107] Two issues were at stake in this theory: it affected not only the possibility of securing ade-quate healthcare for blacks but also the use of biomedical knowledge to legitimatize their second-class social status.

In the early twentieth century, most black physicians were well aware that they were almost powerless against racialism. They considered the racial susceptibility debate to be a waste of time and focused their ef-forts on the urgent and practical issue of improving their communities' health using the strategies of institution building and integrationism.[108] Yet, these reservations notwithstanding, others believed that challenging sociomedical racialism on its own terms might have the pragmatic bene-fits of combating claims used to justify racist practices in the healthcare sector and beyond it. As McBride describes, the first few decades of the twentieth century "witnessed the rise of a small cadre of black medi-cal specialists who were important contributors to the theoretical and clinical movement against medical racialism" and who "lashed out at the idea of black constitutional inferiority."[109] These doctors, social scientists, and reformers—professionals with both the knowledge and credentials to challenge the racialism in mainstream medicine—mounted a cam-paign of critique and counterinterpretation—a politics of knowledge—in specialist journals, the press, and civil rights–oriented publications.[110]

Recontextualization

The politics of knowledge was a pillar of black health activism; as a re-sponse to sociomedical racialism, this tactic often took the specific form of "recontextualization." In an essay titled "Appropriating the Idioms of Science: The Rejection of Scientific Racism," Nancy Stepan and Sander Gilman discuss how Jewish and African American intellectual activists challenged racial science. They identify recontextualization as an important political device toward this end.[111] Recontextualization refers to the creation of a "scientific counterdiscourse" using positivist reasoning to "prove that the supposed factual data upon which the stereotypes of racial inferiority were based were wrong," to generate "new 'facts,'" or to scrutinize the standard "explanation of the facts."[112] The intellectual challenges advanced by the Howard University dean and mathematician Kelly Miller and the pathbreaking sociologist W. E. B. Du Bois—in response to biased research on black mortality rates—exemplified this approach.

In 1896 Frederick L. Hoffman, an autodidact statistician, published *Race Traits and Tendencies in the American Negro,* a study commissioned by the Prudential Insurance Company. In this study, characterized by the historian Beatrix Hoffman (no relation) as the "most influential scientific racist tract of its time," claimed that mortality rates of American blacks were higher than those of whites owing to their racially weak biological inheritance and the ill-effects of emancipation (for which blacks were presumably unprepared).[113] She argues that this report "appealed to an American insurance industry that sought to identify poor risks for life insurance."[114] Frederick Hoffman's claims legitimized discrimination in insurance for blacks who, having been constructed as susceptible to disease and death and therefore, a capricious investment, could be denied coverage or overcharged for it. Miller and Du Bois countered Hoffman's report with data and analysis that exposed both its empirical weaknesses and its barely veiled racism. Miller assembled his own statistics to demonstrate that, far from dying off, the black population was growing and that the birthrate of blacks was increasing at a greater rate than that of white Americans in some cities. Additionally, Miller reevaluated Hoffman's data comparatively and found that the high rates of tuberculosis among blacks cited by Hoffman as evidence of looming black extinction were comparable with those of white workers in Europe. Miller concluded that "high rates of disease and death were a function not of innate racial susceptibilities but of social conditions" in the United States and Europe.[115]

Du Bois's critique ran along similar lines. For his part, the sociologist exposed the incomplete nature of Hoffman's study, including contradictions in how and which data were assembled. Hoffman made claims about African Americans' supposed propensity to illness (and subsequent mortality) on the basis of records from a few cities in the

United States. At a time, in the early twentieth century, when a significant portion of the black population still lived in rural regions rather
than in cities and those living in urban settings in aggregate fared better
than Hoffman's report suggested, Du Bois declared these data as woe-
fully incomplete. Du Bois excoriated the limitations of Hoffman's work
with an instructive European analogy. He wrote:

> Of course no careful student would think of judging the death-rate
> of Germany from that of Munich, or of arguing that an increase in
> the death-rate of Paris showed an increase in the death-rate of France.
> Yet Mr. Hoffman commits very similar mistakes; he bases his ar-
> guments as to the threatened extinction of the Negro almost solely
> on city death-rates, and argues that an increase in these death-rates
> means an increase in the general Negro death-rate. Such logic would
> be erroneous, even if Mr. Hoffman proved that, following the recent
> rush of Negroes into cities, their death-rate there had increased. Even
> this point, however, the author assumes on insufficient proof.[116]

Du Bois also confronted the arbitrariness of the American racial
categories. The investigation of black well-being to which he contributed
and that he also edited, *The Health and Physique of the Negro American*,
was another example of recontextualization deployed as a politics of
knowledge. Published in 1906, it was the eleventh part of an eighteen-
volume series of proceedings from conferences convened by Du Bois at
Atlanta University on various aspects of African American life, including poverty, employment, entrepreneurship, religion, education, and
class. *Health and Physique* was among the first sociological studies of
black health and of African American life, more generally.[117] In the preface to the volume, Du Bois assembled theoretical, craniometrical, and
sociological data to calibrate the health status and physical condition of
American blacks. Before examining the quantity and quality of black
doctors, pharmacists, and healthcare and training facilities, Du Bois
exhaustively deconstructed prevailing social scientific—predominantly
anthropological—theories of race and biological fitness. These were
not simply abstract theories but models of difference that Du Bois felt
had significant bearing on both the corporeal and social well-being of
African Americans. In his words, the study took up the issue of "the
physical condition of Negroes, but enlarge[d] the inquiry beyond the
mere matter of mortality."[118] Du Bois showed that processes of racialization were explicitly linked to health and medicine in this period and

also the degree to which the stakes of the politics of knowledge were more than physical fitness. "Health" signified both physical and social well-being and served as a site for his antiracist politics.

In *Health and Physique* several interpretive interventions were made. First, Du Bois outlined major conceptualizations of race, theories of racial hierarchy, and the biometric techniques that undergirded some of these. In rebuttal, he presented his own methodologically similar studies of one thousand students at the Hampton Institute, a historically black college in southern Virginia.[119] Armed with this data (taken from a sample purposely larger than any past surveys in which the authors claimed to provide evidence of black biological inferiority), Du Bois challenged racially based craniometric studies—many performed by white southern physicians, including most notably Samuel Morton, whose findings were discredited by Stephen Jay Gould in the *Mismeasure of Man*—that put forth the hypothesis that blacks were biologically inferior owing to their supposed low cranial capacity relative to that of whites.[120] Du Bois pointed out the illogic of such theories in the face of the diversity of "Negro types" resulting from generations of "race-mixing" and slavery. This history, Du Bois implied, rendered the categories of black and white arbitrary, at best. Then, stressing the importance of social variables, Du Bois contended that research that linked race and brain mass was flawed in that it took "almost no account . . . of age, stature, social class, occupation, nutrition, and cause of death; each which separately or all together affect both the weight and structure of the brain."[121]

In *Health and Physique* Du Bois (and his colleagues) also turned their attention to the pragmatics of black health, taking up the excessive rates of black morbidity and mortality. Based on a strategy similar to that used by Miller several years prior, the study revealed that the black community's most prevalent health problems were a function of poverty and social deficiencies rather than inherent racial frailty. Du Bois wrote: "The undeniable fact is, then, that in certain diseases the Negroes have a much higher rate than the whites, and especially in consumption, pneumonia and infantile disease. . . . The question is: Is this racial? . . . the difference in Philadelphia can be explained on other grounds than upon race."[122]

Du Bois and his collaborators did not so much question morbidity and mortality rates as reinterpret their significance. At this time, consumption (tuberculosis) was the most deadly epidemic facing black communities.[123] Compiling evidence from vital statistics offices, the Bureau of the Census, U.S. Army recruiting examination records, and life insurance companies, among other sources, and (like Miller) comparing these data with comparable figures among working-class whites in major U.S. cities and in Europe, the study concluded that tuberculosis "was not a racial disease but a social disease" linked to poverty, housing conditions, and working conditions.[124] In reexamining existing information on tuberculosis rates, Du Bois and his colleagues produced evidence that high rates of the epidemics among blacks were a function of the disproportionate numbers of blacks living in poverty, inhabiting substandard housing, or working jobs with high risks of exposure. Turning his attention to infant mortality and using similar methods of analysis, Du Bois concluded that the high frequency of childhood deaths in the black community "was not a Negro affair, but an index of social conditions."[125]

In addition to the strategies of reinterpretation evident in *Health and Physique*, this multifaceted study was important because the authors, through their approach to the health of American blacks, introduced many of the themes taken up in future health activist projects, including those of the Black Panther Party. They dealt with the issue of health institutions: the quantity and quality of medical facilities for African Americans; and medical training schools for black physicians, nurses, and dentists. They made healthcare access and what are now termed racial health disparities a key cause of concern, even as they questioned links between blackness as a racial category and biological inferiority. They articulated that poverty and social marginalization were the causes of black illness and implied as well that racism was a correlate of this community's compromised mortality and morbidity rates.

Across the twentieth century, African American health activists applied a panoply of strategies to improve black well-being. The use of the tactics of institution building, integrationism (or inclusion), and the politics of knowledge were vital to this undertaking. The employ of these three often overlapping interventions reflected the unique stakes of health activism for blacks for whom the domains of health and medicine had been zones of dominance and de jure exclusion, with potentially life-threatening consequences.

As subsequent chapters elaborate, the Black Panther Party's health politics reflected the tactical approaches described in this chapter. While the Panthers' activism surfaced after formal desegregation was accomplished, racial discrimination, economic inequality, and forms of de facto segregation endured. As a result, the Party's tactics reflected the influence of this prior tradition of African American health activism, even as the organization ventured in new directions. The Party deployed the politics of knowledge, for example, to recontextualize scientific and social scientific information about sickle cell anemia and genetics research. This approach, in which social explanations were often counterposed to scientific or epidemiological explanations or alternately used to make them more robust, prefigured the Panthers' social health perspective. Also central to the Party's efforts was an emphasis on demystifying biomedicine and medical expertise and the concomitant valuing and developing of black community participation. Its network of neighborhood-based health clinics exemplified institution building. Working in this vein, moreover, the Panther organization borrowed from a long history of black health politics and also bridged to the more immediate health initiatives of SNCC. Lastly, surprising for an organization that came to be characterized by its strident and audacious resistance to the status quo, the Black Panthers also sought inclusion into mainstream medicine; much like its ventures into electoral politics, the Party would at times seek to change the medical–industrial complex both from within and from without. As the next chapters describe, the Party mobilized many lines of attack to dismantle forms of medical discrimination and to foster social health for the black poor.

2

ORIGINS OF BLACK PANTHER PARTY HEALTH ACTIVISM

A s the ranks of the Black Panther organization rapidly swelled after its founding in 1966, community service became progressively central to its mission. In 1968 Party headquarters mandated that all chapters inaugurate "serve the people" programs. Within two years, attention to medical issues and the provision of healthcare played a considerable role in the Party's service endeavors. By 1970 the establishment of People's Free Medical Clinics was a chapterwide requirement. In 1972 Huey Newton and Elaine Brown revised the Party's ten-point platform and program, adding to it an explicit demand for "completely free healthcare for all black and oppressed people."[1] How did it come to pass that the Black Panther organization within six years of its founding became involved with health concerns to such an extent that its leadership amended its core principles? The previous chapter began to shed some light on this process: as would be borne out by the strategic repertoire employed in the Party's work around issues of medicine and well-being, it was heir to a legacy of African American health advocacy. From this perspective, the Panther health "turn" was an extension of the long civil rights movement rather than a strategic about-face.

Like the organization itself, Party health politics was at the same time a referendum on proximate civil rights legislation and attendant policy developments. The passage of the Civil Rights Act and the Economic Opportunity Act in 1964, and of the Voting Rights and the Social

Security Act the following year, was intended to solidify civil citizenship and extend social citizenship for vulnerable groups, including the poor, the elderly, and racial minorities. Spurred on by an efficacious overlap of antiracist activism (e.g., SNCC, NAACP, and their many allies), judicial rulings and the support of liberal politicians (most notably presidents John F. Kennedy and Lyndon B. Johnson), these laws and policy initiatives were heralded by many as marking a thoroughgoing societal transformation.

The Party soundly disagreed. It was skeptical about the possibility of social equality for oppressed groups under the conditions of capitalism. Through its activism, the organization exposed the limits of civil and social rights for the black poor in particular. Pointing to declining industrial bases, entrenched poverty, residential segregation, racially motivated "law-and-order" policing, and deficient social services in Oakland and elsewhere, Bobby Seale and Newton founded the Party to address abiding barriers to equality despite recent legislative strides. Social welfare concerns were therefore intrinsic to the organization's very formation. The Party's demand for health rights in its 1972 platform was a new articulation of a long-standing matter of concern, as the organization's ideological blueprint always included attention to social issues. As Party minister of education Ray "Masai" Hewitt asserted in 1969, the germ for the "People's Health Plan" was "always in the . . . 10-point program."[2]

Moreover, the actualization of Party health politics arose from a nexus of institutional, tactical, and ideological influences. First, Newton's and Seale's critical appraisal of both federal antipoverty programs and public higher education inspired the formation of the Party as a political and institutional alternative: the Party's founders had firsthand knowledge of community action projects intended to alleviate urban poverty and, as a result of these experiences, became sharp critics of them. As depicted by the Party, these War on Poverty programs extended the federal government's promise of the "maximum feasible participation" for local community cooperation in the administration and oversight of these initiatives while undermining this very possibility.[3] Furthermore, Newton and Seale contended, these programs failed to generate appreciable improvement in the lives of poor, black populations. The emergence of the Party also reflected the founders' frustration with campus activism. Newton and Seale rejected what they perceived as the fecklessness of the cultural nationalism that was gaining prominence among black students; this style of advocacy, the future Panthers believed, focused on cultural expression at the expense of realpolitik. The formation of the Party and indeed the successive establishment of its medical clinics, health initiatives, and other service programs was a direct rejoinder to what the activists deemed incomplete institutional and cultural approaches to the betterment of black life.

Second, while the Party had been primed from the beginning to be a vehicle of community service, its concentration on this focus owed also to political exigencies that prompted a shift in the group's tactics. Specifically, the incarceration of Newton after his arrest for the attempted murder of a police officer in 1967, and other Panther members' often fatal encounters with law enforcement, decimated the group and threatened to erode community support for the organization. In response, the Party reoriented the emphasis of the two issues that defined it—protecting local communities through armed resistance to police harassment and protecting local communities by providing social services. In bringing health-based activism and other social welfare programs to the fore of its mission, the Party leadership was making a strategic calculation to literally and figuratively stay alive. As former Party chairwoman Brown reiterated in her memoir, *A Taste of Power*, these "successful [serve the people] efforts spawned a *true survival program* for the Party, as confused police and FBI had to regroup, bury their old assault plans, and invent new tactics to attack us."[4]

Lastly, the Party's social welfare politics displayed the foundational influence of the political theorists Ernesto "Che" Guevara, Frantz Fanon, and Mao Zedong. The ideas of these thinkers are widely acknowledged as formative to the Party's vanguardist organizational structure and its espousal of guerrilla tactics and revolutionary violence, among other matters. Here I suggest that concepts and theories drawn from these theorists—two of whom were physicians—likewise collectively supplied the Panthers with a storehouse of health political ideology. The Party's articulation of the repressive potential of medical authority as well as the revolutionary possibilities embodied in dispensing health-care services reflected this influence.

Serving the People as a Response to Cultural Nationalism

The confluence of geographic context, historical contingency, political currents, and dynamic, charismatic leadership that conditioned the formation of the Party has been established by recent scholarship. Here I retrace some of this familiar terrain to draw out how and why the "serve the people" or "survival" programs, in general, and health activism, in particular, came to play a key role in the Panthers' endeavors. It is my contention that in revisiting the foundational narrative of the organization through the prism of its social programs, we come to see how the Party expressed citizenship claims and political demands—on behalf of blacks and the poor—through the discourse of fundamental human rights and needs. In doing so, we also gain new perspective on the intrinsic factors that primed the Panthers' social welfare activism and the extrinsic forces that pulled it toward the community service pole.

The historian Komozi Woodard maintains that like other black social movements of the late 1960s and early 1970s, the creation of the Black Panther organization was conditioned by the structural processes of migration, urbanization, and deindustrialization that exerted considerable influence on the social, economic, and political climate of postwar Oakland.[5] In the 1950s both Newton and Seale, as children, migrated from southern states with their parents, who were both in search of employment opportunities in San Francisco Bay Area defense industries and in flight from Jim Crow.[6] Newton's and Seale's families had followed a route to Northern California that was typical among blacks from the westerly southern states of Louisiana and Texas, respectively.[7] The future Panther leaders were therefore children of the Great Migration, that mass movement of blacks from the segregated South to the northern and western United States in two waves between 1910 and 1970.[8]

The generation of Newton's and Seale's parents established a foothold in Oakland's employment sector. The Party founders, however, were members of a generational cohort of young black men and women in the Bay Area for whom jobs were less readily available. In fact, by 1960, 75 percent of persons in Oakland under the age of twenty were unemployed.[9] Reacting to the presence of this large, unemployed, "rapidly growing[,] and disproportionately young migrant population," the historian Donna Murch explains, local law enforcement officials "developed a program to combat 'juvenile delinquency' that resulted in high rates of police harassment, arrest and incarceration."[10] The interrelated issues of bleak job prospects and the criminalization of Oakland youth were compounded by the decline of the manufacturing industry in the city as jobs moved to other nearby cities and suburbs.[11] The white middle class (and a significant portion of the city's tax base) followed industry and business out of Oakland, creating a "spatial mismatch" between the locations of employers and employment opportunities.[12] Thus, by the mid-1960s, impoverished, segregated, and predominantly black West Oakland was crisscrossed by highways and public transportation routes that led to more prosperous, postindustrial regions. Goods, services, and jobs literally bypassed Oakland.

Against this backdrop of recent migration and dire economic straits, the concept for the Party was incubated at two important Oakland institutions: Merritt Junior College and the federally funded North Oakland Neighborhood Anti-Poverty Center. Newton's and Seale's experiences at these sites directly shaped their future direction and their shared vision for a fledgling Panther organization. Essential as well for the development of the Party's health initiatives and other social welfare programs, the leaders' encounters at both this college and the community anti-poverty center led the activists to advance, by contrast, the Party's plans for a "revolutionary" alternative.

Drawing our attention to the fact that, like SNCC, the Party was effectively a student movement (and as discussed in chapter 1, there were also important health activist intersections between the two groups), Donna Murch's recent book, *Living for the City*, suggests that a network of students, campus groups, and political contests over school curriculum at public higher education institutions in the Bay Area undergirded youth activism in the black power era.[13] More particularly, Murch complicates the widely accepted notion that civil rights struggles of the 1950s and 1960s gave birth to black studies.[14] Although "we often think of Black Studies as the product rather than the catalyst of postwar social movements," she writes, "in the Bay Area[,] fights over curriculum and hiring in the early 1960s were integral to the emergence" of black power activism.[15]

Black student organizations channeled and catalyzed Seale's and Newton's interest in social transformation yet also frustrated it. The Party founders met in the early 1960s at Merritt Junior College, where both took classes. At the college, they became involved in a political study group as well as other black student activities. They also participated in the Afro-American Association, a Bay Area student group established in 1961 that, for a time, was an eclectic, ecumenical organization with a membership that variously championed cultural nationalism, electoral politics, and the black radical tradition, among other political perspectives. Newton also took an interest in the Merritt Black Student Union's campaign to instate black history classes and African American faculty at the college. Newton proposed an attention-grabbing rally and march to be held on the occasion of Malcolm X's birthday and at which black students would brandish weapons before an audience of invited local press and community members.[16] His peers in the union demurred. Nevertheless, the contours of the Party's distinct method of social engagement were visible.

Newton found the union to be too beholden to political moderation. The future Panthers were similarly disturbed by student acolytes of black cultural nationalism. The sharp and bitter chasm that existed in the black power era between revolutionary nationalists and cultural nationalists was evident in the bad blood between the Panthers and the US (as in "us" vs. "them") Organization. For the Party, groups like US were wrongly preoccupied with proper comportment, right mannerisms, and the adoption of a romantic notion of putatively "African" lifeways into black American culture.[17] Newton took up this issue directly:

> Cultural nationalism . . . is basically a problem of having the wrong political perspective. . . . The cultural nationalists are concerned with returning to the old African culture and thereby regaining their identity and freedom. . . . The Black Panther Party, which is a revolutionary group of black people, realizes that we have to have an identity. We have to realize our black heritage. . . . But as far as returning to the old African culture, it's unnecessary and it's not advantageous in many respects. We believe that culture itself will not liberate us. We're going to need some stronger stuff.[18]

As Newton's comments implied, the Party deemed cultural nationalism too abstracted from material reality and too apolitical to be of benefit to poor black communities.[19] Newton and Seale were also wholly dissatisfied with their peers' unwillingness to directly confront or respond to the serious issues troubling Oakland's schools and neighborhoods.[20]

The Merritt College experience nevertheless served the purpose of helping the first Panthers distill their own ideology. Newton and Seale eventually advocated direct confrontation with the forces of racial and economic oppression with a gun *and* a helping hand. They believed that social transformation could be effectuated through both approaches.

Cultural nationalists were dismissive of the Party's aspiration to serve the people and doubted the revolutionary potential of doing so. Echoing a common critical refrain about the Panthers' social welfare programs, US's leader Maulana Karenga declared that community service was "not a revolutionary act." "To set up a free clinic is no novel idea. Medicare has preceded that with much more money and much more technical organization . . . to set up a kitchen and put out food for people, the welfare does that, the bureau of public assistance."[21] What Karenga failed to appreciate was that the Panthers carved out a political niche in contradistinction to both campus-originated black cultural nationalism and state-sponsored social welfare programs.

Serving the People as a Response to the War on Poverty

The service programs were instituted as parallel alternatives to the Johnson administration's antipoverty scheme. Many African Americans shared the belief, summed up in a 1970 editorial in the *L.A. Sentinel,* that "the vast majority of Black people have yet to experience any significant change in their way of living despite the passage of civil rights legislature and the promises of anti-poverty programs." With its programs to serve the people, the Party sought to remedy the practical and ideological deficits of civil rights "progress" as it was embodied in the War on Poverty. Established in 1964 through the Economic Opportunity Act, and administered by the then new Office of Economic Opportunity, the War on Poverty was partly composed of an array of federally funded Community Action Programs (or CAPs); by 1965 these included the community health centers program, Job Corps, Head Start (a comprehensive social service program for children), and Volunteers in Service to America (or VISTA, a national service program now part of AmeriCorps).[22]

In the summer of 1966 Newton and Seale worked at a Bay Area CAP, the North Oakland Neighborhood Anti-Poverty Center.[23] At the Center, they developed a close-quarters critique of the War on Poverty. By October of that year, their ruminations had produced a name, the Black Panther Party for Self-Defense (later shortened to the Black Panther Party),[24] and a mission statement, the ten-point platform and program.[25] Newton and Seale availed themselves of the antipoverty center's resources: from this perch they formulated plans for the Black Panther organization. Its library provided the law books Newton and Seale used to educate themselves about the finer points of the California legal system. The center's office was the Party's first headquarters.

It was also at this antipoverty center that the Party's guiding principles were developed. Seale and Newton had in mind a two-pronged approach to social transformation—a practical program undergirded with an ideological one. Accordingly, Seale recalls,

> Huey divided [the ten-point platform and program] into [two sections] "What We Want" and "What We Believe." "What We Want" are the practical, specific things that we need and that should exist. At the same time we expressed philosophically, but concretely, what we believe. . . . [The platform] puts together concisely *all the physical needs and all the philosophical principles.*[26]

Newton and Seale sought to construct an organization whose commitments were more evenly divided between theory and practice, in contradistinction to cultural nationalism and, that distinct from federal antipoverty programs, would truly reflect the priorities of local communities.[27] The Party's platform and program was in point of fact a demand for full economic citizenship ("We Want Full Employment for Our People") and related social rights—those benefits guaranteed in principle by citizenship status (e.g., "We Want Land, Bread, Housing, Education, Clothing, Justice And Peace").[28]

Well after the Party officially came into being, Newton and Seale continued to instrumentally "use the poverty programs" for their own ends.[29] They recruited members at the center: Robert (Li'l Bobby) Hutton, the Party's first member, was recruited by Seale, with whom he had worked in a summer program at the center in 1966. (Hutton, who was the group's first minister of finance, was killed during a fatal shootout with Oakland police in 1968. He was eighteen years old.) Newton and Seale worked with the center through 1967. In this year, the Panther cofounders joined its advisory board and from this position successfully lobbied municipal authorities to place a streetlight at a dangerous intersection in the community.[30]

In addition to the group's leaders, several members of the rank and file had experience as either a staff member or a client of a War on Poverty project. Cleo Silvers, a Philadelphia native, was a VISTA volunteer and eventually joined a Party chapter in Manhattan's Harlem neighborhood; as a Panther, she conducted neighborhood health surveys and worked as a patient advocate. In 1968 Brown worked in an "outpost field operation" of the Office of Economic Opportunity in Los Angeles, the Watts Happening Coffee House, that she described as "a rivulet of the Johnson Administration's new-deal . . . dubbed the War on Poverty."[31] Working to change these programs from the inside out and with the conviction "that blacks now have concentrated in the cities . . . in such numbers that they can take over governments," as the *New York Times* put it, Party members Erika Huggins, William Roberts, Andrea Jones, and Herman Smith were elected as board members of a Berkeley anti-poverty program in 1972. Party members also were elected to six of eighteen seats on the West Oakland Model Cities governing board.[32]

Party chapters' interaction with federal antipoverty programs persisted for much of the organization's life. Although the activists drew on a range of resources from the CAPs and other initiatives, this was a deeply equivocal association: the serve the people or survival programs were partly modeled on the War on Poverty, and some of the antipoverty projects in many ways made the parallel Panther projects possible. However, the radicals did not merely copy the state's program, for its social welfare concern derived as well—and perhaps more centrally—from its Marxist-Leninist politics. For this reason, the activists were harsh critics of the CAPs and easily drew ideological distinctions between the Party's social welfare work and that of the federal government.

For the Panthers the two important considerations that distinguished its work from that of the state were the organization of the programs and the anticipated outcomes of them. Its ten-point platform and program demanded "the Power to Determine the Destiny of Our Black Community." Federal antipoverty programs, the Panthers complained, gave lip service to the full participation of the poor in administering these programs, but in practice, owing to ideological differences and local political struggles, constrained communities' self-empowerment.[33] As Newton explained, "I don't think black people should be fooled . . . because everyone who gets into office promises the same thing. . . . The Great Society; the New Frontier. All of these names but no real benefits."[34]

The diverse CAP initiatives shared the underlying principle that local community involvement in planning and implementing social programs was crucial to their success.[35] Indeed, Title II of the Economic Opportunity Act mandated that these programs be "developed and conducted with the maximum feasible participation of the residents of the areas."[36] Yet as Senator Daniel Patrick Moynihan wrote in 1969, debates over actualizing community control would lead to "maximum feasible misunderstanding."[37] Brown gave voice to this misunderstanding when she bitterly recalled that the CAP center she worked at in Los Angeles "was *supposed to be* a cultural center operated by and for the black residents of Watts."[38]

Soon after the War on Poverty programs were rolled out, it became apparent that some poor blacks interpreted the concept of community control differently from the federal government, local authorities, and, frequently, even middle-class blacks.[39] While the Johnson administration envisioned the management of the CAPs as a partnership between community leaders, the poor, and government administrators, many African Americans interpreted local control as social, political, and economic autonomy, or in the parlance of the black power era and the Party, as self-determination. The Party regarded the War on Poverty as a plan that would not end poverty but merely amount to control and surveillance of the poor. With its community service programs, the Party had a more ambitious, revolutionary end in mind, a process that Fred Hampton, head of the Chicago Party chapter, encapsulated in this way: "First you have free breakfasts, then you have free medical care, then you have free bus rides, and soon you have FREEDOM!"[40] The Panthers believed that serving the poor and enabling local communities to help themselves had transformative potential.

These programs were, furthermore, vehicles to enlist the community in the Party's political causes. Chief of Staff David Hilliard illustrated how the Party understood this process when he described the political effects stimulated by the "Community Pantry," also called the Angela Davis People's Free Food Program. The "food serves a double purpose, providing sustenance but also functioning as an organizing tool: people enter the office when they come by, take some leaflets, sit in on an elementary PE [political education] class, talk to cadre, and exchange ideas."[41] As such, the community service programs were, as one Oakland Panther, Carol Rucker, explained, "another tactic for revolution" alongside armed self-defense.[42]

CAP initiatives like the North Oakland Neighborhood Anti-Poverty Center, according to the historian Daniel Crowe, "unwittingly supported and trained a new generation of black radicals that included the co-founders of the Black Panther Party."[43] The Johnson administration was alarmed to discover that the resources it provided to wage the War on Poverty were being used to radicalize and organize black community activists.[44] As Moynihan explained in his analysis of the failings of the federal antipoverty campaign of the late 1960s and early 1970s, government officials did not share this view. "Washington has an entirely different, almost antithetical view of the style and function of 'community action' from that of its proponents in the field," he wrote.[45]

This battle over the boundaries of community participation at the Office of Economic Opportunity's community health centers—launched in 1965 as part of the War on Poverty—typified the "misunderstanding" between poor blacks, activists, African American elites, the state, and other stakeholders over the definition of "maximum feasible participation." The community health centers operated through federal grant monies given to medical schools and teaching hospitals that in turn organized and directed primary care and basic healthcare services.[46] Although the centers had community advisory boards and also drew staff from local areas, the historically vexed relationship between black communities, academic hospitals, medical schools, and the public health system and the scientific authority embodied in even these small-scale neighborhood institutions meant that these clinics were destined to court controversy in some quarters.

Teaching hospitals emerged in the early twentieth century, when doctoring was becoming a "profession" and medicine a "science."[47] This transition of medical education in the United States to a teaching hospital system included "university-based" medical schools, "faculty . . . engaged in original research," and students, who "participate[d] in 'active' learning through the laboratory study and real clinical work" with disproportionately poor or otherwise vulnerable patients.[48] The expansion of biomedical science through this new vision of medical education at times came at a particularly high cost for marginalized groups. In the shift from medicine to biomedicine that began around 1910, "African American, indigent, and low-income working class patients were still required to virtually sacrifice their bodies in exchange for treatment," the scholars of race and medicine Linda Clayton and W. Michael Byrd pointedly note.[49]

In the mid-twentieth century, patients at teaching hospitals such as the Johns Hopkins Hospital in Baltimore—where Henrietta Lacks's cervical cells were taken without her permission by a biomedical researcher in 1951[50]—were made to contend with "certain indignities and discomforts," including long waits for care; impolite hospital staff; and "underfunded, understaffed, overcrowded and poorly maintained" facilities.[51] Racial discrimination further compounded the problems of teaching hospitals. During Jim Crow, "frank racism," in the form of segregated facilities and wards, "was not uncommon at teaching hospitals," the medical historian Kenneth Ludermer argues.[52] At some institutions black patients were only ever seen by medical students. In the late twentieth century, uninsured and underinsured poor and minority communities and welfare recipients not infrequently received substandard care at teaching and public hospitals. In the 1970s, for example, there were numerous controversies involving poor women of color who received shoddy care or authoritarian treatment or both at teaching hospitals. As well, unnecessary and often coercive hysterectomies were performed on women of color at teaching hospitals.[53] During this time, the *Black Panther* was replete with accounts of the pitiable and at times fatal healthcare doled out to the Party rank and file and members of the local community at both teaching and public hospitals.[54] As Panther volunteer Marie Branch expressed, "We were battling a lot of things. . . . [doctors] told women that if they removed part of the uterus, they could still have a baby. . . . We were fighting the partial hysterectomy myth and sterilization attempts."[55] Thus black activists' demands for "community control" of healthcare facilities was also a call to change an often harrowing, disrespectful, and unaccountable culture of medical practice.

By placing large teaching hospitals in charge of the community health centers program, the federal government did not inspire the confidence of marginalized groups. In addition, debates about "community control," while certainly concerned with both patient and local autonomy, voiced objection to the lived experience of racism and poverty. As Crowe explains, "low-income residents throughout the Bay Area interpreted . . . the War on Poverty [as] part of the black struggle for civil rights." In contrast with federal reformers, these communities believed that the "CAPs should serve as vehicles for protest" and "should be on the front lines in the battle against racism."[56]

The Party founders had a social and ideological vision—Seale characterized this perspective as "revolutionary, community, socialistic"[57]—that was different from that of the Great Society imagined by LBJ.[58] Newton's and Seale's experiences at the antipoverty center thus impressed on them the limits of state-sponsored reform and black citizenship after the (re)codification of African American civil rights and compelled them to forge an alternative path. At its originary moment, the Party drew on its members' experiences with the War on Poverty programs in conceiving its own community service platform. These programs responded to the perceived failure of U.S. welfare state programs to meet poor African American communities' needs and reflected the activists' sense that black well-being could not be achieved without self-determination.[59]

From Self-Defense to Self-Determination

Despite its initially broad vision and forays into other community issues, the Party's early activism focused on armed surveillance of Oakland law enforcement—through "defense patrols"—to quell harassment from law enforcement.[60] The intimate knowledge the Panther leaders gained about firearms regulations and arrest procedures in the state influenced their use and endorsement of armed militancy.[61] These patrols used tape recorders and cameras to record police brutality. More famously, the Party deployed armed members to "police the police." In doing so, the Party followed to the letter an obscure California law that permitted citizens to carry loaded arms in public. A Republican state legislator, Don Mulford, responded to the Party's audacious tactics by proposing a bill to prohibit the public bearing of loaded weapons. On May 2, 1967, the day that the bill was to be discussed on the floor of the state legislature, Newton dispatched Seale and several other openly armed Party members to the state capitol in Sacramento to protest the proposed legislation.[62] Though the Party's protestations garnered national press attention, the California state assembly ratified the Mulford Act prohibiting the possession of loaded weapons in public in July 1967.[63] Seale was arrested for his participation in the protest at the California state capitol and was sentenced to a six-month jail term in August 1967.[64]

All the same, Party members continued to carry loaded weapons, and run-ins with Bay Area police persisted. On October 27, 1967, Newton was arrested for a shooting incident with Oakland police during which he and an officer were injured and another officer was killed. After this incident, the Panther leader was jailed while awaiting a court date and during his subsequent murder trial. Newton's incarceration and Seale's brief stint in jail for his involvement in the dramatic Party protest at the California statehouse created a leadership vacuum in the organization.[65] Though Seale was the "titular head" of the Party and could have resumed his role as leader after his release from prison in December 1967, Minister of Information Eldridge Cleaver's power had grown in Seale's (and Newton's) absence.[66] Concurrently, media coverage of the California capitol demonstration and the "Free Huey" campaign galvanized black communities' support for the Panthers across the United States and caused the Party's membership ranks to swell unexpectedly (despite its cofounders' incarceration). Under Cleaver's direction, violent encounters between the Party and local authorities escalated. In April

1968 Cleaver allegedly instigated a shoot-out with Oakland police, during which Hutton was killed.[67] Cleaver and Hilliard were arrested and jailed after this incident.[68]

The Party was forced to confront the implications of its armed militancy. In 1967 the organization dropped the phrase "for Self-Defense" from its name because as Seale put it, the Panthers "didn't want to be classified as a paramilitary organization."[69] Newton was convicted of voluntary manslaughter in September 1968. With his fate determined for the next two to fifteen years, from prison he instructed the Party to devote more of its attention to programmatic issues and creating local institutions. The Party cofounder had grown concerned by the violent direction the Party had taken. (The price of freedom that Newton paid as a result of his own violent encounter with the Oakland police was perhaps not lost on him.) In his words, Newton "wanted to emphasize the community development aspect of the party. . . . I felt that we should turn away from the arms because too much had been made of them."[70] With somewhat similar sentiment, Seale argued also that negative views of the Party had been exaggerated by inaccurate "preconceived opinions" about the organization and its aims. Newton and Seale accordingly shifted the balance of the organization's commitments, bringing the Party's attention and energies to bear on aspects of its platform that had been eclipsed by their other activities. "The gun itself does not symbolize a revolutionary," Newton declared in an interview with the *Los Angeles Times*. "Fascists also carry guns."[71]

Dr. Terry Kupers, an MCHR member and close collaborator with the Southern California chapter of the Party chapter, recalled that after the murders of Alprentice "Bunchy" Carter and Huggins at UCLA resulting from the bitter feud with the US Organization, "there was a question . . . what could people do to . . . keep the Panthers going and being active and getting their message across . . . that fit the Panther platform?"[72] Kupers, then a psychiatry resident at UCLA, led the formation of this clinic with Marie Branch, an African American nursing professor at the university, Party chapter leader Brown, and other Panther cadre. It was not a coincidence that this chapter soon launched its Bunchy Carter PFMC. From the perspective of the MCHR, Kupers argues that the clinic "was an attempt to keep the Panthers and their positions alive after the COINTELPRO attack on them in Chicago, LA and elsewhere."[73] One tragic reflection of how violence spurred the creation of the Party's social welfare politics is suggested by the fact that, as in Los Angeles, PFMCs were often named for "martyred" cadre, for example, the George Jackson People's Free Medical Clinic in Berkeley and the Fred Hampton People's Health Clinic in Portland, Oregon.[74]

Although Newton, Seale, and other members of the Party leadership began to reorganize the Party's structure and rethink its strategies, the heightened emphasis of the service program did not amount to the Party's complete abolition of armed self-defense.[75] Rucker, who worked at the Oakland PFMC (when she was not waitressing at the Party's Lamp Post bar), recalled that "nobody in the Party was about to give up guns."[76] Rucker underscored the "contradiction" inherent to the Party's community service strategy: police were in neighborhoods "looking for us" and "kicking in doors." "Can we claim to serve the people, body and soul, and scare them to death at the same time?" she asked.[77]

The centerpiece of the Party's renewed community service strategy was a diverse, evolving set of programs and initiatives. Newton's prior attempts to develop the Party's community programs had created tension in his relationship with Cleaver, who preferred to conceive of the Party as an armed underground resistance movement of urban guerrillas rather than social workers.[78] Ironically, not entirely dissimilar from Karenga's critique of the "serve the people" campaign, Cleaver viewed the programs as attempts to reform the existing system rather than to completely transform or revolutionize it, and vocally protested their implementation. Newton, on the other hand, contended that "you can't very well drop out of the system without dropping out of the universe . . . you contradict the system while you are in it until it's transformed into a new system." Cleaver eventually resigned from the Party over precisely this clash of vision about the direction of the Party. However, as late as 1967, even he backed the survival programs as part of a larger revolutionary strategy and notably penned a piece affirming them in the *Black Panther*: "If we can understand Breakfast for Children, can we not also understand Lunch for Children, and Dinner for Children, and Clothing for Children, and Education for Children, and Medical Care for Children?" Cleaver wrote.[79]

In late November 1968 Cleaver went into exile to avoid an attempted murder charge, and Seale instituted the community programs as he and Newton had envisioned them. In this same month, Seale announced the launch of the Party's expanded slate of community service programs in the pages of the *Black Panther*.[80] With this announcement, preexisting neighborhood service programs and new initiatives were bundled together into an impressive array of locally controlled alternative institutions that harked back to a tradition of community institution building in the long medical civil rights movement, evinced the Panthers' frustrations with the War on Poverty and facets of the black power movement, and, as I describe below, operationalized political theories that were their groundwork. Grouping these programs under the umbrella of the service campaign, the two-year-old Party served notice that it was shifting the emphasis of its endeavors. While in keeping with the initial seed ideas contained in the ten-point platform, which sought to balance political ideology with the needs of the people, the expansion of the community service programs marked a shift from armed self-defense to social self-defense.[81]

Keeping in mind Rucker's mention of the "contradictions" of the Party's community service strategy, the expansion of the survival programs should be interpreted also as a signal from the Party to the poor, predominantly black neighborhoods with which it worked that it appreciated that some shift in emphasis was warranted. Kent Ford, head of the Portland chapter, has commented that the programs succeeded in gaining both admiration and legitimacy for the Panthers in the eyes of local communities.[82] Rucker concurs, saying that "we realized that we were alienating a lot of the community that we needed to reach—that we wanted to help. . . . We . . . start[ed] going into churches and just reaching out . . . the Survival Programs were going well but we wanted to branch them out—[to] start a clinic."[83]

Crafting a Critique of Medicine

In addition to responding to the contemporary policy terrain, intraracial politics, and the many tolls of violence and state repression, the groundwork for the Party's health activism was supplied by the writings of several theorists who unequivocally linked medicine and politics.[84] Although the Black Panthers' heightened attention to community programs had been compelled by tactical exigencies and influenced, partly, by its leaders' experiences with federal antipoverty programs and their rejection of cultural nationalism, the Party had arguably been primed for this shift in register since its inception. The ideas of several "Third World" intellectual-activists, who linked revolutionary theory to the material needs of a society, were formative.

Chroniclers of the Party acknowledge its indebtedness to a few important political thinkers, especially Mao Zedong, the former leader of the People's Republic of China; Ernesto "Che" Guevara, an Argentinean medical doctor and leading figure in the Cuban revolution; and Frantz Fanon, a Martinican psychiatric doctor turned Algerian revolutionary.[85] Party memoirs, moreover, commonly testify to the importance of these thinkers in both formulating the organization's theory and shaping its actualization into practice. In Newton's autobiography, *Revolutionary Suicide*, for example, he writes that "we pored over these books to see how their experiences might help us to understand our plight. We read the work of Fanon, particularly *The Wretched of the Earth*, Mao Zedong's four volumes, and Guevara's *Guerrilla Warfare*."[86] Numerous other Panthers, including Seale, Hilliard, and Brown, likewise acknowledge the profound influence of these writers on the Party's endeavors.[87] Collectively, and as is widely recognized, the political ruminations of Mao, Guevara, and Fanon provided a blueprint for the Party's revolutionary praxis, as well as an equally important if less acknowledged context for its community service programs.

Less appreciated is the fact that the ideas of these theorists provided the ideological foundation for the Party's health activism. Two of these thinkers were physicians, and each of the three advanced a unique health political outlook that would in some way shape that of the Party. Guevara's stress on the need for social movements to build total institutions to meet all of a society's needs was rendered in the Party's vision for its health programs. Similarly, Fanon's analysis of medical oppression in colonial Algeria became a template for the Party's criticism of the United States. Mao's emphasis on "the masses" as the source of political and epistemological authority—exemplified by the People's Republic of China's "barefoot doctors" initiative—found voice in the Panthers' commitment to having lay locals play a role in administering the PFMCs and providing healthcare services at them. The expansion of the Party's communitarian orientation into health activism, moreover, was inspired by its adherence to the ideas of these political thinkers who offered a readily available ideological bridge between social revolution and "revolutionary medicine."[88]

As the Party leadership and membership were close students of Guevara, his writings helped give ideological contour to its health programs and other community service initiatives. The Party's focus on poor black communities' basic needs drew on the model of War on Poverty programs and the activists' critical reaction to these. However, it was also influenced by the activists' simultaneous engagement with the ideas of Guevara, who, two years after completing medical school, was a leader in the Cuban revolution. Among Guevara's political writings is a meditation on his personal evolution from a young man who sought "to become a famous scientist or mak[e] a significant contribution to medical science"[89] to a "fighter–doctor,"[90] who recognized the broad intersections of corporeal and social well-being. Guevara's account of the events leading up to the Cuban revolution depict a moment at which this fighter–doctor had to literally choose between retrieving a box of medical supplies or one of ammunition. He selected the latter.

Guevara nevertheless insisted that health workers had a vital role to play in revolutionary struggles. In the early stages, "revolutionary medical workers" provided comfort and care to guerrilla fighters. Once revolution was accomplished, these same health cadres were needed to establish healthcare institutions and supply medical training. A new society required social welfare programs, including a public health infrastructure.[91] More particularly, and writing somewhat metaphorically, he described the job of health workers in the postrevolutionary moment as being "to find out what diseases [the people] have, what their sufferings are, what have been their chronic miseries for years."[92] After revolution, Guevara maintained, "the doctor, the medical worker, must go to the core of this new work, which is to treat "what has been the inheritance of centuries of repression and total submission."[93] The Argentinean doctor–activist drew an inextricable link between individual health and collective health, writing that

> the principle upon which the fight against disease should be based is the creation of a robust body; but not the creation of a robust body by the artistic work of a doctor upon a weak organism; rather, the creation of a robust body with the work of the whole collectivity, upon the entire social collectivity.[94]

Guevara thus established health work as a bedrock of social transformation, and his observations resonated in the Party's activism beyond standard depictions of his *Guerrilla Warfare* and its influence on seventies radicals. Guevara's writings expressed a political-cum-medical philosophy of well-being that would be refracted in the Party's activism as its social health perspective.

Like Guevara, Fanon conveyed the social and political import of health and medicine.[95] His observations also offered an intellectual template for the Party's critique of medicine. Fanon's trenchant dissection of racialized medical oppression in colonial Algeria, detailed in *The Wretched of the Earth*, inspired the Panther organization's analogous critique of the U.S. medical–industrial system as an instrument of social control.

Members of the Black Panther Party were profoundly affected by *The Wretched of the Earth*: Newton, who was first introduced to Fanon's ideas by Seale, insisted that Party members be close readers of the book, and Cleaver referred to the text as "the Black bible."[96] Hilliard claims that "Fanon—and the Algerian Revolution—has provided our most important theoretical model."[97] In considering Fanon's influence, standard histories of the Party have focused almost exclusively on the author's advocacy of violence. Yet, as Party members attest, close readings of *The Wretched of the Earth* also informed the Panthers' health politics.[98] In addition to the discussion of violence with which much of *The Wretched of the Earth* is admittedly concerned, the book contains a seminal discussion of the role of medicine in the colonial situation. Too infrequently discussed by Party scholars—but notably referenced by Cleaver in his book review of *The Wretched of the Earth* for *Ramparts* magazine—is a portion of this work in which Fanon conducts medical diagnosis as political theorizing.

Born in Martinique, Fanon was trained as a physician in Lyon, France, and subsequently practiced psychiatry in the Antilles. In 1953, as an employee of the French government, Fanon was assigned to lead the psychiatry department at a colonial hospital in Algeria. While he was working there, the Algerian war for independence from France began. Fanon's experiences treating Algerian nationals traumatized by colonial oppression, as well as his observations of the devastating psychological effects of war, compelled him to resign his post and begin working on the side of Algerian liberation.

According to the medical sociologist Jock McCulloch, *The Wretched of the Earth*, written in 1961 shortly before Fanon's death, exemplifies a final transition in the author's writing "from psychiatric practice to political theory" and, more specifically, a move toward a "mature theory of decolonization."[99] Nevertheless, as McCulloch explains, a "sociology of mental illness" and a "critique of ethnopsychiatry" run parallel throughout Fanon's oeuvre. Building on work established in two of his earlier books, *Black Skin, White Masks* and *A Dying Colonialism*, in the last chapter of *The Wretched of the Earth*, "Colonial Wars and Mental Disorders," for example, Fanon details how the colonial administration used medical science to classify the colonized population as pathological. He writes, "It was confirmed that the Algerian was a born criminal. A theory was elaborated and scientific proofs were found to support it."[100] In Fanon's sarcastic formulation, "The hesitation of the colonist in giving responsibility to the native is not racism nor paternalism, but quite simply a scientific appreciation of the biologically limited possibilities of the native."[101] During times of war, a more insidious form of ethnopsychiatry emerges: doctors were explicit "agents of colonialism" who administered torture disguised as medicine, which Fanon called "subversive war."[102] The medical "warfare" described by Fanon included administering medication to induce confessions from Algerian prisoners and deploying categories of medical pathology to mark the colonial subject.

In *The Wretched of the Earth*'s concluding chapter, Fanon's critique of colonial medicine and the effects of colonial war in Algeria take the form of medical case histories. Fanon offers these studies as proof of the ravages of colonialism and as confirmation of the abuses of politicized, colonial medicine. By way of introduction to the medical case studies that follow, Fanon writes, "Clinical psychiatry classifies the different disturbances shown by our patients under the heading 'reactionary psychoses.' In doing this, prominence is given to the event which has given rise to the disorder . . . [which] are chiefly the bloodthirsty and pitiless atmosphere [and] the generalization of inhuman practices."[103] After these opening comments, the chapter quickly moves to Fanon's recounting of his specific experiences with French and Algerian patients during the war. In each account, Fanon describes the patient's symptoms and then diagnoses the condition as deriving from extramedical or social, rather than biological, origins. Strident political analysis, critiques of the subjectivity of medical professionals under colonialism, and anticolonial sentiment bracket the case studies in the chapter.

As part of its health politics, the Party took up the Fanonian tactic of the political diagnosis of medical cases in its own publications. The weekly newsletter of the Southern California chapter of the Party, the *People's News Service*, frequently printed articles about health issues of concern to black communities in Los Angeles.[104] A March 1970 issue recounted in detail the experience of a black Angeleno suffering from second-degree burns, attributing his inability to get adequate care to the fact that a capitalist imperative in the healthcare system had over-taken the medical mandate to do no harm. In particular, this man's condition went untreated because he could not afford to pay for ambulance service to the hospital.[105] Another article, titled "Legal and Medical Genocide," told of the experiences of Ronald Freeman, a Party member who was incarcerated in New County jail in Los Angeles and suffered from an undiagnosed and untreated chronic illness.[106] Excerpts from Freeman's medical history were framed by a discussion of what the Party described as the politically fraught and uneven character of health services, and critiques of the treatment of blacks in prison and of the medical–industrial complex.[107] In addition to the medico-political case study, Fanon's influence arguably was present in the Party's 1972 challenge to a psychiatric center proposed by medical scientists at UCLA who planned to investigate biological models of violence with research that focused disproportionately on black and Latino male youth.

A second notable intersection between Fanon's ideas and the Party's health politics was the complex perspective that the theorist brought to his understanding of the social power of medicine. McCulloch argues that the radical psychiatrist believed that "pure" medical science was impossible to achieve in the colonial context.[108] Fanon appreciated that pathology could be constructed to advance the colonial enterprise.[109] At the same time, however, Fanon also understood that ethical medical practice was necessary for healing the wounds that resulted from racism and colonial war. While critical of medicine, Fanon was not *anti*medicine. Extrapolating to the Party's health politics, we can see a Fanonian perspective in its politics of health and race: the activists apprehended the dangers of biomedical power for impoverished blacks living in America's "internal colonies" and, at the same time, sought to extend healthcare services to them—from trusted sources, including itself and its allies.[110]

The People's Doctors: Maoist Health Politics

The impact of Mao's ideas on Party political ideology is often narrowly attributed to its uptake of his adage that "political power grows out of the barrel of a gun."[111] This is somewhat fitting as Newton and Seale famously earned money to build up the Party's coffers and weapons arsenal by selling copies of *Quotations from Chairman Mao* on the campus of the University of California at Berkeley.[112] However, the "little red book" was to provide more than finances and guns.[113] The historians Robin D. G. Kelley and Betsy Esch propose, in particular, that Mao's "China offered black radicals a 'colored,' or Third World, Marxist model that enabled them to challenge a white and Western vision of class struggle—a model they shaped and reshaped to suit their own cultural and political realities."[114] In addition, the Party borrowed, sometimes verbatim, many of its principles and tenets from Mao.[115] One name for its community programs—serve the people—was adapted from a chapter in "the little red book" titled "Serving the People."[116] Also included in this brief chapter were aphorisms that offered guidelines for the relationship of the political vanguard—which the Party considered itself to be—to the community. According to Mao, though it was the vanguard's responsibility to lead, political and epistemological authority was vested in "the people."[117] By inaugurating the practice of using the phrase *the people* to refer to the legitimate political actors of Chinese society, Mao aimed to do away with the stratification that he felt characterized prerevolution China, which was organized into classes of peasants, the proletariat, and the bourgeois—the latter group including bureaucrats and other technical and knowledge elites. In a related gesture, the Party adopted the practice of referring to its many social programs as the people's programs, as in the People's Free Medical Clinics and the People's Free Breakfast for Children Program.

Mao, following Marx, also stressed that "the people's" privileged knowledge derived from their experiences as workers. Such a perspective underlay communist China's "barefoot doctors" program under which urban physicians were compelled to effectively trade places with rural peasantry, with the former required to divide their time between medical practice and agricultural labor (among other projects), and the latter receiving accolades for expertise in traditional healing practices such as acupuncture as well as their acuity with "Western" medicine.[118] The effect was a blurring of boundaries between laypersons and expert elites.[119] Party members received firsthand exposure to the deprofessionalization of medicine in China during two visits there in the early 1970s. In March 1972 a Panther contingent of eighteen persons visited the country by way of Seattle and Tokyo, after being denied entry into Vancouver, Canada, the activists' original jumping-off point to China. The group included the Party's minister of culture Henry Douglas; L.A.-based minister of justice Masai Hewitt; Branch, who helped establish the Los Angeles Party chapter's health clinic; Angela Davis; "Doc" Satchel, who began his days in the Party in Chicago; and Panther medical adviser and physician Tolbert Small. Small learned acupuncture and other traditional Chinese healing practices during this tour; on his return he authored two articles in the *American Journal of Acupuncture* that detailed the physiological bases and uses of this technique in China and its potential implementation in the United States. Small incorporated acupuncture into his medical practice. The China tour also inspired the Party to begin to use vans to bring healthcare services out into the community. "They came back with all the 'barefoot doctor' techniques," Norma Armour explained. "That's where we got the idea for the mobile unit."[120]

The Party and other health radicals embraced this "red versus expert" perspective modeled in Mao's China.[121] Kelley and Esch explain the concept in this way: "The idea that knowledge derives from a dialectics of practice and theory empowered radicals to question . . . expertise . . . Maoists—from black radical circles to the women's liberation movement—sought to overturn bourgeois notions of expertise . . . [and] saw themselves as producers of new knowledge."[122] Hilliard expressed such sentiment in a 1969 interview about the Party's foray into health politics. He remarked that the Party's aim was to cultivate "revolutionary medicine" by "unlock[ing] [the] secrets . . . kept hidden" by medical professionalization.[123] "Doctors are not servants of the people," Hilliard declared, "but professionals." "We want to do away with the bourgeoisie concept of medicine. It should be brought down to the community to teach the people how to practice medicine," he continued.[124] With statements resembling the ideas of Mao and Guevara, Hilliard's comments suggest how political theory conditioned and informed the Party's health activism. The valorization of experiential knowledge and lay perspective was a significant facet of the Party's fight against medical discrimination.

Within several years of its founding, the Party expanded its purview considerably to include a range of service programs. Several factors contributed to the evolution of its health politics. As previously discussed, the Party was successor to a tradition of civil rights health activism that spanned Marcus Garvey's UNIA to SNCC's Freedom Summer. In the next chapter I describe how activists from this and other SNCC campaigns linked the health activism of this southern student organization with that of the Party.

There were institutional and ideological factors organic to the formation of the Party that moved the organization toward community service programs, and health politics more particularly. The Party's commitment to action over black cultural nationalist rhetoric, its rejection of state control, and its service vanguard position vis-à-vis its constituents remained in place, but were reoriented—shifting registers from self-defense to self-determination (via the creation of an array of community programs).

Newton and Seale were Oakland college students when black cultural nationalism was ascendant. The Black Panther cofounders regarded this focus on black consciousness-raising as at odds with what became the Party's Marxist-Leninist politics. The activists' aspirations for the Party—as articulated in its ten-point platform—partly emanated from their disappointment with the cultural politics practiced by student groups. Concomitantly, they desired a realpolitik that could yield practical benefits—better housing, economic conditions, and healthcare, for example—for the urban poor of Oakland and, eventually, oppressed groups globally.

On the other hand, the Party was partly constituted in contradistinction to what some blacks regarded as the thin democracy of the War on Poverty and, to some extent, the lack of efficacy of these programs. While the Johnson administration conceived of antipoverty programs as being operated with the "maximum feasible participation" of the underserved communities in which they were located, in practice this involvement was curtailed by government officials and often politically moderate blacks as well. Given their political commitments to black self-determination and Marxist-Leninism, Newton and Seale wanted poor people to take a leading role in the CAPs. The Panthers' array of "serve the people" programs was instituted as a more democratic and participatory alternative to federal ones. Despite the ideological differences between how the Party and CAP administrators viewed "community control," several key members of the Panther organization cut their teeth as social activists working in these federal antipoverty programs or being served by them. In this way, the War on Poverty was a condition of possibility for the Party's health politics.

The shift in emphasis from self-defense to self-help in the Party was also a manifestation of dynamics that occurred after the Party was inaugurated. Although the organization was established to furnish protection to the poor and black communities most vulnerable to police brutality and social welfare programs, the relative importance of these two foci shifted in light of law enforcement reaction and state repression.

The Party's health "turn" was also augured in the writings of the political theorists who are known to have greatly influenced the activists in other ways. As I have shown here, the impact of Mao, Guevara, and Fanon on the Party was more extensive than typically thought. From these thinkers, whose writings were required reading in the Panthers' political education classes, the Party also received health political tools. The works of Mao and Guevara aided activists in conceptualizing how health and medicine fit with broad political aims. Fanon exposed how medicine was used to repressive political ends in colonial Algeria; the Party found in this an analogy to the healthcare of institutionalized blacks in the United States as well as the medical mistreatment experienced by the larger African American community. At the same time, the ideas of Fanon and Mao suggested that medicine, in the right hands and in an equitable society, could have healing and perhaps even revolutionary potential, and in this way prefigures the Party's social health frame. This dual discourse about medicine was given voice by the Party, when it amended its ten-point platform of 1972 to elaborate and declare, in no uncertain terms, the activists' commitment to health politics and its demand for healthcare access. Part of the new language, the modified point 6, read:

> We believe that the government must provide, free of charge, for the people, health facilities which will not only treat our illnesses, most of which have come about as a result of our oppression, but which will also develop preventative medical programs to guarantee our future survival. We believe that mass health education and research programs must be developed to give Black and oppressed people access to advanced scientific and medical information, so we may provide ourselves with proper medical attention and care.[125]

Calling for universal healthcare, asserting a social health perspective, and noting the import of health education and research, this declaration was a landmark in the Party's health politics. The addition of this elaborated statement on health in the Party's revised platform—in contrast with lesser mention of the issue in the original platform—was the culmination of a process through which the Panthers carried on as community service radicals but did so also as committed health activists.

Now-standard narratives of the Black Panthers' formation privilege a combination of structural factors and political forces. Yet as is demonstrated here, this standard accounting can obscure rich veins of insight about the Panthers. The Party's health activism also emerged at the intersection of the institutional, tactical, and ideological processes. These dynamics paved the way for the specific health outreach, screening programs, preventive care initiatives, and challenges to biomedical authority that the activists undertook. From this revised narrative about the organization, fresh observations about its mission and course are possible as well as evidence of the relevance of the Party's work for present-day concerns about race and health inequality. In the next chapter, I describe how the Party and its collaborators in the radical health movement worked to erect the essential infrastructure of the Party's health politics—its national network of People's Free Medical Clinics.

3.

THE PEOPLE'S FREE MEDICAL CLINICS

> Patients don't get a political rap before they see a physi-
> cian[,] but the very existence of the clinic is political.
>
> —Volunteer, People's Free Medical Clinic,
> "The Free Clinics; Ghetto Care Centers
> Struggle to Survive," *American Medical News*

A February 1970 issue of the *Black Panther* featured two articles that dramatized how mainstream medicine could fail poor communities. One account told of the untimely death of James Anthony Nero, an African American infant, in Brooklyn, New York. Suffering from fever and chest congestion, James was taken to the emergency room of a local hospital. Doctors "hurriedly" examined the baby and allegedly sent him home with medication, but without a proper diagnosis.[1] Several days later, James was discovered unconscious by his mother, Hattie. Taken again to the emergency room, the infant was pronounced dead on arrival. He was four months old. A photograph of baby James in his tiny casket accompanied the story.[2]

The *Black Panther* piece conjectured that getting "to the essence of James' tragic death" necessitated a consideration of the "circumstances surrounding it." Criticism was especially heaped on the failed social service system: the Black Panthers' account of this incident underscored the fact that the Nero family lived in Brownsville, a Brooklyn neighborhood so neglected by municipal services that "garbage piled up," attracting "rats, mice, roaches." The diagnosis that had allegedly eluded James Nero's doctors was then ventured by the Party; the newspaper declared that "pneumonia and flu viruses [run] rampant" in impoverished settings such as this.[3]

A second article employed anecdotal vignettes to depict the dismal state of healthcare services for the underprivileged in the Bay Area. Shining a light on the disrespectful, unprofessional, and even authoritarian encounters between physicians and their patients at San Francisco General—a public, teaching hospital affiliated with the University of California—the piece's unnamed author declared that this public facility should not be regarded as "a charity hospital because there is no charity practiced there."[4] Represented as typical of this hospital were patient–doctor interactions such as the one described here: "The intern who examines you at first at least says hello, but the resident who comes in to check up on him hurts you and ignores you. He talks to you as though you weren't there."[5] Affronts to women seeking reproductive healthcare at S.F. General received extended consideration in the article in its portrayal of the many hurdles and indignities faced by a hypothetical impoverished, pregnant everywoman of color, who was getting by with Medicaid assistance. Shuttled between prurient social workers and public health nurses, poorly managed municipal health facilities, and callous physicians depicted as lobbying expectant mothers to choose abortions over childbirth—and waiting for hours to be seen in each instance—poor women's pursuit of maternal care was presented as a frustrating, coercive, and demeaning affair.[6]

The article spins out from these vignettes to a broader critique of the medical–industrial complex:

> The drug companies, the doctors, the insurance companies and the equipment suppliers take in huge profits from private hospitals . . . [because] they don't have to deal with the . . . poor people in this city. The Department of Public Health is in collusion with these doctors, with the health industry, with the Chamber of Commerce, because it maintains an undersupplied, drastically understaffed, overpoliced, over-social-worked institution—San Francisco General Hospital, which has no respect whatsoever for the privacy and dignity of people who have no choice but to use it.[7]

This account closes with a rallying cry for support for the Party's own healthcare facilities. "Our people are dying of medical miscare—we must all work to make the People's Free Health Clinics a reality."[8]

Running side by side in the newspaper, these two articles encapsulated the activists' interpretation of the challenges confronting medically underserved communities, including inadequate facilities, negligent care, and paternalistic (and sexist) interactions with medical authorities. More particularly, dealing as they did with the pragmatics of healthcare access, the newspaper accounts offered ready justification for forming the Party's *own* clinics. An announcement celebrating the recent opening of a PFMC in Berkeley underscored the necessity of the Panthers' alternative institutions:

> We have initiated a Free Health Clinic to combat the health problems which exist among poor and oppressed people. We realize that a person's health is his most valuable possession. We also realize that health care and inadequate facilities can be used as a tool to perpetrate genocide against a people. We know that as long as the oppressor controls the institutions within our oppressed communities, we will be subjected to institutionalized genocide whether it comes from inadequate housing, the barrel of a pig's shotgun, or from inadequate medical attention. . . . [We] must create institutions within our communities that are controlled and maintained by the people.[9]

In April 1970 Bobby Seale issued an organizationwide directive that all Party chapters establish local, free healthcare facilities. Called the People's Free Medical Clinics, the resulting clinics became the infrastructure for the Party's health programs.[10]

Bobby Seale at the Bobby Seale Free Medical Clinic in Berkeley. In 1970 Seale mandated that all party chapters establish a People's Free Medical Clinic. This PFMC was renamed for George Jackson in the summer of 1971. Courtesy of It's About Time Black Panther Party Archive.

Having established in chapter 2 why health politics came to be important to the Party's activism—and how this politics evolved from a confluence of founding principles, political ideology, and tactical exigency—I illustrate its breadth in this chapter and the two that follow. Here I describe the formation of the organization's network of health clinics. How did Party chapters convert Seale's 1970s mandate into local institutions? What hurdles did Party members confront in creating clinics? How did the PFMCs evince the Panthers' social health perspective?

In the early 1970s creating alternative healthcare facilities, if a radical act, was not a radically new idea. Nor was the idea for the PFMCs crafted out of whole cloth by the Panther leadership. The formation of the clinics reflected, on the one hand, a tradition of African American institution building as a form of recourse to health inequality. On the other, the Panther clinics were part of a broader New Left activism scene in which establishing independent clinics became a calling card of the radical health movement.[11]

The inspiration for the PFMCs, however, also arose directly from the Panthers' inimitable political perspective. With its clinics, the Party sought to remedy the lack of sufficient, affordable, and respectful healthcare services for the disadvantaged, who were often relegated to teaching hospitals and their often inexperienced staff. These sites also provided trustworthy alternatives for the vulnerable poor who were especially at risk for medical discrimination, ranging from disrespectful or incompetent treatment to unethical experimentation, in both private and public healthcare settings. As community-based operations, the Panther clinics offered a local option in contrast to health facilities that were often at great distances from black communities. Norma Armour described the spatial segregation and psychic distance—that served as a hurdle to healthcare access in Los Angeles—in this way:

> You know, in those days, we didn't travel far. I never went west of Western Avenue, if I even went that far. Maybe Vermont Avenue. I don't think I went west of Vermont until I was in college. . . . USC General Hospital was all the way in East L.A. That's where you had to go [if you were poor or uninsured]. No car? Then you met somebody for a ride or said "let's get on the bus and get over there."[12]

Offering services at no cost to clients, the clinics were also imagined as an alternative to profit-driven healthcare.

In addition, the PFMCs were experiments in a different culture of healthcare; medical authority was demystified at the clinics, as lay people—including many of the Panthers—were vital to their operation. The Party, like other radical health activists, valorized this nonexpert wisdom from members of the community, both patients and volunteers, who brought valuable experience and knowledge to the clinic. In this same vein, at Party clinics volunteer medical professionals trained community health workers to provide basic healthcare; this transmission of expert knowledge was central to the Panthers' health politics.[13] Thus in addition to offering needed treatment, the clinics also embodied the Party's critique of medical authority, professionalization, and the medical–industrial complex. At the same time, because health activism of the kind that the Party was engaged in depended on forms of expertise, the operation of the clinics would have been impossible without collaboration with its *trusted experts,* such as members of the MCHR. As the Panthers' health work bore out, the Party did not reject medicine outright; rather, it sought to provide and model respectful and reliable medical practice.

The clinics also served as a broad base of operation for the Party in at least two ways. First, the PFMCs were the organizational and administrative infrastructure for its platform of health initiatives. Second, given the Panthers' attention to the "circumstances surrounding" illness, in the case of baby James and more generally, their brick-and-mortar clinics were unsurprisingly also put to the purpose of broader social welfare needs. In keeping with the Party's social health prerogative, its clinics were ecumenical spaces in which medical care was the central but not the sole aim; the PFMCs had wide-ranging missions. Local residents could receive assistance from a "patient advocate"—a Party member or volunteer—on such matters as physical health, housing issues, and legal aid. In this way, the clinics were also bases of operation for the Panthers' wider "serve the people" agenda. This interpersonal support epitomized the advocacy the Party hoped to provide on a larger social scale. The clinics embodied a critique of mainstream social programs and the medical care system by exposing what Huey P. Newton called the "contradiction" between what the Panthers could accomplish with will and few resources and what the state did not accomplish with much more. Material embodiments of the Party's critique of both the healthcare state and the commodification of medicine, "the very existence of" the PFMCs was "political," as a staffer at the Chicago chapter's clinic declared.[14]

Clinic Culture and the Radical Health Movement

To fully realize its health politics, the Party worked with others to put these theories into action. Somewhat unique among modes of political mobilization, health activism may require mastery of biomedical information or the acquisition of technical skills and, therefore, frequently involves collaboration between activists and persons with expertise in medicine and science.[15] The Panthers partnered with health activists who were able to impart the knowledge necessary to administer Party initiatives and who also shared its commitment to patient empowerment to demystify medicine, to the deprofessionalization of medical practice, and to a conception of healthcare as a human right, rather than a commodity.

Others in the radical health movement aided the Party in developing its health politics, including medical professionals who supported its work but were not affiliated with the group, for example, Tolbert Small and members of social movement organizations such as the MCHR and the Student Health Organization.[16] Both the MCHR and the SHO regarded community health service as central to their missions; the MCHR, in particular, played a key role in advancing the Party's health-based activism.[17] Notably, these activist–professionals often came to the aid of the Panthers themselves, serving as personal physicians to cadre. In turn, the Panthers helped these activists realize their own political aims to assist medically underserved communities by allowing health workers entrée into those communities most in need of their assistance. In addition to linking volunteer experts and underprivileged groups, as former Harlem Panther Cleo Silvers explained to me, the Party also sought to "reeducate" the medical professionals who partnered with them by exposing them to the ideas of Mao Zedong, Frantz Fanon, and other political thinkers.[18] These writings helped convey the Party's political perspective to its collaborators. Collective reading of these works also helped communicate the life perspective of the mostly black and poor lay activists to their mostly white and elite allies. Stressing the necessity of this second objective, Silvers explained, "essentially . . . people in the medical establishment . . . come from privileged backgrounds and, usually they don't have a clue as to the culture of the people they are supposed to be treating. They didn't understand what our conditions were."[19] The political reeducation that the Party required of its expert collaborators was intended to build a bridge of understanding.

The Party's clinics must be understood in the context of the "neighborhood health centers," "community health centers," or "community clinics" movement that was also taking place during this time.[20] In addition to the Panthers, the radical health movement of the 1970s included feminist groups; hippie counterculturalists; leftists such as Students for a Democratic Society and Health/PAC; politicized medical professionals and students, including the MCHR and the SHO; and the Party's allies in the "rainbow coalition," most notably, the Young Lords Party.[21] This multifaceted radical health community was a decentralized aggregate of groups, collectives, and organizations with distinct missions that sought to transform medicine, institutionally and interpersonally. In keeping with the DIY spirit of the era, the activists enacted the better world they imagined by establishing their own independent healthcare initiatives and institutions; the radical health movement modeled practices that, in the slogan of the Berkeley Free Clinic—a Party collaborator—valued "Health Care for People Not Profit."[22]

Boston's Franklin Lynch PFMC, located in a trailer parked on a city street. Clinics varied by chapter and according to each chapter's resources. Courtesy of It's About Time Black Panther Party Archive.

This mission was frequently manifested as activist-run no-cost or low-cost clinics, such as the Panthers' PFMCs. Consistent with the period's antiauthoritarian zeitgeist, activists encouraged patients to have a voice in the medical encounter and urged laypeople to claim the mantle of expertise by taking a hand in their healthcare—and, sometimes, in producing medical knowledge as well. The democratization of both medical practice and biomedical knowledge, often in the clinic setting, was a tactical cornerstone of radical health politics. Members of the radical health movement worked in solidarity—and sometimes, in tandem—to provide inexpensive alternatives to mainstream medicine. The free and low-cost clinics that were founded to fulfill the healthcare needs of underserved groups reached a critical mass in the early 1970s.[23] By 1972 this phenomenon was considerable enough to spur the formation of the National Free Clinic Council. The council's first meeting, held that same year in Washington, D.C., was attended by over eight hundred activists, representing more than two hundred health facilities across the United States.[24] The majority of these clinics were organized by and served feminist and minority groups like the Party.[25]

Although communities and collectives had long established their own medical facilities in response to nonexistent or inadequate healthcare services—African Americans' efforts to establish healthcare facilities in the early twentieth century is a case in point—this renaissance in alternative-institution making was more immediately inspired by the health programs launched as a part of the Freedom Summer initiative in 1964.[26] This renaissance flowered alongside the free clinic movement that arose from hippie culture in San Francisco beginning in 1967.[27] The network of activist relationships and collaborations that arose from these developments became the scaffolding for the broader radical health movement.

The emergence of activist-run health facilities such as the Panthers' PFMCs was deeply influenced by Freedom Summer. In some cases, the link was direct: both Stokely Carmichael and H. Rap Brown, each of whom went on to serve roles in the Party as honorary prime minister and minister of justice, respectively, participated in the Freedom Summer as members of SNCC.[28] For this campaign, SNCC joined forces with the politicized health workers of the MCHR because, as the historian John Dittmer notes, its leadership recognized that the arrival of thousands of activists from the North to Mississippi would "increase the level of violence in the state."[29] Doctors, nurses, surgeons, medical and nursing students, pharmacists and lab technicians, and others were therefore needed to provide emergency medical treatment and "attention for problems resulting from stress" in addition to tending to "normal ailments."[30]

As summer faded, so too did this particular SNCC campaign, but the struggles for racial justice and health equality intensified. MCHR members were stirred further to action by their experiences in Mississippi. Several of these volunteers, including the physicians Alvin Pouissant and H. Jack Geiger, continued to work with the poor in the South.[31] In the period immediately after Freedom Summer, the MCHR was thus transformed from "medical presence" for southern civil rights struggles to "the medical arm of the New Left," mostly in the urban North and East.[32] In this latter capacity, the MCHR became a vital player in the radical health community, helping the Panthers, the Young Lords Party, feminist groups, and others to staff (and, in some cases, coordinate) clinics and other healthcare projects as it extended its efforts to other regions of the United States.[33] Following Freedom Summer, Geiger would play a prominent role in the development of the federal community clinic program. With more than one million dollars in funding from the Office of Economic Opportunity, he established successful clinics in Bayou Mound, Mississippi, and Boston. The facilities that Geiger spearheaded were a source of inspiration for the Party. In Branch's words, Boston "had a wonderful clinic plan that we wanted to adopt."[34]

On top of the formative influence of the Freedom Summer health programs and projects closely modeled on them, the model of San Francisco counterculturalists, who instituted primary healthcare services during the so-called Summer of Love, encouraged the growth of the health radical clinic network. Hippies, who came to the city by the tens of thousands for several weeks beginning in 1967 to "turn on, tune in [and] drop out," in LSD-enthusiast Timothy Leary's memorable phrasing, were in need of care that could be delivered inexpensively and in a nonjudgmental setting for drug-related illnesses, sexually transmitted diseases, and other ailments. The counterculture free clinic was the brainchild of Dr. David Smith, an internist at the University of California, San Francisco Medical Center.[35] The creation in June 1967 of the first such facility, the Haight-Ashbury Free Clinic, was, in Smith's words, "a political statement . . . [about] inadequacies in the health care delivery system."[36] This clinic begot others sponsored by counterculturalists and members of the New Left, including many in the Bay Area such as the still-functioning Berkeley Free Clinic, and added both substance and velocity to health radicals' drive to develop alternative healthcare sites as a form of political critique. Berkeley and its surrounding communities became major sites of health politics in the 1970s. The former Panther Armour, who worked in the Party's clinics in both Southern and Northern California, recalls that the Bay Area was home to an active "health consortium" of which the Panthers, the Berkeley Free Clinic, feminist health collectives, and other members of the local radical health movement were members.[37]

Trusted Experts

Consistent with its vanguardist principles, the Party viewed and represented itself as standing in for the interests of "the people"—its health-underserved urban constituency.[38] Like SNCC in the South, the Panthers (as well as the Young Lords Party and other groups) necessarily facilitated the community service aspirations of its health radical allies. The Party was a "bio-cultural broker" that mediated between medically underserved poor, black communities distrustful of mainstream medicine and medical expert health radicals, who sought to use their skills to bridge health inequality.[39]

This trust warrant was symbolically performed in the New Left and counterculture health radical communities. Here it was deemed appropriate that the appearance of the doctors, nurses, and others working with this population more closely resemble their patients than their colleagues.[40] Patients and practitioners were supposed to "share the same values and life styles. . . . Professionals [did] not hide behind the symbols of uniforms or authoritarian roles," observed a report on a San Francisco Bay Area free clinic.[41] Hippie health workers wore jeans and T-shirts under their white coats, if they wore white coats at all.

The white coat of medical science could have a different connotation in black communities. Because the Party worked with populations that historically had not had regular contact with medical professionals, the white coat, worn by trusted experts, could be a welcome sign of long-sought access to quality healthcare *as well as* an emblem of the potential excesses of medical power. Accordingly, at the Party's clinics, community volunteers, health workers, and Panther health cadre alike donned this symbol of medical science that had evolved from late-nineteenth-century lab coats.[42]

Even if they were not expected to undergo a sartorial transformation, activist health professionals who joined forces with the Party were often

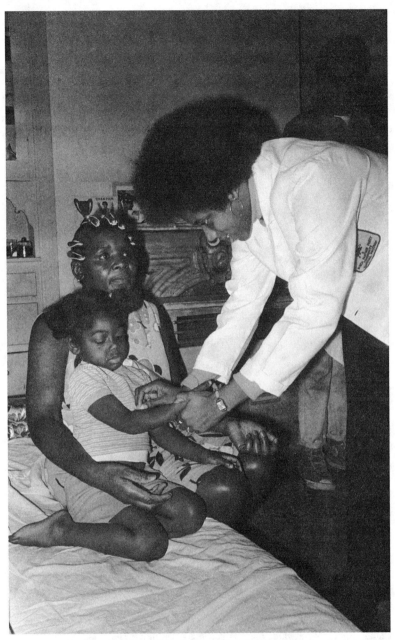

Wearing a white clinician's coat with a badge that reads "Black Panther Party Community Survival Programs," Party member Norma Armour made a house call to check the result of a TB test given to a girl in Oakland. Courtesy of Steven Shames.

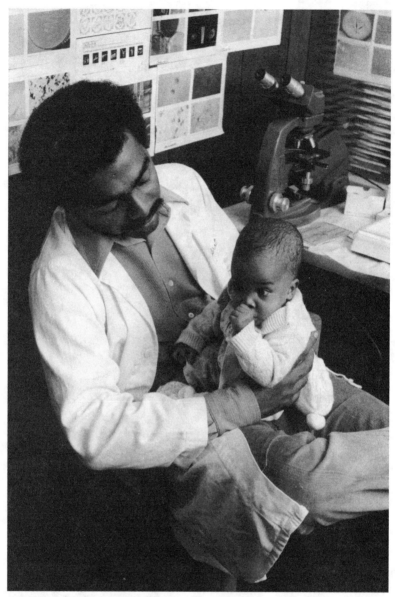

Henry "Smitty" Smith was a leader of the Black Panther Party health cadre. At its George Jackson PFMC in Berkeley, he conducted electrophoresis analysis for the local chapter's sickle cell anemia program. Courtesy of It's About Time Black Panther Party Archive / Billy X. Jennings.

required to participate in political training. For some of the Panthers' allies in the radical health movement, ideological indoctrination was the price of trustworthiness, a sign of solidarity. The physician Fitzhugh Mullan remembered that during his time as part of the Lincoln Hospital Collective in the Bronx, New York, the Panthers and the Young Lords Party required that activist doctors take PE classes from them.[43] In these sessions, works by writers such as Joshua S. Horn, Mao, and Fanon were read, scrutinized, and committed to memory.[44] Although Mullan grew to find the required rote learning of these and other texts pedantic and tiresome, he also conveyed that the experiences were important political and ideological "stimulants" for himself and other radical health workers.[45] The education was mutual. Silvers explained how this reciprocal interchange between medical professionals and Panthers worked:

> I was responsible for giving political education to the doctor's collective [that] had agreed to work with us . . . [and] they taught us. The doctors taught us to use the equipment. We didn't come up with these ideas about the results of the ingestion of lead poisoning [by] ourselves, the doctors who did the research brought the [information] to us. We broke it down and explained it to the community and acted on it: We did this as a group. We had a doctor, a nurse, and a community person and a Young Lord or a Panther.[46]

The Party thus held a pivotal place in the radical health community, linking the medically underserved and the wider health movement. Although the Panthers could count on the assistance of some African American health workers such as Branch, at a time when black women and men made up a mere fraction of the total number of physicians and nurses in the United States, the organization relied heavily on a multiracial cast of medical professionals to carry out its preventive healthcare projects and other initiatives.[47] Concomitantly, the vanguardist Panthers facilitated the activities of these and other health radicals among poor people of color who were historically neglected by mainstream medicine and remained distrustful of it, while also vouching for these trusted expert collaborators.[48]

The Demystification of Medical Power

"We are training some of the young people to do laboratory urinalysis and blood tests and teams of people from the community are organized to canvass the neighborhood and bring the center to the people. . . . Our teams take their blood pressure, medical histories, and in general determine if people are suffering from illness."[49] So explained Sylvia Woods, a nurse volunteer at the Chicago Party's clinic in 1970. Through such expansions of responsibility for health outreach and medical treatment from professionals to community members, the Party put a check on medical authority by transforming its standard practice. This course of demystification took at least two paths: first, the valorization of nonexperts' experience over physicians' expert knowledge, and second, and related to this, the promotion of the practice of self-help healthcare, or "self health." As with other health radicals (most notably, women's health activists), the Party held that "the people"—be they the impoverished, the uninsured, pain sufferers, genetic trait carriers, or racialized and gendered bodies—had access to a special and valuable perspective on disease and illness. A mode of expertise based on the distinctive standpoint or vantage obtained through life encounters and personal observations, experiential knowledge was a central tenet of the Party's health politics. This knowledge reflected the premium placed by the activists on the potential of community members to be both health workers and health educators, building from the standpoint of their own lives. The Black Panther organization endeavored to give voice to patients' experiences partly by privileging the judgment and perspective of those individuals or communities over that of healthcare professionals. At Party clinics, health cadre underscored the fact that professional volunteers largely served at the pleasure of their patients.[50] In free clinic examination rooms in Berkeley and elsewhere, patients learned to ask questions of the health professionals who treated them; they "frequently challenge[d] the behavior of professionals" if they found it to be inappropriate and, furthermore, were encouraged to do so.[51] Additionally, during the height of the radical health movement, it was not uncommon for health workers to be dismissed from activist-run clinics if they were deemed disrespectful to patients.[52] "We . . . require[d] the best from the doctors," Armour recollected. "People started complaining about . . . one pediatrician that came to work for us. The parents were complaining about some things that he said about their kids. . . . Have you ever heard of firing a volunteer? I had to tell him we didn't need his services anymore!"[53]

This experiential knowledge tack was partly a remedy to what health radicals diagnosed as the "built-in racism and male chauvinism" of mainstream medicine.[54] Medical patriarchy was a concern of feminist health radicals in particular, who argued that women too often found the mostly male, mostly white physician cohort typical of this era to be "condescending, paternalistic, judgmental and non-informative."[55] The Young Lords Party and the Panthers further highlighted the problems of racial discrimination and class inequality inherent in the medical encounter.

This ideal of lay expertise among health radicals extended to the very exercise of medicine.[56] Along with patients' increased agency, at its healthcare clinics the Party encouraged the transfer of technical skills from health professionals to nonexperts. Activists and patients alike engaged in larger and more active roles in a quite literal sense, taking the provision and delivery of healthcare services "into their own hands."[57] These self-health activities included and could also well exceed the bounds of what might be expected to transpire at typically rudimentary clinic settings.

Self-health was an important and transformative practice among feminist health radicals. The work of the women's health centers comprised not only rape counseling, birth control services, midwifery, and such "self-help gynecology" as cervical self-examination but also obstetric procedures and, in some rare cases, abortions.[58] The Panther health cadre also engaged in self-help reproductive health practices alongside local community members. "Know your body, know thyself. Own your own speculum. Do your own examinations," Armour remembered. She continued, "We practiced doing Pap smears on each other. And then, we sent them to the lab [for results]."[59] This would prove a life-saving practice for Armour, who was able to detect her own cervical cancer at an early stage. "Had I not been doing [self-examination], I might not even be here today," Armour revealed to me.[60]

Self-health was even promoted by those health radicals with the most to lose—credentialed healthcare workers like the Party's collaborators Woods, Branch, and Terry Kupers, an MCHR physician, whose professional authority was challenged by this realignment of power. While radical physicians and students of nursing and medicine could be deeply committed to their professional identities, many also recognized that systematic change in medicine was long overdue.[61] For example, in a September 1971 "position paper on national healthcare," the MCHR recommended that health facilities, including clinics, hospitals, and medical schools, should be administered by trained health workers as well as "community-worker councils" made up of "patients and health workers."[62]

Seale conjectured that self-health also planted seeds of political transformation. "Another aspect of the 'survival programs' is that we have drawn a good many community people into them. . . . We are now training community people to do sickle cell anemia testing. The people themselves have become very involved in running these programs. . . . At some point or another, the people can actually choose to defend . . . those clinics that they know they have a right to as decent human beings."[63] For the Party, then, in addition to providing concrete medical services, lay expertise also represented revolutionary possibility. Self-health was thus a multivalent tactic that provided real benefits, demystified medical authority, and as Seale suggested, potentially exposed both the deficiencies and the priorities of the U.S. welfare state.

Clinics for the People

In the spring of 1970 Seale ordered that community service work of all Party chapters should minimally consist of a Free Breakfast for Children Program and a health clinic. This directive was partly an effort at centralization responding to the fact that as the Panthers gained national notoriety, Party chapters were springing up across the United States (and internationally), sometimes without permission or oversight from the organization's leadership. More importantly, for the purposes of this discussion, this mandate confirmed health politics as a core element of the Panthers' work.

With the formal establishment of a national network of PFMCs, health politics came to have an integral role in the Party's plan to "serve the people, body and soul." The plan to expand the clinic program was first announced by the Party's minister of education Ray "Masai" Hewitt at a press conference in the fall of 1969.[64] PFMCs were launched as early as 1968 in several cities, including Kansas City, Missouri; Chicago; and Seattle, with Portland following suit in 1969.[65] The Los Angeles chapter's Alprentice "Bunchy" Carter Clinic, located in the Watts neighborhood, opened in late December 1969.[66] Soon after the clinic mandate was handed down, Panther clinics were launched in New York, Cleveland, Boston, Winston-Salem, and Philadelphia.[67] The New Haven clinic, located at 27 Dixwell Avenue, opened in February 1971. The Party medical clinic located closest to its Oakland headquarters—the Berkeley-based Bobby Seale PFMC (later renamed for George Jackson)—would not open until April 1971.[68] The Party headquarters opened its clinic after several

THE BLACK PANTHER PARTY

ANNOUNCES.....

THE GRAND OPENING OF

THE BOBBY SEALE PEOPLE'S FREE HEALTH CLINIC

SATURDAY
APRIL 24th 1971
2:00 P.M.

3236 Adeline St. Berkeley

A persons' health is their most valuable possession. Improper health care and inadequate facilities can be used to perpetrate genocide on a people. The present facist, racist government used its facilities for that purpose -- the genocide of poor and oppressed people. The people must create institutions within our communities that are controlled and run by the people in order to insure our survival. With this in mind, the Black Panther Party announces the opening of our first Free Health Clinic in the Bay Area.

ALSO.....FREE FOOD & CLOTHING ON OPENING DAY

For further Information contact

Black Panther Party···Berkeley Branch

2230 10th St. Berkeley···Phone 848-7740

A flyer announces the opening of the Bobby Seale PFMC in Berkeley in April 1971. This Black Panther Party headquarters clinic was established later than some of the other clinics. Courtesy of It's About Time Black Panther Party Archive / Billy X. Jennings.

other chapters had formed PFMCs. Small, an African American physician who volunteered with the Party, recounted that "it was kind of an embarrassment for the Oakland chapter of the Black Panther Party that although the Party had free clinics . . . they didn't have one in the Oakland area. So . . . we got together with the Berkeley branch of the Panther Party and we opened the Berkeley clinic."[69] The Washington, D.C., chapter's clinic was launched in 1973.[70] The Panther clinics eventually spanned thirteen cities, with New York City and Portland each having more than one.[71]

As this uneven rollout of the Party clinics implies, although Party leadership mandated that all of its chapters establish clinics, it was not able to offer direct support toward this end. Thus the clinic mandate—that required at the very least a location, equipment, personnel, and supplies—presented a great challenge to most chapters and frequently required considerable ingenuity on the part of the Party rank and file. Formation of clinics in cities throughout the United States necessitated the acquisition and mobilization of many human and economic resources, not to mention real estate and supplies. Attempts to set up a PFMC in Milwaukee, for example, floundered altogether when the chapter disbanded in 1969.[72] Hewitt, who held a national position in the Party but was based in Los Angeles, acknowledged the difficulties the chapters might face in setting up medical clinics: "Finding places in underprivileged areas where we can do the job" was difficult.[73] This being the case, Panther membership often had to repurpose spaces, such as storefronts or trailers, by renovating the sites and converting them into workable clinics.[74]

The challenge of finding sites appropriate for PFMCs was often compounded by the fact that clinic real estate often required adequate security. Hewitt noted that owing to police harassment of the Black Panthers, safety concerns had to be taken into account. The PFMCs "can't be structured like Harlem Hospital. We have to be conscious of the problems of sabotage and security," he expressed in a press interview.[75] In Seattle the chapter's headquarters and clinic initially shared the same space: an examination table and medical supplies were located a room that also contained security paraphernalia, and "sandbags lined the walls, boards covered the windows and a couple of rifles leaned against a doorway" as defense against a police raid.[76]

Of the thirteen Black Panther clinics established during the late 1960s and early 1970s, all contained examination tables, offered pri-

Boston's Franklin Lynch PFMC. Courtesy of It's About Time Black Panther Party Archive / Billy X. Jennings.

mary healthcare, collaborated with medical professionals, and relied on donations of supplies and labor. These PFMCs were decidedly grass-roots institutions. Each chapter had to garner independently the re-sources necessary to found a PFMC. The healthcare services offered at a given Panther clinic were thus indicative of the resourcefulness of a Party chapter, the extent to which the chapter was supported by the sur-rounding neighborhood, and the availability of local supplies. Portland's Fred Hampton Memorial PFMC, for instance, was the only chapter to provide dentistry because it developed a working relationship with an area dental school. PFMC services thus both responded to the needs of particular communities and relied on their succor.[77]

"Woe to he who behaves as though his body were his own."
This chapter outlines how the Party operated the clinics that were a cornerstone of its health politics. Just as the PFMCs were structurally necessary to the group's health interventions, the able hands and healthy bodies of its membership were consequential to the organization—and in-dispensable to its sweeping broader mission. Accordingly, the healthcare

access that the Party sought for marginalized communities was also essential for the activists, who emerged from the same underserved communities. Individual well-being—understood in a social health frame—was stressed by the Party. As Armour explained, "We had a slogan: 'Woe to he who behaves as though his body were his own.' [It meant that] your body belongs to the revolution, so you have to take care of it."[78] The activists' healthcare needs were incorporated into the Party's vision for a "people's medical plan."[79] The proposal for this plan asserted that "the maintenance of health among the BPP is presently very low in priority"; this state of affairs was characterized as a "contradiction both to the aspiration and practice of the liberation struggle."[80]

Panther field marshal Don Cox noted some of the health problems that burdened the membership: "Party members have some of the worst health in the country. . . . They suffer from inadequate rest, improper diet. In New York[,] there are five sisters who are anemic. Two have sickle cell anemia. . . . Two brothers have been to the hospital to find out why they have been passing out . . . but they're not being treated."[81] On top of this, "ulcers and pneumonia [were] recurrent problems."[82] Some of these health problems likely stemmed from the stressful conditions under which the activists lived and worked. "There are no part time Panthers," Newton frequently emphasized.[83] But it was also the case that Party members commonly worked *more* than full time.

In addition to the physical toll of Party service, the group's communal living arrangements could exacerbate the spread of illness. As a consequence, the activists developed their own internal public health system to contain infectious disease and less serious communicable illnesses. For example, in the early 1970s, the Party's Oakland Community School—where up to three hundred students boarded in dormitories during the week—experienced an outbreak of shigella, a highly contagious bacterial infection that typically affects children. To staunch the infection's spread, Armour, Ericka Huggins, and others designated one of the Party's homes as a "quarantine dorm," where persons with shigella were housed until the epidemic passed. There was "a whole house," Armour described. "Everybody that was sick had to go there. The doctor would come daily to check that everybody was there, to see how they were doing (do cultures, make sure there was no blood in the stool, and stuff like that). We had developed really, really good relationships with the physicians."[84]

In the "free love" seventies, the Party also had to contend with the presence of sexually transmitted diseases among its membership. The Party developed the "freeze list" to prevent the spread of STDs. The list was a public document, and all members were required to keep track of the names on it and, by doing so, to play a role in health surveillance: Panthers monitored each other to ensure that required medications were being taken and that individual behaviors were aligned with the goal of a healthy community. Brown relayed the purpose and operation of the freeze list in this way: "We decided as an organization that we had to take precautions regarding disease, we couldn't afford to have disease in the community." She continued, "People could call the clinic and ask if a certain person was on the list. Women would mostly call about the brothers. Don't be on the list and drinking alcohol [that might counteract the effects of the medication]. Norma [Armour] and [Sheba] Haven mostly managed the list."[85] To describe someone in the Party—usually a man—as "on the freeze" was to say that the person was taking a course of medication for treatment of an STD and was therefore not available to engage in sexual intercourse. "If a brother was on the freeze, he didn't get 'any,'" a former Party member elaborated. The list "became institutionalized in the organization," Brown recounted.[86]

Staffing

The primary responsibility for the staffing of the PFMCs fell to Party members. The Washington, D.C., clinic was reportedly run with "the part-time efforts of 35 or 40 members."[87] In 1970 the medical staff of the Chicago chapter's clinic consisted of "10 doctors, twelve nurses, and two registered technicians" as well as interns "from medical schools around the city."[88] In Oakland, for several years, Carol Rucker's principal responsibility as a Party member was working as a nurse at the George Jackson clinic. Small, the Panthers' medical adviser, described the staffing arrangement as similar to military service. "Being in the Party was a lot like being in the Army," he observed. "It wasn't like you chose to do something. . . . They would select people to do various things. Some of the [members] expressed an interest in working in the clinic, too, which is why they got in."[89] The Panther Nelson Malloy, a leader of the Winston-Salem Party's health-related programs (and presently a member of the city council there) had paramedic training. When the many chapters of the Black Panther organization were consolidated at the national headquarters beginning in 1970, after Newton's release from prison, Malloy and two members of the South Carolina chapter—his girlfriend, Maria

Moore, and Charles Zolacoffer—moved to the Bay Area. (The chapter's other leader, Larry Little, remained in Winston-Salem and became an influential local politician.) In Oakland Malloy worked alongside Rucker and other Party members at the group's Berkeley clinic.[90]

The Party health cadre was mostly composed of black women. This is unsurprising given that Seale estimated that within three years of the Party's founding approximately 60 percent of its members were women activists.[91] On the national and local level, women filled many of the ranks of the Party leadership. They included Elaine Brown, who was the Party's chairperson between 1974 and 1977; Ericka Huggins, who was head of the Intercommunal Youth Institute; and Kathleen Cleaver, who for several years in the late 1960s was the group's communication secretary and press agent.[92] Women's presence was also considerable at the local chapter level. Black women made up about one-third of the Portland chapter's fifty members.[93] Additionally, women Panthers often organized the Party's highly successful breakfast programs.

The labors and leadership of Panther women were also essential to the operation of the clinics. Branch, a registered nurse, was "the *only* black medical professional" who volunteered her services in the Southern California chapter's clinic. In New York City the Panther Assata Shakur worked in the "medical cadre" of the Harlem chapter under the supervision of Joan Bird, a nursing student.[94] (Shakur was also involved with this chapter's Liberation School and its Free Breakfast for Children Program.) In Washington, D.C., the registered nurse and Party member Catherine Showell was the "health coordinator" for that chapter's PFMC.[95] New Haven Panthers Frances Carter, Carolyn Jones, and Rosemary Mealy are credited with conceiving of and launching the Panther free clinic in that city.[96]

The historian Tracye Matthews argues that women's participation in the service programs might be regarded as "an extension of 'traditional' roles for women in the family: nurturers, caretakers of children, transmitters of morals, etc."[97] These programs fit squarely with conventional ideas of "women's things" like "feeding children" and "taking care of the sick."[98] Matthews's observations were clearly borne out by the Party's health activism, and it was also the case that women both envisioned and led these programs, in addition to making up a large percentage of the organization's rank-and-file membership.[99]

A second important source of staff at the PFMCs was volunteer medical professionals (e.g., physicians, nurses, pharmacists, lab technicians, medical technologists, and medical students). The Bay Area optometrist Elichi Tsuchida, for example, in a letter to Newton, offered to provide vision care services at the Berkeley PFMC.[100] In Seattle students and faculty from the University of Washington's medical school volunteered their services and helped the Sydney Miller PFMC obtain supplies.

As the former Panther JoNina Abron noted, "Medical cadres in the Party received first aid training," but "the survival of the health clinics depended upon health professional workers such as African American physician Tolbert Small, to donate their time."[101] A native of Coldwater, Mississippi, Small was reared under Jim Crow. As a young adult, he was involved in civil rights activities. He was a member of Friends of SNCC. He was also involved with the Mississippi Freedom Democratic Party and counts serving as a driver for Fannie Lou Hamer when she went on fund-raising tours at southern churches as one of the prouder moments of his life. Small would also be on hand when Hamer and other members of the Freedom Party attempted to unseat the Democratic Party's segregationist delegates and stood vigil with scores of other activists outside the Atlantic City convention center.

Small spent his summers in Mississippi after his family moved north. He was educated in Michigan, first at the University of Detroit and then at medical school at Wayne State University. It was in 1968 when the young doctor moved to Oakland to take an internal medicine internship and residency at Highland Hospital.[102]

Rather than join the Party, Small came to his work with the Black Panthers independently and, moreover, initiated what would become a long-standing and substantial collaboration with the Party. Soon after he began working at Highland, Small offered his assistance to the Party. In early 1970, he remembered, "I drove by Grove Street and just left my name and said 'If you ever need a doctor, give me a call. I'm available.'"[103] Never formally a Panther, the doctor helped establish, with the Panthers Claudia Grayson and Rucker, the Bobby Seale People's Free Medical Clinic in Berkeley (later renamed after George Jackson) and served as its director until 1974. He was also the Party's medical director from 1970 until 1974 and, during this time, supervised its sickle cell anemia outreach.[104]

In Portland a white organizer and health radical named Jon Moscow played a formative role in organizing that chapter's PFMCs. A former member of the Congress of Racial Equality, Moscow became inspired by the work of Health/PAC while working for another organization on a report about the New York City hospital system. After he returned to Portland to resume college, he formed Health/RAP, "a research and action project," on the model of Health/PAC. Working with the local Party leader Kent Ford, Moscow played a formative role in creating the Fred Hampton Memorial PFMC.[105]

Other trusted experts were often affiliated with the MCHR, which was SNCC's "medical arm" during the Freedom Summer campaign of 1964. Some volunteers in the summer program remained in rural Mississippi to help cultivate a rudimentary healthcare system. Others returned to their places of origin and continued the work they had begun in the South closer to home, particularly in urban settings in the Northeast, West, and Midwest.[106]

The Party gave the MCHR "much credit" for the advisory role the health professionals played in the "formulation of its [health] program.[107] Its collaboration with MCHR members was multidimensional and reciprocal; lay and expert radical health activists needed each other both in practical and in ideological terms. Party chapters called on members of the MCHR when they needed to establish clinics or when they required medical care.

Such was the case with the physician Michael Wilkins. Having recently completed medical school in the Midwest, Wilkins moved to the borough of Staten Island in New York City, where he worked at Willowbrook State School, a state institution for mentally disabled children.[108] At this time he also began attending MCHR meetings with his fellow physician and Vietnam veteran David McClanahan.[109] Wilkins and McClanahan were contacted by Neil Smith, minister of defense for the Staten Island Party, about helping that chapter establish a health clinic. "He just called us up and said, 'You know, we heard you work with the Medical Committee for Human Rights, and we'd like to know if you would work with us and develop a clinic.'"[110] Soon after, Wilkins signed on; the clinic opened in a storefront on Jersey Street on Staten Island, with Wilkins working there at least one evening a week.

These health professionals also tended to the health of Party members. The physician Phillip Shapiro, chair of the prison health committee of the Bay Area chapter of the MCHR, advocated on behalf of David Hilliard when the Panther was incarcerated in the California Medical Facility at Vacaville. Shapiro protested "the negligence of medical care afforded" to Hilliard and drew attention to his deteriorating health and inadequate treatment, recommending that he "be granted parole at the earliest possible date so that necessary therapy not available at the CMF might be obtained" from "a physician of his own choice."[111] Small was the personal physician to Newton and many Bay Area Party members. In this capacity, he visited George Jackson and Angela Davis when they were incarcerated. He also treated the rank and file and their children for a variety of illnesses, both at the clinic and in their homes.[112]

Community volunteers were also important to the functioning of the PFMCs. Some of these volunteers were political progressives who had training in the health professions; others were laypeople. Party members and lay volunteers at the Chicago and Berkeley clinics were taught by health professionals and more experienced nonexpert volunteers to take medical histories, vital signs, and blood pressure, and to do lab work, including urine and blood analysis.[113] "We would train them to work to some extent like paramedics or physician's assistants," Small explained.[114] "We actually trained some of the women to do pelvic [examinations] and gonorrhea screening. . . . You had a lot of sharp people who learned things very quickly."[115] In some instances this training was quite extensive; some of the individuals trained at the Portland clinics, for example, reportedly developed skills that sufficiently prepared them to work as lab technicians and dental assistants.[116]

Volunteers and health cadre did administrative work in the clinics as well. They were in charge of the day-to-day operations, from making phone calls, doing clerical work, and receiving and organizing supplies to scheduling patient appointments; scheduling doctors, nurses, technicians, and other volunteers; arranging referrals to other clinics, hospitals, or medical specialists as necessary; keeping patient records; and doing basic lab tests.[117] Survey teams of volunteers also made home visits during which they recruited members of the community to come to the clinic for health services.[118]

In administering its clinics, the Party valorized the experiential knowledge of "the people" by transmitting technical skills from medical professionals to laypersons and, in doing so, sought to empower communities.[119] The Los Angeles PFMC, for example, invited "doctors, nurses, pharmacists and other medical technicians to donate their time and skills," emphasizing that these volunteers would also train community members in first aid and basic medicine so that the clinics could "be turned over to the people because all programs and institutions should be controlled by the people and run as they would have them run."[120]

Similarly, an article for the second of two clinics in Portland founded by that Party chapter explained that the People's Health Clinic would "initially . . . be run jointly by the Black Panther Party and HEALTH-RAP; [but] as soon as possible, control will be handed over to the black and white communities."[121]

Clinic staff worked rotating schedules, often balancing clinic duties with paid work, schoolwork, or home responsibilities. The clinics were typically open in the afternoon and evenings—when the people they served were most likely to be able to come to them. The Portland and Seattle clinics were open for three or four hours a day on most weekday evenings.[122] The Los Angeles clinic initially opened all day on Saturdays.[123] By 1971 the booming Chicago Spurgeon "Jake" Winters PFMC claimed fourteen hundred registered patients and averaged more than fifty patients per week (although it was not open every day).[124] In 1970 Portland's Fred Hampton Memorial PFMC claimed a substantial staff that included "27 doctors, plus nurses and medical students."[125]

The Berkeley clinic, staffed by Small and other medical and community volunteers, was open several days a week, mostly during the evening.[126] "The clinic hours were supposed to start around six. But sometimes Dr. Small wouldn't get there until ten because he was coming from his job at Highland Hospital. So, if we were busy, the clinic would be open until midnight or one or two in the morning. Besides the evening clinics, we had weekend clinics. . . . Whenever [health workers] were available, that's when we had the clinic," explained Armour.[127] Twice a week, during the day, this site offered pediatric services with the help of medical residents from nearby Oakland Children's Hospital. This clinic opened every day of the week, even when expert volunteers were not present. "If the doctor wasn't there, we were open for health education and referral information," Armour said. "When things were slow at the clinic we used to practice on each other. . . . I learned to draw blood, give injections. . . . We also learned to do Pap smears. . . . We used to have people at the clinic who were corpsmen in the Vietnam War and they taught us a lot," she recalled.[128] At the Los Angeles PFMC, Branch and Kupers worked in the clinic themselves and solicited assistance for the clinics from their UCLA colleagues. "I would have people from work . . . nursing friends and some of my [other] friends, come and help the clinic," Branch recalled.[129]

When plans for the organization's clinics were just getting under way, Hewitt publicly declared that getting "'personnel is no problem.' . . .

THE

BLACK PANTHER PARTY

FREE
HEALTH CLINIC

THE BLACK PANTHER PARTY HAS OPENED A FREE MEDICAL CLINIC AT 173 20th AVENUE. THE HOURS ARE MONDAY THRU THURSDAY 5:30 to 9:00 PM.

THE BLACK PANTHER PARTY REALIZES THAT THE FASCIST NIXON REGIME HAS NO CONCERN FOR THE HEALTH AND WELFARE OF THE PEOPLE OF THIS COUNTRY AND IT IS CLEAR THROUGH IT'S ACTIONS HERE IN AMERICA, IN VIETNAM, AND THROUGHOUT THE WORLD THAT THIS COUNTRY HAS NO INTENTIONS OF CORRECTING IT'S OPPRESSIVE, EXPLOITATIVE WAYS. THE BLACK PANTHER PARTY REALIZES THAT THE BASIC NEEDS OF THE PEOPLE MUST BE MET. AND WE WILL MOVE FORTH WITH THE SUPPORT AND HELP OF THE PEOPLE TO MEET THOSE NEEDS THROUGH FUNCTIONAL AND PRACTICAL PROGRAMS LIKE THE FREE BREAKFAST PROGRAM AND THE MEDICAL CLINIC.

WE SAY LATER FOR PIG NIXON AND ALL THE REST OF HIS LACKEYS WHO WILL NOT AND CANNOT MEET THE NEEDS OF THE PEOPLE THROUGH THE EXISTING CAPITALISTIC SYSTEM THAT IS BASED ON INEQUITIES

SEIZE THE TIME

POWER
TO THE PEOPLE

Flyer advertising that the Seattle PFMC was open four evenings each week. Courtesy of Black Heritage Society of Washington State.

Offers [from] volunteer medicals 'are pouring in.'"[130] Many of the Black Panther medical clinics were indeed well-staffed and many prospered, with a handful of these remaining open well into the late 1970s. However, for other chapters, the staffing hurdle sometimes proved too steep at times or was altogether debilitating. The Kansas City Party's Bobby Hutton Community Clinic opened in August 1969. Yet by several accounts, the clinic was barely operable by 1970 and offered screening only for sickle cell and high blood pressure on an ad hoc basis.[131] Staffing issues frustrated this chapter's efforts. The MCHR members and Wilkins, who had collaborated with Staten Island Panthers in the formation of its clinic before moving to the Midwest in late 1971, made several unsuccessful attempts to help Pete O'Neal, the leader of the Kansas City Party, "find a . . . radical doctor that would run the clinic."[132] Despite great effort, the Houston Black Panthers' struggles to start a medical clinic were utterly thwarted by a potent combination of limited human and financial resources and relentless police repression that diminished the group's ranks and the support of the surrounding communities.[133]

Even the Seattle chapter, which ran one of the more successful clinics, the Sidney Miller PFMC, also experienced "staffing problems." These issues were attributed to health professionals' waning interest after the novelty of the effort had worn off and the fact that working in the "inner city" was inconvenient for some physicians based at suburban medical practices and hospitals.[134] This made the clinic's services unreliable. According to former Seattle Party head Elmer Dixon, "Sometimes we had a roomful of patients waiting to be seen and the doctor wouldn't be there."[135]

Donations and Supplies

The equipment necessary to operate the PFMCs was begged, borrowed, purchased, scavenged, and sometimes just appeared on the doorstep.[136] Businesses, churches, and other organizations provided financial support for the Party's health programs. Pharmaceutical companies donated drugs to the Black Panther clinics in Oregon.[137] Corporate donations were similarly an important source of support for the Seattle chapter.[138] Kupers, who helped shape the Los Angeles chapter's Bunchy Carter People's Free Medical Clinic, and Small sought donations from medical supply and pharmaceutical companies on behalf of the Panthers. Small personally solicited donations from Bay Area medical and laboratory supply companies, including Bischoff's Medical and Libby Lab.[139] The pastor of St. Matthew's Roman Catholic Church in Brooklyn, New York, held a benefit featuring a Trinidadian steel drum band to support the local Party chapter's clinic and breakfast program in the Brownsville neighborhood.[140] In Connecticut, students from the University of New Haven made a substantial monetary contribution to that city's PFMC.[141]

Healthcare services were coupled with other social services at the PFMCs, as shown on this flyer from 1970 advertising Los Angeles's Alprentice Bunchy Carter clinic. Courtesy of Dr. Marie Branch.

The Panthers' Washington, D.C., clinic opened in the spring of 1973, "with a shoestring budget."[142] Chapters requested donations of all kinds via flyers, newsletters, and the press. In a local alternative newspaper, the Chicago Panthers put in a request for "anything anyone can give—time, money, talent . . . food for the breakfast for children program . . . medical supplies for the clinic."[143] Party chapters also gained some funds through the sale of the group's national newspaper.[144] Fund-raising efforts were carried out by Party members and volunteers through door-to-door neighborhood solicitations and events and outreach on college campuses.[145]

The PFMCs were also supplied through the generosity of physicians via donations of small medical equipment such as needles and syringes, as well as drug samples. Kupers, who was also a psychiatry resident at UCLA, sought out his teachers' assistance to keep the clinic stocked. "I would just go to my professors and I would say 'This is what we're doing in South Central and we need your help. Can you give us

```
     Now open in Southeast Los Angeles and serving the people,
is the Alprentice Bunchy Carter People's Medical Center, located
at 3223 South Central Avenue.  The Medical Center is sponsored
by the Black Panther Party.  Like all of our other socialistic
programs, services provided at the facility are free, because
we fully understand the medical conditions in our Black communi-
ties and how difficult it is to receive medical attention when
you don't have money, right then, to pay for it.
     Some of the services we provide are:  physical examinations,
child immunizations, laboratory work (blood tests, urinalyses,
pap smears), minor surgery, treatment of common ailments (such
as anemia, bronchitis, sinusitis, detection and treatment of ven-
eral diseases).  Most medicines are free.  On Wednesday evenings
at 7:30 first aid  and health classes are held at the Clinic.
     Besides regular medical doctors or general practioners, we
also provide a pediatrician (baby doctor) and a surgeon.
     Community as well as medical professional help is needed.
If you are interested in helping with the Clinic, call 233-7044
or 636-1763.  For appointments and more information call 233-7044.

ALL POWER TO THE PEOPLE !
Health to those who have been deprived
for so many years!
```

Healthcare services offered at the Alprentice Bunchy Carter PFMC included gyneco-logical screening, childhood immunizations, and minor surgery. Courtesy of Dr. Marie Branch.

your samples of medication?'" He continued, "People were happy to help."[146] The Party also had friends in the pharmaceutical industry. As Armour recalled from her time in Los Angeles, "Black folks who worked for pharmaceutical companies would bring us [drug] samples and we would use these" in the clinic.[147]

The Oakland Party also relied on the generosity of other health radicals. A colleague from another community clinic in the city helped keep the Party clinic stocked with supplies. "A pharmacist who worked at the West Oakland Health Center [a Bay Area community clinic with which Small was affiliated] would come down . . . occasionally to take a look at the pharmacy," to see if there were drugs that were needed.[148] "We had a regular pharmacy [at the clinic]. We had a whole wall of medications that we attempted to keep supplied,"[149] Small explained. With donated medications, some PFMCs were able to assemble adequately stocked clinic pharmacies.

Although the Seattle Panthers' small real estate initially served as both an administrative hub and a medical clinic, its Sidney Miller PFMC moved to a separate location when "a building for the clinic was donated by its millionaire owner."[150] Donations were also acquired in unexpected ways. Sometimes equipment arrived at the PFMCs through the generosity of those working in solidarity with them. Supplies from radical health clinics that ceased operation were sometimes donated to the Party chapters. Branch recounted that when a free clinic in Los Angeles's Willowbrook neighborhood closed, its sponsors "loaded up their equipment and brought it to our clinic."[151] In 1969 equipment and supplies left over from the mobile medical units used at the historic Woodstock concert in upstate New York were delivered to the Harlem Party.[152] In California the UCLA medical center daily discarded supplies that were still usable. These items became part of the supply cache at the Bunchy Carter PFMC: "We would just take them and we were given them," Kupers reported.[153]

Some chapters were able to secure municipal, state, or federal funding to support their initiatives. Doing so was initially frowned on by Party higher-ups and was regarded as antithetical to the organization's mission of "show[ing] what people can do for themselves without government assistance."[154] The Party, moreover, regarded its PFMCs as necessary alternatives to those of the federally backed community clinic movement funded by War on Poverty monies. An article in the Party's *Community News Service,* a publication of the Los Angeles chapter, lamented, for example, that "there are many government financed 'Free' clinics. These clinics are therefore required to adhere to the directive of the government."[155] In contrast, this article underscored the fact that services at the Bunchy Carter PFMC were *free.* Its healthcare services were supplied at no cost "by doctors, nurses, and community workers whose primary interest is to serve the People."[156] In this context, *free* here also intimated that the Black Panthers' clinics functioned with an autonomy that state-sponsored clinics could not.

On the other hand, there was sentiment among some in the Party that it was perfectly reasonable to appropriate the government's money and make better use of it. As Armour, who wrote several successful grant applications for public funding during her time in the Party, put it, "We sought resources from wherever we could get them . . . as long as it didn't go against our ideology."[157] The Portland Panthers accepted state funding. Its People's Clinic, the outcome of "a coalition of social actions groups" and health radicals that included the Panthers and Health/RAP, was established with state, federal, and private grant monies.[158] The activists, however, also raised contributions for the operation of the clinic, which was supplied with donated equipment and run with volunteer labor by members of the community and health professionals.[159] The Party's Seattle chapter reportedly received grant funding from the Boeing corporation to support its health clinics.[160] By 1974, when Elaine Brown took over as leader of the Party, grant writing at Party headquarters was de rigueur. The organization regularly wrote grant applications to garner support for its community service programs, even soliciting money from unexpected sources, like criminal justice agencies that typically funded police interests. Brown relished the Panthers' success in appropriating and redirecting state money. The Portland Panthers benefited from the largesse of a private dentistry society that donated equipment to its dental clinic, for example.[161] The clinics were also supported with government grants. Indeed, when this city's health centers ceased operation in 1980, it was attributed to a decline in funding from the state. "As soon as [President Ronald] Reagan got in there," Portland head Ford maintained, "we just couldn't sustain the funding anymore."[162]

Services

Panther clinics mainly provided basic healthcare. First aid and basic services—including testing for high blood pressure, lead poisoning, tuberculosis, and diabetes; "cancer detection tests"; physical exams; treatments for colds and flu; and immunization against polio, measles, rubella, and diphtheria—were available at many PFMCs.[163] In some instances, clinics screened for sickle cell anemia and offered optometry services, well-baby services, pediatrics, and gynecological exams.[164] For the most part, Party health cadre attended to basic health needs that might have otherwise gone unconsidered or untreated. Kupers, who with Armour, Brown, Branch, and Hewitt launched the Los Angeles chapter's clinic, acknowledged that the facility "couldn't handle anything very serious."[165] He continued, describing the types of ailments that PFMC staffers were likely to come across: "We did a lot of kids' infections, sore throats, and that kind of thing. We did basic work-ups. We were basically a triage system."[166]

Nevertheless, the PFMCs also tried to make preventive healthcare available. As Kupers explained of the L.A. clinic, "We had a lot of people who had chronic illnesses that were not life threatening—things like hypertension, ulcers, [and] diabetes—who, just because [they gave their health] a low priority or did not receive enough attention from health professionals, weren't taking care of themselves. And, I would say to somebody, 'You know, your blood pressure is really too high. . . . You would really do well to do some exercise and lose a little weight.'" Kupers concluded that "it was the subtle everyday preventive medicine that I think we were most effective at. We got people more conscious about their health . . . we got a lot of people to start thinking about it and start changing."[167]

When treatment for more complex or serious healthcare issues was required, the PFMC workers, in a manner not dissimilar from an insurance system, made an effort to provide referrals to other facilities or other medical professionals. Patients needing more extensive care than the Portland clinic could provide, for example, were referred to contacts at the University of Oregon Medical School, where the client could receive care at no or low cost and the treatment was ideally provided by students or teaching faculty who shared the activists' health political commitments and even volunteered at the PFMC in their spare time. The Portland PFMC also referred its clients for private specialist care. "We have specialty referrals to private offices on a free basis in surgery, internal medicine, dermatology, hematology, neurology, pediatrics and cancer therapy," Moscow wrote in an alternative press article announcing the opening of the Portland clinic.[168]

On some occasions at the L.A. clinic, the Panthers were able to arrange for "specialist[s] of one kind or another—a surgeon, an orthopedic surgeon, a cardiologist—to come and drop by [on] a certain day of the week . . . and then [we'd] line up all [the] patients" needing specialized care, Kupers remembered.[169] The MCHR had a dense network of health workers, and referrals to specialists could also readily be arranged with members of that organization. Physicians, nurses, and medical students from this group came to the Party clinic to see patients needing more extensive care than what the PFMCs typically provided. At other times, patients—often escorted by a member of the Party medical cadre— would be seen by MCHR senior medical professionals and specialists at their medical offices.[170]

In a contemporaneous account of the Black Panthers' activities, an observer commented that the Party's health activism in Seattle could amount to little more than referrals when the chapter's clinic and head-quarters were housed together: "A doctor helped to found and operate the clinic, which was open two days per week, a former Seattle Panther said, but lack of privacy and the presence of Panthers with guns tended to discourage community use of the facility. Services offered involved

PANTHERS OPEN   FREE CLINIC

DENNIS LEVITT

Saturday, December 27, the Black Panther Party opened a free medical clinic for the benefit of the community. It is named the Alprentice Bunchy Carter Free Clinic, in memory of Panther Bunchy Carter who was gunned down on the UCLA campus January 17. The clinic will provide the community with free medical service from 4111 So. Central Ave., two doors down from Panther Headquarters.

Organizing and planning of the clinic has been going on for some time now, since before the December 8 raid on Panther Headquarters. At the time of that raid, the building was very severely damaged by gunshot and heavy doses of tear gas. At 4111, the gas was so heavy two weeks after the raid that it was impossible to work there. Volunteer helpers could not prepare the building in time for the opening of the clinic. So on the day of the opening, most patients had to be treated in a VW bus parked on the street.

Besides providing medical care, the Panther program includes a number of classes in Natural Medicine and General First Aid. The teaching began weeks ago, but had to be stopped after the December 8 raid. The class in Natural Medicine will deal basically with helping people to help each other. A passing on of information about what to do until the doctor comes, how to recognize certain types of illness, child care, etc. What the class in General First Aid will deal with is self-explanatory. But due to the political situation in the community, the class will deal with one area not normally covered in first aid classes. That area being tear gas exposure. A

number of people who live in the area of Panther Headquarters have been affected by tear gas recently. Bloodshot and swollen eyes from gas exposure are commonplace. One five month old baby had to be hospitalized. The problem is very real.

A personal clinic which can relate to the needs of the people is very much needed because county hospitals have alienated the people. County General, the closest public hospital although many miles away, is much too large and a six hour wait in the

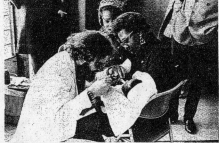

Al Prentice Bunchy Carter Free Clinic Watts — Treating the patient is Dr. Terry Kupers.
Photos by Andrew Kent

receiving room is not uncommon. Treatment is very impersonal and leaves much to be desired. Marie Branch, a nurse at the clinic and one of its organizers, described an instance where "a baby who was treated for tear gas exposure at University Hos-

pital ended up with diarrhea and vomiting and had to spend four days in Childrens Hospital." Due to this situation, people with minor ailments sometimes ignore the ailment rather than go to the county hospital. The ailment then gets worse and treatment becomes more difficult. Carter clinic can help these people and avoid those kinds of problems.

Dr. Terry Kupers, one of the coordinators, says the clinic will also have a political effect in the community. Dr. Kupers says the clinic will "educate people to what health care can be like... and what kind of health care they are entitled to. They are theoretically entitled to it at county hospital, but they don't get it." Dr. Kupers went on to say that once people become educated to this, they can begin to demand the kind of care they are entitled to.

In the community, reaction to the project seems to be very good. One interested observer, whose daughter was treated for a cold at the clinic, said, "If it can be maintained without too much outside harassment, it'll be a real good thing for the community." He felt the treatment his little girl received was very good and quite professional.

The coordinators of the clinic plan to keep it open every Saturday and eventually everyday. But they are having their problems. The Panthers are being threatened with eviction from the clinic building as well as from their headquarters. But the clinic personnel say the clinic will remain open and continue to function, either in VW buses as on December 27, or at a new location.

Group forms in Berkeley to defend Black Panthers

"Citizens to Defend the Black Panther Party" is a newly formed Berkeley coalition of groups concerned that the recent attacks against the Panthers in Chicago and Los Angeles indicate a national drive which might soon manifest itself in a raid upon the Panthers' national headquarters on Shattuck Avenue in Berkeley.

The group was called together Dec. 11 by Frank Daar of the Berkeley Coalition, Conn Hallinan of the teaching assistants union at UC, and ASUC President Dan Siegel. The meeting included members of the three campus unions, the Oakland Black Caucus, the American Civil Liberties Union, the National Lawyers Guild, the Economic Opportunity Organization of the Berkeley Area, the Committee of Concerned Asian Scholars, the Welfare Rights Organization, and the Communist Party, USA.

After discussions with members of the Black Panther Party, the following demands were presented to the Berkeley Police Chief Bruce Baker on Dec. 15;

paign of destruction against the Black Panther Party, we demand:

"1. That in light of Black Panther Party Chief of Staff David Hilliard's order that police with proper warrants are to be admitted into Panther office without resistance, but no secret night-time raids be carried out against Black Panther offices.

"2. That no warrant for the arrest of any member of the Black Panther Party or for a search for weapons be served until it is made public or communicated to a person chosen by the Black Panther Party, that no warrant be served at Party Headquarters unless it is so directed on the face of the warrant, and that the judge issuing the warrant or a member of the private bar chosen by the judge accompany police serving the warrant at Black Panther Headquarters.

"3. That the police make public all contingent plans for attacking the Black Panther Party headquarters and all instructions from and communications with the FBI, the Justice Department,

concerning attacks upon the Black Panther Party.

"4. That no weapons ever be used against black people by members of the Berkeley Police Department unless absolutely necessary for the preservation of life.

"5. That the Berkeley police be put under genuine community control."

Chief Baker said that he was well aware of the latest police raids upon Panther offices and was concerned about preventing similar incidents in Berkeley. He stated that it was his intention not to conduct secret or predawn raids against Panther headquarters and he agreed to the proposal that Berkeley Police contact the Black Panther Party or its attorneys before attempting to serve a warrant at Party headquarters or upon an individual Panther sought by the police.

He also agreed with the suggestion that if the judges agreed a judge or member of the private

pany police serving any warrant at Panther headquarters.

Baker also claimed that the Berkeley Police Department possesses no attack plans for Party headquarters and that the plan

More on LAPD atrocities

MICHAEL HANNON

The next time I hear some wind bag pontificating about the Great American Principle that a man is "innocent until proven guilty," I fear the politest response I will be capable of will be a derisive laugh.

On any day, there are hundreds of men and women, who have been accused but not yet convicted of any crime, being punished in the medieval dungeons euphemistically called the Los Angeles County Jail. Yet because no bail has been set, or because they lack the money for the bond premium, or because they do not own real property to put up as col-

recently published in local newspapers was simply a set of notes dealing with the possibility of a gun battle between Panthers and a rival black group.

lateral, they sit in jail and are treated like convicted prisoners. Just as if he had a right to do so, the sheriff imposes rules that reduce their contact with the outside to a bare minimum, feeds them on slop and thoroughly regiments and orders their lives.

The only legal purpose for pretrial confinement is to insure the appearance of the accused in court. Yet the sheriff uses pretrial confinement as an excuse to punish and punish he does.

The jail atrocities committed against the Panthers arrested Dec. 8 are only slightly more sharp and blatant than the usual

---

Marie Branch (above) was a UCLA nursing professor who helped run the Alprentice Bunchy Carter PFMC outside the clinic. Dr. Terry Kupers (below), a UCLA resident and MCHR member, worked at the Alprentice Bunchy Carter PFMC. From Los Angeles Free Press, January 1970. Courtesy of Dr. Terry Kupers.

'referrals' more often than treatment."[171] The Sidney Miller PFMC subsequently moved to a new location where it was led by the Panther Carolyn Downs. The fact that today a county clinic pays tribute to this Party medical clinic and to Downs suggests that Seattle's health politics became more efficacious over time.

In instances when advanced treatment required patients under the Black Panthers' canopy to seek care at a local public health facility or county hospital, Party cadre or patient's advocates were dispatched to accompany the person seeking healthcare. The patient advocate system that was most developed in Chicago but present in several Party clinics was a clear example of how the clinics were envisioned to do broader work of social transformation and reflected the organization's social health perspective.[172] The advocate, often a member of the Party, translated medical diagnoses and procedures to patients. This person also informed clients of their rights as a patient. At the Los Angeles chapter, patient advocates often did the work of ensuring that those in the community needing care beyond what the Party could provide received it: "If we found something [serious], then what we would do is advocate," explained Kupers. "Panther members would be the advocates. We'd send someone with them to stand up for them. If necessary, these advocates represented the interests of the patient, ensured that he or she did not have to wait extensively to be seen by making a fuss, or insisted that a patient be treated respectfully by appropriate medical personnel."[173]

Modeling the type of care that the community should expect, the clinics served not only to treat the ill but to also "educate people about their healthcare" and to empower them; at the PFMCs members of the community were instructed to "stand up to their doctors" and demand their rights to respectful and suitable care."[174] Dr. William Davis, a medical adviser to the Portland PFMC, echoed this sentiment: the clinic was about "becoming aware of your healthcare condition . . . and doing something about it. Enabling you to do something about it . . . a place . . . where the Afro-Americans and poor people could [have] a little less formal atmosphere and they would not be intimidated."[175]

The clinics also conveyed aid distinctive to a chapter's resources or a community's specific needs. In the fall of 1969, after Los Angeles Party headquarters was raided by police, resulting in injuries to Party members and volunteers, the Bunchy Carter PFMC began offering classes on how to treat tear gas exposure; this California clinic characteristically also dispensed natural medicines and remedies.[176]

In Winston-Salem emergency medical services were "often distributed on a racial basis rather than on the basis of need."[177] Sick or injured persons requiring medical transportation were allegedly vetted by callous ambulance dispatchers who were instructed by their supervisors not to send assistance to poor blacks who might be unable to pay. If callers could not prove that they were ill to a dispatcher's satisfaction or that they had the resources to pay for the service, they were denied transport to the hospital.[178] In instances in which county ambulance service was dispatched, it might arrive late or medics might refuse to transport a person in need of care to the hospital. An occasion in which this medical discrimination proved fatal was the death of a black teenager from a gunshot wound. The municipal ambulance service took thirty minutes to arrive on the scene and then refused to provide treatment or transport to the emergency room. The youth later died. The Panther Larry Little complained that "we had people who died because these ambulance employees, who were county employees, determined these people were not in an emergency situation."[179]

In response, the Winston-Salem Party initiated a service to provide free medical transport. In 1971 the Panther repurposed a late-model hearse as an ambulance. At the same time, Party members took classes to become proficient in first aid and some became certified emergency medical technicians,[180] as part of its People's Free Ambulance Service. This program began in 1972 using a donation from a deceased Panther, Joseph Waddell, who died in prison under suspicious circumstances and had named the Winston-Salem Black Panther chapter as the beneficiary of his life insurance policy.[181] The ambulance service was suspended briefly during this year when the vehicle's insurance premiums proved too high for the chapter to maintain. The formerly part-time service resumed in 1973—after the Panthers received $35,700 in financial backing from the national Episcopal Church—and they began serving the community twenty-four hours per day with a new ambulance obtained through these monies, with Malloy as its director and a staff of emergency medical technicians and drivers.[182] The renamed Joseph Waddell People's Free Ambulance Service was in operation until 1977 when Malloy moved to Oakland.[183]

The Portland Party's health activities were notable for the fact it operated three PFMCs. Its Fred Hampton Memorial PFMC was dedicated to general medical care, and a second location housed its Malcolm X People's Free Dental Clinic, which opened in March 1970. The success

In June 1971 the Black Panther *announced the start of the Winston–Salem chapter's unique "Serve the People" Program—The People's Free Ambulance Service. Courtesy of It's About Time Black Panther Party Archive / Billy X. Jennings.*

of the healthcare PFMC encouraged Ford and another Panther, Sandra Britt, to establish a second healthcare facility—the People's Clinic—in that city.[184] At the dental clinic located around the corner from the chapter's medical facility, free emergency and preventive dental care was dispensed by students and faculty affiliated with the University of Oregon

Dental School.[185] Members of a professional society of dentists also volunteered at the Black Panthers' only clinic dedicated to oral health and donated equipment and supplies.[186] The oral care program was coordinated with Portland's Free Breakfast for Children Program. Volunteer dentists and dentistry students gave presentations to children about proper care for their teeth.[187]

The diverse constituencies of the radical health movement were, for the most, consistent in their goal of overturning health inequality by improving healthcare services and putting a check on biomedical authority. Offering alternatives to mainstream healthcare, at their clinics these activists supplied urgently needed services. With their support for the practice of self-health, the radical health movement sought to give patients a measure of agency in their healthcare decisions and medical treatment. Activists also undermined medical professionals' elite status. Transferring this authority, in turn, to trusted experts, community volunteers, and to patients themselves (by valorizing experiential knowledge), health radicals hoped to empower some of those most in need of healthcare.

Toward this end, at its clinics the Panther organization supplied a range of services to local communities. Because the health activist tactic of institution building is especially resource demanding, requiring both outlays of capital and access to (trusted) expert collaborators, the Party's clinic program was a mixed endeavor.

The Black Panthers' PFMCs were a centerpiece of its health activism and engendered the support and approval of the communities they served. Thus police and public health agencies that sought to discredit the Party often took aim at its clinics. Human and financial resources aside, repression and regulatory hounding by authorities presented a formidable challenge to the success of the PFMCs. An urban renewal plan that never came to fruition forced the Portland chapter to be evicted from its clinic site. The local sheriff cleared out equipment and medical supplies from the site before the activists were able to do so. Nevertheless, this chapter was able to reestablish its clinic in a nearby location.[188]

City police, likely working with the FBI, destroyed the Chicago clinic during a police raid in the summer of 1969. Also in Chicago, home to large numbers of radical health movement free clinics,[189] the health board cited the Party for violation in 1970 because its clinic "'was not adequately set up under the terms of the city ordinance.'"[190] The MCHR physicians Alfred Klinger and Quentin Young, who helped launch the

Chicago clinic, deemed this "harassment" by "some political forces in the city [that] are trying to demolish anything the Panthers do."[191] The Party rejected this gambit. The Chicago chapter refused to apply for a license from the health board to dispense healthcare services because doing so would have permitted "city [health] inspectors to make at-random checks at the clinic."[192] Several months later, the Chicago city council considered an ordinance to "regulate free health care centers" there. Because existing laws were not applied to all health clinics, at least one councilmember charged that this was an effort by the city to "selectively . . . discriminate against free clinics established by political groups such as the Black Panthers and Young Lords."[193]

Other chapters were also forced to untangle bureaucratic red tape. For example, the Portland Public Solicitations Commission in charge of approving individuals and organizations that did public fund-raising, for example, initially denied the Black Panther Party the permit necessary to solicit monies.[194] After an outcry from the local community, a permit was granted to the chapter. Oakland police, at the behest of the FBI, routinely harassed the local Party chapter for soliciting money to support its clinics and sickle cell anemia screening initiatives without proper permits. Clinics also drew seemingly more "positive" attention from the state. The success of the New Haven PFMC brought the notice of the Nixon administration, which sent an envoy to the clinic to observe its workings. The government's suggestion to take over the clinic was rebuffed by the Panthers, who feared co-optation by the state.[195]

In Los Angeles the Party headquarters and nascent clinic located at 4115 South Central Avenue came under fire by a police raid before it was fully realized. The attack, on December 8, 1969, left the facilities destroyed, a score of Party members injured (and imprisoned), and three police officers wounded.[196] The previous evening Branch, several Party members, and Party supporters had gathered at the Los Angeles headquarters to finalize clinic planning.[197] The police raid delayed, for a time, the opening of the clinic a few doors away at 3223 South Central Avenue, because the building had been "very severely damaged by gunshot" in the raid on the headquarters.[198] But within a few weeks, the Bunchy Carter PFMC was open for business. The clinic opened in the shadow of a year of catastrophic violence—both the Panther killed on the campus of UCLA in January 1969 in an altercation with the US Organization, for whom the clinic was named, and the destructive, fatal December 1969 encounter that this Party chapter had with the police.

The launching of the clinic thus signaled the Party's perseverance and foreshadowed its turn to rededication to community service.

By 1971 the Black Panthers had established a national network of health clinics. In this and other ways, the Party encouraged the poor and predominantly African American communities on whose behalf it advocated to take some measure of control over their healthcare.[199] Traditionally, doctors alone set the tone and agenda of the medical encounter. Health radicals empowered patients to be agents in these interactions. The Party's health activism evidenced the multilayered interactions and the sometimes overlapping commitments of the radical health movement. Certainly, then, the Party's health politics was not a brand-new idea. It was part of a larger health political terrain. The Party's health activism, both within and beyond its clinics, was distinctive in its attention to class, health, *and* race. The organization combined elements of radical health activism with an extant tradition of black communities' responses to myriad forms of health inequality. Moreover, the Party brought to the efforts of the radical health movement its own social health perspective. This agenda, reflecting the formative influence of the social medicine tradition, assumed a holistic view of disease and illness and incorporated antiracism, Marxist-Leninist ideology, and a critique of medical authority. Conceived as sites of social change, Party medical clinics attended to more than just narrowly defined health needs.

4.

SPIN DOCTORS

The Politics of Sickle Cell Anemia

On March 29, 1972, in Oakland, California, the Party launched a three-day Black Community Survival Conference at De Fremery Park, known to the Panthers as Bobby Hutton Memorial Park after the first member of the Party besides Newton and Seale.[1] This park held much meaning for the group. "Defremery was a tattered park," Elaine Brown recalled. "Its thinning grass reflected the poverty of West Oakland, where Bobby . . . lived and died. But it was our park now, the people's park. It had come to be called 'Bobby Hutton Memorial Park.'"

The *Black Panther* reported that conference attendance over the three days topped sixteen thousand.[2] Of these attendees, some eleven thousand people were purportedly screened for sickle cell anemia, an incurable and ultimately fatal genetic disease that causes typically round red blood cells to take a sickle shape, depleting their ability to circulate oxygen through the body. Encouraged by positive reception to its screening program, the Party's newspaper boldly predicted that by 1973 the organization would have tested as many as one million possible carriers of the trait or unwitting disease sufferers using mobile medical units to extend the health services provided by its network of chapter-based PFMCs.[3] This scenario did not come to fruition. In fact, by the following year, the Party came to play a diminished role in efforts to raise public consciousness about sickle cell anemia when federal authorities, working with state public health agencies, brought the regulation of the genetic condition under their purview after years of inattention to the disease. At the same time, the condition became a rallying cry for other representatives of the black community, ranging from more moderate civil rights organizations to soul music radio stations. The inclusion of sickle cell anemia in the national healthcare agenda represented a bittersweet success for the Panthers who, with their campaign, sought to shine a light not only on the plight of disease sufferers but also on the inequities of a profit-driven U.S. healthcare system sustained by publicly funded biomedical research.

In the spring of 1972, the Party's sickle cell anemia initiative was a hallmark of its health politics. This campaign epitomized the Party's social health perspective, highlighting both the biological and the extramedical circumstances that contributed to the prevalence of sickle cell anemia among African Americans and to the disproportionate burden of disease borne by blacks more generally. A genetic disease primarily affecting persons of African descent, sickle cell anemia also proved a particularly effective vehicle for Party political ideology. As a condition of the blood, sickle cell anemia evoked consanguinity and racial kinship. This kinship entitled the Party to speak to and for the experiences of black suffering and to ground these experiential claims in the history of the African diaspora. The Panthers' attention to the needs of sickle cell trait carriers and disease sufferers was thus an especially powerful symbol of its affiliation with and service to African American communities.

The Party's sickle cell health politics involved two interdependent emphases: *health education,* imparted by the activists via a variety of media, including newspapers and television, that combined lessons in genetic disease inheritance with ideological framing and political instruction; and free *genetic screening* for sickle cell anemia traits and disease administered in private homes, at its chapter-based clinics, and at public events, all carried out under the auspices of the mostly titular People's Sickle Cell Anemia Research Foundation (PSCARF).[4] In keeping with the egalitarian principles of the Party's health politics, the genetic screening program relied on the labor of Party cadre and community members in addition to the work of volunteer medical professionals. In addition to the sickle cell screening it carried out in intimate settings (such as homes, schools, and its health clinics), the Party conducted large-scale testing at community gatherings using Sickledex, a recently introduced, inexpensive, and portable test that allowed preliminary sickling diagnoses to be made outside the laboratory.

The Black Panther Party's sickle cell anemia screening program was carried out at its clinics, parks, and other public venues. Courtesy of Steven Shames and Department of Special Collections and University Archives, Stanford University Libraries.

In addition to genetic screening, the sickle cell campaign included education of the public about the disease through the distribution of written information such as the flyer held by this woman in 1972. Courtesy of Steven Shames and Department of Special Collections and University Archives, Stanford University Libraries.

The health education dispensed by the Black Panther Party contextualized sickle cell anemia within a matrix of mediating factors that included not only biology but also racism and poverty. The Party's explanation for the disease's origins strategically reworked earlier and often racially essentialist associations between sickling and blackness that had emerged in 1910 beginning with the initial diagnosis of a case of sickle cell anemia in an Afro-Caribbean man. Drawing on theories from anthropology and population genetics, which suggested that sickling offered resistance to malaria in sub-Saharan Africa, the Party developed an etiological narrative for sickle cell anemia that triangulated biology with social environment and political ideology. The group's social health frame did not deny the significance of disease inheritance—indeed, its newspaper featured pieces that detailed the genetic transmission of sickle cell anemia. Rather, the Party's explanation for the persistence of sickle cell anemia foregrounded the history of racial slavery, contemporary racism, and the vagaries of a profit-driven healthcare system that it alleged privileged revenue over healing. The Panthers were, in effect, "spin doctors," who politically diagnosed illness. In drawing attention to sickle cell anemia and the plight of those suffering from it, the Party worked not only toward preventing the disease but also toward eradicating the societal ills that enabled its persistence and exacerbated its effects.

Although its social health frame was distinctive, the Black Panther Party was not alone in its efforts to bring attention to the plight of African Americans suffering with this blood disease, which is characterized by "crises" or bouts of chronic pain.[5] The term "crisis" also aptly describes the bouts of ideological debate and political posturing that would unfold around the issue of sickle cell anemia. These debates were precipitated by a 1970 *Journal of the American Medical Association (JAMA)* article by a physician named Robert B. Scott that stressed the relative invisibility of sickle cell disease, compared with other genetic diseases. Moreover, the article exposed disparities in federal funding for research on genetic diseases,[6] revealing that the U.S. National Institutes of Health devoted considerable resources to the study of genetic conditions common among white Americans, but that the funding the agency provided for research on treating and preventing sickle cell anemia, which predominates among (but is not exclusive to) African Americans, was nominal by comparison. For the Party, this article was paradigmatic. It provided the Panthers with support for its contention that the administration of President Richard Nixon failed to equitably support the healthcare needs of all U.S. citizens and, furthermore, strengthened their claim that the state's disregard of black health was both acute and deliberate.

This widely publicized and circulated *JAMA* article was also partly responsible for fueling a contest among sickle cell stakeholders, particularly activists and politicians, seeking to take credit for meeting the heretofore neglected health needs of poor black communities.[7] The Nixon administration, other civil rights organizations, and a nascent sector of sickle cell philanthropies, such as the National Sickle Cell Disease Research Foundation, among others, vied with the Panthers to prove their dedication to African American constituencies by garnering resources for treating and preventing a disease that affected them disproportionately. Sickle cell anemia activism was one of the primary sites through which the Party established its legitimacy in black communities and among the broader public. Unsurprisingly then, as the visibility of sickle cell anemia increased, Party leaders' worries about losing their ability to shape the disease's political significance also grew, as competing stakeholders with political agendas diametrically different from their own angled to influence the meaning of the disease. The Party's anxiety over its diminishing influence was voiced in several articles in the *Black Panther* in which organizations and government agencies that had taken up the cause of the sickle cell disease were fiercely criticized.

The Party's apprehensions were borne out when the Nixon administration, with a storehouse of fiscal and political resources at its disposal (despite its austerity politics), effectively resolved the sickle cell "crisis." Within a few months of the Party's De Fremery Park event, after a year of testimony and public debate, the U.S. Congress passed the National Sickle Cell Anemia Control Act of 1972, to establish a national program for genetic counseling and for the diagnosis and treatment of sickle cell anemia, and to fund scientific research on the disease with the aim of finding its cure. This expression of federal support for what had historically and imprecisely been understood as a "black disease" blunted somewhat the Party's accusation that the state neglected African American health concerns and, as a result, also diminished the organization's ability to persuasively frame the disease in a social health context.[8] Although this social health perspective would lose none of its credence, its political utility to the Panthers was depleted when public health agencies attended to sickle cell anemia and African Americans were indexically incorporated into the U.S. healthcare polity.[9] The symbolic inclusion of blacks in the nation's health infrastructure established their "biological citizenship"—individuals' claims on the state based on illness status (instead of the "social" and "economic" citizenship the Party had sought for oppressed communities since its founding)[10]— even as it failed to stem race- and class-based health inequality.

Bringing the "Invisible Malady" into Relief

In the early twentieth century, sickle cell anemia was widely known in scientific circles. Aspects of this "first molecular disease" were studied by hematologists, chemists, geneticists, and social scientists.[11] Yet the disease remained "invisible" to many outside these professional communities, including those most likely to be affected by it.[12] Although the severity of African American health issues was acknowledged before

World War II—what are now called "racial health disparities" had long been a fact of black life—neither public health agencies nor the black press extensively publicized sickle cell anemia as a "disease of significance among blacks" before the 1970s.[13] The October 1970 *JAMA* article, however, appreciably boosted sickle cell anemia's visibility.[14] Scott's article, "Health Care Priority and Sickle Cell Anemia," exposed glaring funding disparities for research on genetic diseases and, in the process, brought national attention to sickle cell disease.[15]

This piece was a noteworthy source of inspiration for the Party. However, sickle cell anemia was on the Party's radar screen at least one year before the publication of Scott's critique. In June 1969 Field Marshal Don Cox announced that the disease was among the issues that the Party would address in its health programs. In the same month the *Black Panther* published a short article on sickle cell anemia, "Medicine and Fascism," that anticipated some themes of the sickle cell anemia campaign, especially unacknowledged and unaddressed black pain and suffering. Sickle cell disease was also identified as a topic of concern in a health workshop at the Party-organized Revolutionary People's Constitutional Convention of September 1970.[16] Nevertheless, the *JAMA* article stoked the activists' interest in the disease and furnished a stark and specific example of medical inequality that was readily importable into its health politics.

Scott, at the time a researcher at the Medical College of Virginia Health Services Center in Richmond, declared sickle cell anemia "a major public health consideration."[17] The disease would proliferate, Scott argued, as long as fiscal and social resources dedicated to it remained insufficient. He prescribed screening and genetic counseling as ways to decrease the disease's prevalence.[18] The article suggested that more could be done to prevent sickle cell anemia on at least two additional fronts: advocacy and fund-raising. Scott reasoned that sickle cell advocacy groups needed to be more effective in raising both consciousness and money. He called on black communities, in particular, to work to aggregate the few existing local philanthropic organizations dedicated to sickle cell anemia into a national effort capable of applying additional resources to the goal of ending the disease. "There is no nationwide volunteer organization devoted to sickle cell anemia," Scott wrote.[19] "There are groups in cities throughout the country which are active and no doubt increasing in effectiveness, [but they are] not coordinated nationwide."[20]

Although the Party came to criticize the plethora of charitable organizations that sprang up in response to the sickle cell "crisis" precipitated by the publication of Scott's article, in 1971 the group formed PSCARF[21] and worked with the Mid-Peninsula Sickle Cell Anemia Foundation, a research initiative and philanthropy initiated by Stanford medical student Donald Williams and his peers.[22] Despite the Party's claims to the contrary,[23] there is little evidence that the PSCARF carried on scientific investigations of the disease. The establishment of this foundation was nevertheless important because it shored up the larger sickle cell anemia initiative by allowing the Party to augment its grassroots credibility among underserved communities with scientific authority.[24] Specifically, the foundation, led by the physician Tolbert Small, already facilitated the Party's affiliation with several prominent medical researchers and scientists whom Small recruited as members of its advisory board.[25]

Importantly, the formation of this advisory board was necessary for the PSCARF to secure nonprofit status and receive charitable donations.[26] Donations to the foundation to support the Party's sickle cell screening and educational outreach were solicited in the *Black Panther*; one such solicitation asked for "people [who] can contribute their time, effort and money toward educating other people and finding a cure" for sickle cell anemia.[27] Monetary support was also sought at Party-sponsored rallies and social events and by Party members in front of local businesses.[28] The sickle cell anemia campaign received support from other philanthropies.[29] In-kind donations also spurred interest in the sickle cell initiative. In Portland, Oregon, for example, the owner of a local McDonald's franchise supplied the Party chapter there with coupons for a free hamburger, fries, and soda that were given to members of the community who took part in the genetic testing program.[30]

One member of the PSCARF's board of advisers was the renowned scientist and avowed Communist Linus Pauling, whose research with collaborators in 1949 used electrophoresis, a common biochemical laboratory technique, to establish the molecular basis of sickle cell anemia disease.[31] Electrophoresis analyzes the structure of molecules by observing their migration in an electrical field. The hemoglobin molecule comprises four polypeptide chains, two alpha and two beta subunits. The mutation that results in sickle cell anemia occurs when one amino acid on the beta chain, glutamic acid, is replaced by another, valine. As these amino acids have different electrical charges, the former charged and the latter uncharged, observing the molecule in an electromagnetic field yields information about the structure of hemoglobin.[32]

William C. Davis, the brother of the activist–actor Ossie Davis, who held a PhD in biochemistry from the University of Idaho, also served on the board.[33] In the early 1970s, after his doctoral training, William Davis moved to Oregon to take a job as the director of clinical research at United Medical, a commercial laboratory; from this vantage, he was able to assist Portland Black Panther leader Kent Ford in establishing a medical clinic and with sickle cell anemia screening and education outreach efforts.[34] Davis stressed that the sickle cell anemia campaign was not just testing but also "educational outreach . . . telling them about the disease, what it was, and what they should do in terms of treatment." Davis, too, felt that the state's neglect of sickle cell anemia was "an epidemic attack . . . an attempt to decrease the number" of blacks in the United States. Davis, who directed the medical lab at Emmanuel Hospital in Portland, Oregon, was never a member of the Party, but his affiliation with the Panthers resulted in harassment from federal authorities; shortly after moving to Oregon, he was visited at his home by an FBI agent who suspected that Davis was going to lead the local Party.[35]

The Washington, D.C., pediatrician Roland B. Scott (no relation to *JAMA* author Robert B. Scott) was a member of the PSCARF board as well. Chairman of the pediatrics department at Howard University Medical Center at this time, Scott also founded the Center for Sickle Cell Disease there in 1972.[36] Dr. Charles Whitten, a leading sickle cell anemia researcher based at Wayne State University School of Medicine, where Small had been a student, and a founder in 1971 of the Sickle Cell Detection and Information Center and the Sickle Cell Disease Association of America, also advised the Party.[37] Although the board never met as a body, the Party's affiliation with Small, Pauling, Davis, Scott, and numerous other advisers imparted credibility to the Panthers' health politics, as the authority of these doctors and scientists was symbolically extended to the Party's sickle cell initiatives.[38]

PSCARF lent a patina of scientific credibility and in turn advanced the Panthers' efforts to garner financial donations for its sickling initiatives. Although much of the Party's financial support continued to come from the sale of its newspaper in the United States and abroad, the foundation was an important fund-raising conduit. Donations to support the foundation's work were solicited regularly in the *Black Panther* between 1971 and 1972. A solicitation in the newspaper, for example, encouraged readers to send money to the Party headquarters in Oakland in support of sickle cell. The Party claimed that 80 percent of the funding necessary to conduct its sickle cell anemia campaign was provided through donations. While this figure is impossible to verify, the fact that the FBI specifically targeted the Party's fund-raising for its sickle cell anemia campaign—for example, the FBI instructed the Oakland police department and other Bay Area police authorities to "arrest for unlawful solicitation the Black Panther Party members who sought public donations for the [sickle cell anemia] program in public places"—suggests that this initiative may have inspired substantial financial backing.[39]

The *JAMA* commentary that inspired the formation of PSCARF influenced the Party in another important way. By exposing a substantial biomedical research funding gap by disease, it supplied the Party with hard evidence in support of the activists' assertion that the general lack of public awareness about sickle cell anemia was abetted by the federal government's racially motivated fiscal neglect of black health. "In 1967," Robert Scott detailed, "there were an estimated 1,155 new cases of SCA, 1,206 of cystic fibrosis, 813 of muscular dystrophy, and 350 of phenylketonuria. Yet volunteer organizations raised $1.9 million for cystic fibrosis, $7.9 million for muscular dystrophy, but less than $100,000 for SCA. National Institutes of Health grants for many less common hereditary illnesses exceed those for SCA."[40] Despite the fact that sickle cell anemia occurred in a "similar order of magnitude" to many other genetic diseases, Scott complained, the disease had not received comparable private interest or public funding.[41]

Of note was the fact that the genetic diseases Scott compared might be understood to have distinct racial "identities":[42] cystic fibrosis, muscular dystrophy, and phenylketonuria predominate among persons of European descent, while sickle cell anemia is most common among persons of African descent. The author, however, never explicitly charged that racism lay behind the lack of attention that sickle cell anemia had received to date. The implication of his analysis was nevertheless unmistakable; the social status of the sufferers of the respective diseases shaped both public sympathy and levels of government funding. The Party was not alone in viewing the health disparities that Scott disclosed as issues of racial politics. A similar interpretation of the Scott article was made by Senator John Tunney of California, a cosponsor of the bill that became the National Sickle Cell Anemia Control Act: "I think it is fair to say—and research figures prove the fact—that if sickle cell anemia afflicted primarily white people instead of black, we would have made the commitment long ago to end this disease."[43]

Echoes of Scott's argument reverberated in the pages of the *Black Panther*. These Party news items magnified the racial bias that was merely insinuated by Scott. For example, one article complained that sickle cell anemia "has not received the attention or consideration from public agencies" despite the fact that it "is as crippling, as painful and as deadly" as diseases that "primarily affect white people."[44] Small, an architect of the sickle cell anemia campaign, recalls that in 1971 when he and Party member Ronald "Doc" Satchel embarked on a speaking tour of several Party medical clinics to drum up publicity for the initiative by holding press conferences and to instruct health cadre in how to establish education and screening initiatives, he quoted liberally from the *JAMA* article "to document the neglect of the United States government in dealing with sickle cell anemia."[45] The rehearsing of Scott's analysis thus formed a pillar of the sickle cell anemia initiative. The Party found in Scott's revelation of the state's disparate dedication to its citizens' health needs the building blocks of a powerful critique that it hoped would resonate with black communities and simultaneously mobilize them around its sickle cell anemia initiative and its political philosophy.

"The People's Fight against Sickle Cell Anemia Begins"

The Party announced the formal start of its sickle cell anemia campaign in May 1971 in an article in the *Black Panther* titled "The People's Fight against Sickle Cell Anemia Begins." With this item, which ran accompanied by two photographs of volunteers (likely affiliated with its Chicago chapter, which had begun a sickle cell anemia campaign one month prior) administering sickle cell tests to black children in a classroom, the Party unveiled the ambition and breadth of its initiative. The organization declared its intention to raise awareness about the disease as well as its plan to expand the alternative health infrastructure initiated with the PFMCs to include its sickle cell anemia prevention efforts—through the interlinked activities of health education and genetic screening.[46] This response to the sickle cell "crisis" was not, however, a public health campaign in any conventional sense; it was a social health praxis in which ideas and action were united to expose the political stakes of sickling.

"A Massive Educational Campaign":
Panther Health Outreach and Education

The Party's ideational aims were advanced, in its words, in "a massive educational campaign" through which information about the "nature," "origin," and "effects" of sickle cell anemia, "its prevalence among Black people," and "why the racist U.S. government had done nothing to help" was circulated to black communities.[47] To this end, its educational outreach included basic instruction in the genetic transmission of sickling, yet extended beyond this focus; the Party offered up scientific information about the disease together with social critique and political analysis. The group endeavored to place sickle cell anemia in a broader context by advancing a conception of the disease as a simultaneous biological, historical, and sociopolitical phenomenon.

Much of this work of framing sickle cell anemia transpired via a range of media that served as conduits for the Party's health ideologies.[48] In commentaries, self-published pamphlets and brochures, and local chapters' newsletters; at the PFMCs; and at political rallies, Party members and their collaborators embarked on an educational crusade.[49] Between 1971 and 1974 the Party published editorials and interviews that described the mechanics of sickle cell anemia in detail in addition to dozens of other items on the topic, ranging from solicitations for donations to announcements of events and sites at which it would offer free genetic screening for sickle cell anemia.[50] The Party additionally made use of other media outlets at its disposal—including broadcast television and the alternative press—to expose the failings of the U.S. public health system and to publicize the Party's alternative ameliorative efforts in its stead.[51]

Typical of the science-based health information disseminated by the Party was an article in the *Black Panther* titled "Black Genocide: Sickle Cell Anemia." The cover story of the April 10, 1971, issue, this article ran alongside striking photographs of normal and sickled red blood cells. It described the genetic transmission of the disease and illustrated this biological process as well through an accompanying pedigree chart that visually depicted how sickle cell disease may be transmitted to a child if both parents carry recessive genetic traits for sickling.[52] Other items in the newspaper limned sickle cell anemia as "a blood disease" resulting from the presence of "Hemoglobin S," an "abnormal" form of "the matter in the red blood cells which gives the red coloring to the cells and which carries the oxygen in the body."[53] Scientific explanations

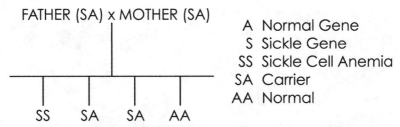

FATHER (SA) x MOTHER (SA)

SS   SA   SA   AA

A Normal Gene
S Sickle Gene
SS Sickle Cell Anemia
SA Carrier
AA Normal

Educating the public about the genetic inheritance of sickling was an important facet of the Party's campaign; a chart like this one accompanied an article about sickle cell anemia published in April 1971.

for the bouts of pain that tormented sufferers of the disease were also circulated.

With the Party's educational outreach, technical information about sickle cell anemia was frequently couched in a form of ideological editorializing, through which health promotion and science literacy were combined with political education. This approach was on vivid display in February 1972 when Seale; Marsha Martin, a Party member and Mills College student body president; and Donald Williams, a Party ally and Stanford University medical student, appeared on the popular, nationally televised variety program *The Mike Douglas Show* to discuss sickle cell anemia.[54] Seale and his collaborators were invited by the artists John Lennon and Yoko Ono, to whom Douglas turned over hosting duties for one week. The constellation of controversial artists and activists guaranteed wide circulation of the Party's sickle cell anemia campaign among the public.

The respective presentations of Seale, Martin, and Williams underscored several aspects of the stakes of sickle cell anemia. Martin, who was heavily involved in the planning of the Party's survival conference that took place one month later, used this platform to decry the lack of healthcare services available to the poor and the uninsured. She lamented the fate of those blacks who "for money reasons . . . aren't able to go to hospitals" and expressed sympathy for those "parents [who] are unable to provide proper medical care for their kids." Many African Americans "are unaware of a lot of diseases . . . there are a lot of people who know nothing about [sickle cell anemia]," she continued. Martin's comments also highlighted the social inequality, including poverty and inadequate healthcare services, which made black self-help initiatives such as the Party's sickle cell anemia campaign urgently necessary. The

FIGHT SICKLE CELL ANEMIA

PEOPLE'S MEDICAL RESEARCH HEALTH CLINICS,
SICKLE CELL ANEMIA RESEARCH FOUNDATION,
A BLACK PANTHER PARTY COMMUNITY
SURVIVAL PROGRAM.

HELP DESTROY ONE OF THE ATTEMPTS TO COMMIT

BLACK GENOCIDE

GENOCIDE: THE SYSTEMATIC KILLING OR
EXTERMINATION OF A WHOLE PEOPLE.

The above photo is of Sonny Jones, age 11, who is a positive sickle cell
case. He is standing in front of a magnified illustration of red blood
cells taken from a patient in a sickle cell crisis. The cells are sickled,
stretching away from their normal donut shape.

TAKE ONE

FIGHT SICKLE CELL ANEMIA

SEND CONTRIBUTIONS TO: DR. BERT SMALL, CHAIRMAN, PEOPLE'S MEDICAL
RESEARCH HEALTH CLINICS, SICKLE CELL ANEMIA RESEARCH FOUNDATION,
P.O. BOX 8642, EMERYVILLE, CALIFORNIA 94608. CALL (415) 653-2534 OR
848-7740.

BLACK GENOCIDE

The Black Panther Party created media to disseminate information about sickle cell anemia and appeal for donations. This stand-up poster from 1972 featured Sonny, Otistine Jones's son who suffered from the disease, against a backdrop of sickled cells.

Party programs to be featured during the upcoming conference were intended to help "people not to [have to] rely on the local government, [or] the establishment," she explained, differentiating between the trustworthy "authentic expertise" provided or vouched for by the Party and the scientific authority that oppressed communities should regard skeptically.[55]

Clad in Afrocentric attire, physician-in-training Williams followed Martin and used his time in the spotlight to define sickle cell anemia in terms of molecular biology. In answering Lennon's and Douglas's questions ("Does this show up in a normal, everyday physical?" "How is it diagnosed?"), he explained the mechanics of the genetic disease. (The descriptions were so technical that, at one point in the conversation, Douglas sarcastically quipped, "Oh, you fellows with those medical terms!") Lingering on the bleak state-of-the-science with regard to preventing and treating sickle cell anemia, Williams also appealed to authentic experts, and for more and more ethical scientific research into the disease, in contradistinction to "the kind of experiments that were done with the Tuskegee experiment [beginning] in 1932." Drawing this contrast, Williams confirmed that the Party's sickle cell anemia campaign unfolded against the backdrop of this notorious research program into the effects of late stages of syphilis, several months *prior* to the July 1972 news article that brought it national infamy.

Williams next spoke about the work of the Mid-Peninsula Sickle Cell Anemia Research Foundation, which he founded and ran with other Stanford medical students. The foundation worked with the Party and others to "educate the entire black population in this country about sickle cell anemia."[56] Williams also mentioned G6PD deficiency, another genetic disorder associated with malarial resistance. As part of its health outreach, the Party distributed a brochure titled "Two Common Diseases of Blacks: Origin of Sickle Cell Anemia and G6PD Deficiency," created by Williams with other members of the foundation. Williams exhibited this brochure during his appearance on *The Mike Douglas Show*. Williams's presentation and indeed his very presence underscored the importance of *trusted experts* to the Party's health initiatives. Such experts conveyed appropriate health education to black communities and conducted ethical biomedical research studies.

When Seale joined the hosts and Martin and Williams onstage before a white Philadelphia studio audience, he expounded on how the

Black Panthers Bobby Seale and Marsha Martin and Black Panther Party collaborator Donald Williams appeared on The Mike Douglas Show *on February 16, 1972, to discuss sickle cell anemia with Douglas, Yoko Ono, and John Lennon.*

sickle cell anemia campaign exemplified the Party's extensive survival program platform as well as its political commitments. He offered the campaign as a "concrete example" of how collective effort could produce social transformation, describing how free medical care and free genetic testing coordinated by the Party (and administered with the help of local communities) modeled "freedom" in the form of an alternative vision of U.S. society in which human needs were provided for and human rights were guaranteed. Seale, in this way, amplified the points about black health raised by Martin and Williams and additionally situated these issues in the organization's broader social health mission.

Seale, Martin, and Williams articulated three sickling "discourses": local and federal governments' neglect of poor black communities' health that in turn obliged their self-reliance; the necessity of trusted sources of health information, healthcare services, and biomedical expertise; and a unique conception of African American well-being that ranged from the individual body to society as a whole. Drawing our attention to the interpretive flexibility of sickle cell anemia, the anthropologist Melbourne

Marsha Martin explained that genetic screening for sickle cell anemia would be provided free of charge at an upcoming Community Survival Conference.

Donald Williams described the molecular structure and genetic transmission of sickling to Mike Douglas in detail.

Tapper observes that throughout the twentieth century there have been numerous "discourses" of the genetic disease; it has stood in for myriad issues and ideas, including race, citizenship, and scientific progress.[57] Extending Tapper's insight to the Party's educational outreach reveals that the activists also forged an overarching message about sickle cell anemia from several discourses. Frequently disposed in unison, the themes of the Party's educational platform were plot points of a social health metanarrative that served as a backdrop to the genetic testing it provided. These discourses about the stakes of sickle cell anemia were transmitted by the Party in several venues besides television and frequently joined a few others—namely, charges of state-backed genocide through medical neglect and mistreatment; plaints of protracted black suffering, from slavery to sickling; and the valorization of the experiential knowledge accumulated as a result of this painful history.

Accusations of government negligence arose repeatedly in the Party's rhetoric around sickle cell anemia. Evidence of this neglect—such as that supplied in Scott's *JAMA* article—established the exigency of the Party's sickle cell anemia campaign and other community service programs. This was one intent of a special September 1974 issue of the *CoEvolution Quarterly* (a "supplement" to the Bay Area counterculture publication the *Whole Earth Catalog*) guest edited by the Party—mostly by Brown, who had been recently appointed Party chair by Newton and served as editor of the *Black Panther* for several years prior.[58] At ninety-five pages, this publication was a compendium of the Party's more than one dozen survival programs, developed to "meet the needs of the community" until such time as "social conditions" were improved for poor blacks.[59] A section of the special issue devoted to the group's sickle cell work enumerated the technical and human resources required to run the sickle cell anemia campaign. Precisely detailing the many services it supplied to black communities, the organization indicted the state for all of the services it did *not* provide, for its inattention to the basic necessities of all of its citizens.[60]

The state's failure to prioritize an incurable genetic disease predominantly affecting African Americans (and black health, more broadly) was, for the Party, but one tactic of a larger, systematic strategy to eliminate African Americans that also included fatal incidents of police brutality, the unchecked proliferation of drugs in black communities, and attempts to temper procreation through the abusive, compelled sterilization of African American women.[61] The fact that the few existing genetic counseling programs regularly recommended that two sickle cell trait carriers not bear children together—lest the offspring of the two carriers have the misfortune of having the disease, a possibility for which there is a 25 percent chance—also heightened African Americans' concern that medical professionals, working at the behest of the state, were more committed to eliminating blacks than to eradicating the disease.[62] The Party's accusations of genocide expressed its awareness of what Michel Foucault theorized as "biopower," the modern state's authority to both "let live" and "make die."[63] Sickle cell anemia was not merely a debilitating condition, the Party contended, but also the state's biological weapon. The neglect of the disease was alleged to amount to a "plan of genocide upon Black people."[64]

Charges of state-sponsored genocide were not new to black power–era social movements. Such claims had a long history in African American political culture. At prior moments in the twentieth century, similar accusations had been levied. In 1951 the Civil Rights Congress leader and attorney William L. Patterson spearheaded the publication of *We Charge Genocide*, a chilling account of the racist abuses suffered by blacks in U.S. society and an impassioned appeal for international intervention to the United Nations Convention on the Prevention and Punishment of the Crime of Genocide (a panel established a few years prior in response to the atrocities of the Holocaust). Submitted to the UN by Patterson and the activist–actor Paul Robeson, the report decried the tenuous circumstances of black life in the United States that included "the willful creation of conditions making for premature death, poverty and disease."[65] The report's conclusion that blacks "suffer from genocide as the result of the consistent, conscious, unified policies of every branch of government" was echoed by the Party.[66] Not only did accusations of state-sponsored genocide against African Americans predate the allegations of black radicals in the 1970s, these suspicions were also held in many quarters of the black community. Citing an unnamed (but presumably African American) Howard University Medical School faculty member who confessed, "I have fears myself," a 1972 *Wall Street Journal* article on the sickle cell "crisis" noted that "accusations of 'genocide' come from . . . sophisticated black medical men" as well as "angry community leaders [and] Black Panthers."[67] In the face of what the Party (and, indeed, many others) deemed the state's calculated disregard, and its persistent discriminatory social policies despite recent legislative civil rights victories, the sickle cell anemia campaign was rhetorically situated by the Party as a "fight" against the disease that at the same time struck a blow against "racist and genocidal policies."[68]

Another predominant theme of the Party's sickle cell educational outreach was the protracted history of black suffering. To realize this argument, the Party "dramatized" sickling.[69] This origin narrative forged a link between the historical injury of racial slavery and blacks' contemporary suffering from sickle cell anemia and between the ecological "fit" of blacks with an African homeland and their corresponding incompatibility with a U.S. society stratified by race and class. One such instance was the article "Black Genocide"; the centerpiece of this item was a politico-etiological account of sickle cell anemia that construed the disease as a corporeal consequence of the slave trade:

> In Western and Central Africa, where there is a high incidence of Malaria . . . a natural immunity against this dreaded disease was built up by some of the People. . . . The actual shape of the red blood cells in these people began to transform. Instead of being the normally round, donut shape, their blood cells became elongated into a sickle-like shape.
>
> When Euro-american slave traders invaded the African continent and forcibly removed the people from their homeland to the U.S., the people naturally began to be affected by this new environment. That is, what was once an advantage in their homeland, became a disadvantage in this foreign environment. Those who had the sickled red blood cells . . . began to suffer terrible consequences of their transplantation from one continent to another. . . . Black People in the U.S began to suffer from anemia from these sickled red blood cells.[70]

This depiction suggested that the pain of slavery continued to assert itself in the present as sickling crises.

The Party's version of the etiology of sickling exhibited the unnamed author's familiarity with the prevailing evolutionary account of the disease, first advanced in the 1950s by Anthony C. Allison, a British researcher trained in biochemistry and in genetics. After several years' investigation in Uganda, Allison determined that the sickle cell *trait* was a genetic mutation that afforded protection from the malarial outbreaks endemic in some regions of Africa.[71] This strategic use of Allison's explanation conflated sickle cell trait *with* sickle cell anemia disease to emphasize that the genetic mutation was beneficial to blacks in their "natural" African environment and became deleterious after the forced migrations of the slave trade placed them in biologically and socially hostile new worlds. This framing of sickle cell anemia in relation to African origins represented something of a political departure for the Party. One way that the Party distinguished itself first from black cultural nationalism and later from the Panthers in New York City was by arguing against idealizing "Africa" as the basis of African American political culture. As the historian Robert Self puts it, the Party felt that "Black people suffered as a nation, but their homeland was not Africa."[72] Yet, in its understanding of the stakes of sickle cell anemia, Africa played a central and formative role.

While it drew on evolutionary theory, the activists' account was most centrally a sociopolitical one that subsumed biology under the larger veil of black suffering, in the process analogizing slavery and sickling.[73] Sickle cell anemia symbolized the injurious consequences of slavery but, importantly, with this narrative, also came into view as a symbol of black perseverance in the face of the basest practices of racial domination.[74] Or, as Williams asserted, invoking a social Darwinist maxim, sickle cell anemia was evidence that "only the strong survive."[75]

The conservative Memphis congressman Dan Kuykendall invoked a similar paradigm during hearings for the National Sickle Cell Anemia Bill. In a move that mirrored President Nixon's appropriation of black power as black capitalism, Kuykendall argued, "Being a carrier of the sickle cell trait is not a weakness. It is not a stigma. Actually, it is a historical strength. The sickle cell trait is a historical protection from malaria." Overstating his case, he continued, "An individual who has sickle cell trait and desires to become a missionary in Africa would never have to worry about malaria. He is stronger in that area than other people are, and I wonder why we do not use some of the strengths and the positive aspects of this trait instead of emphasizing the 'disease.'"[76]

The Party's construal of sickle cell anemia as a somatic sign of the fortitude of slave descendents reversed pejorative associations between blackness and sickling that had existed since the disease's discovery in the blood of an Afro-Caribbean man by the physician James B. Herrick in 1910.[77] In the early twentieth century, racist physicians and scientists found in sickle cell anemia scientific proof of the immutable peculiarity of African Americans and biological justification for de jure racial segregation in the United States.[78] In 1943 the southern physician A. G. Ogden argued that the fact of sickle cell anemia—then believed to be transmitted by a dominant genetic trait—suggested the need for anti-miscegenation legislation."Intermarriages between Negroes and white persons directly endanger the white race by transmission of the sickling trait. . . . Such intermarriages, therefore, should be prohibited by federal law," Ogden wrote.[79] Several years later, whites who opposed civil rights for African Americans invoked sickle cell anemia to support their argument that blacks should be returned to Africa, rather than have full citizenship extended to them in the United States.[80]

In the ideological hands of the Party, however, a disease that for decades had been invoked to support specious theories of African American racial inferiority became the basis for a new (disease) identity for blacks. Sickle cell anemia was transformed from stigmata of biological inferiority to exemplar of black fortitude.

In the Party's sickling discourse, resilience in the face of protracted black suffering in turn became a resource in developing experiential knowledge.[81] The Party's valorization of popular wisdom established black and poor people as the definitive authorities on their healthcare needs and on the impediments racism and economic inequality posed to fulfilling these needs. The Party conveyed the primacy of experiential knowledge through the "illness narratives" of disease sufferers.[82] First detailed by the medical anthropologist Arthur Kleinman, "illness narratives" are patients' interpretations of their infirmities that impart "meaning" and "coherence" to the experience of suffering.[83] The illness narratives disseminated by the Party were primarily rendered in the generic form of the interview.[84] A summer 1971 issue of the *Black Panther* featured interviews with two African American women, under the title "America's Racist Negligence in Sickle Cell Research Exposed by Its Victims."[85] Bay Area resident Ozella Keys, described as "a victim of sickle cell anemia," had been an aspiring nursing student before being informed that she had the genetic disease during a standard pre-admission medical exam.[86] (She was subsequently denied admission to the nursing program by administrators wary of bearing insurance liability should Keys take ill while enrolled in their school.)[87] The second woman, Brenda Pennington, a nurse in a San Francisco hospital, carried the sickle cell trait. Although the women's interviewer is not identified, they are shown holding plates of food, one on each side of Seale, who embraces them.[88] Endorsed by Seale, Keys and Pennington are presented, on the one hand, as respectable homemakers and sympathetic sickle cell anemia victims and, on the other, as authorities on the disease in their own right.[89]

In the interview, Pennington, a carrier of the typically asymptomatic genetic trait, and Keys, a sickle cell anemia sufferer, both recounted painful interludes. Pennington remembered how several years prior her carrier status had resulted in her being hospitalized with excruciating aches in her stomach and abdomen.[90] Keys, for her part, described years of suffering and the numerous, mostly ineffective, treatments she had been given in hopes of quelling her pain, including oxygen via a "nasal catheter," "strong narcotics," and "sodium bicarbonate . . . to thin out the blood."[91] Voicing an experience consistent with the historical use of blacks as human research subjects, she reflected that an experimental "urea treatment" produced a "terrible reaction" that was more distressing than the sickle cell crises it was intended to allay.[92] Quoted at length on the topic of the poor medical care they received, the women described their erratic courses of treatment and unpleasant interactions with unenlightened doctors. Pennington recounted that the medical staff was befuddled by the source of her suffering during a hospitalization for pain:

> They took my temperature and blood pressure . . . and did some blood work. . . . I heard people talking about ["]it was probably her gallbladder, we might have to do surgery; or, it might be her appendix or she might have an intestinal obstruction.["] . . . It was [on] the second day that somebody said ["]well[,] why don't we do another blood test.["] And that's when they found I had the trait.

Pennington's pain was eventually determined to be a consequence of the presence of the sickle cell trait, a state that does not frequently result in suffering for the carrier. This episode caused her to contemplate—both as a patient and a nurse—the shortcomings of medical education. Thinking back to her own training, Pennington remembered only a brief mention in a textbook of sickle cell disease "in the end of a chapter on hematology, there was a paragraph, two lines maybe." Likewise making a case for the healthcare system's disinterest in black vitality through the lens of her personal experience, Keys suggested that the therapies used to treat sickle cell anemia were at best, speculative—doctors "don't know the accurate dosage; it's just an experiment," she commented—and at worst, reckless.[93]

The Party circulated other accounts of sufferers lamenting the headaches, chronic fatigue, nosebleeds, relentless pain, disability, and death caused by sickle cell anemia and decrying victims' often harrowing interactions with physicians, hospitals, and the healthcare state. These included an interview with Glenda Cotton of Detroit, Michigan, whose crises persisted despite the consultation of more than twenty different doctors, and another with Otistine Jones, the mother of a boy with sickle cell anemia disease, who was frustrated by the "casual" manner in which doctors responded to the gravity of her son's terminal genetic disease. Ella Bea Munson recounted the experiences of her eleven-year-old son, Woodrow, who, having recently succumbed to sickle cell anemia, could no longer narrate his life as a patient.[94] A photograph of Woodrow lying in an open coffin, which ran together with the Party's interview of Munson, visually alluded to the violent murder in 1955 of another boy, Emmett Till, images of whose battered, swollen body circulated via an iconic postmortem image in the black press. With this photographic analogy, the Party bolstered its accusations of health neglect as racial genocide while linking its sickle cell anemia campaign to the broader fight for racial justice in the United States.

With first-person accounts, the Party championed poor blacks as the *real* experts on sickling. In telling their accounts, Keys, Pennington, Jones, and others gave narrative coherence to their experiences as sufferers in a manner similar to that described by Kleinman. Yet this meaning was epigraphically shaped by introductory comments that preceded each published illness narrative, so that these accounts of pain and untimely death spun out from the individual to the collective. Distinctively for the Party, these individual sufferers' accounts were made to stand in for all sickle cell victims *and* for the well-being of black people, by and large. As the preface to one interview announced, these depictions of sickle cell suffering were concomitant articulations of a more general "lack of understanding [of] and concern for the welfare of Black people."[95]

Kleinman distinguishes "illness" from "sickness" and "disease": illness refers to how a sick person and the community, broadly conceived, "perceive, live with and respond to symptoms and disability," while the anthropologist uses "disease" to describe the "narrow" technical or biological understandings of bodily infirmity most often held by medical professionals.[96] The third concept, sickness, refers to "the understanding of a disorder . . . in relation to macrosocial (economic, political, institutional) forces."[97] Through its sickle cell education, the Party expressed a social health frame similar to Kleinman's notion of sickness. Not only was the individual body indexical to the body politic, but sufferers' bodily pain was situated within a matrix of macrosocial causes and consequences, elaborating discrete illness into social sickness and offering a political diagnosis. We might thus understand one undertaking of the sickle cell anemia initiative as the valorization of "illness narratives" and their subsequent translation into "sickness narratives."

Conveyed through both illness and sickness narratives, the experiential knowledge garnered through individual sickling and collective suffering and exacerbated by institutional racism and economic exploitation established African Americans as privileged authorities on the terms of their healthcare needs and rights. In this regard, the "freedom" to which Seale referred in his television appearance was a freedom to lay claim to sickle cell anemia: to assert a unique understanding of what it means to suffer a "crisis," both literally and figuratively; to demand adequate treatment and declaim medical inequality; and to redefine the association between race and disease from biological inferiority to discrimination and neglect.

Genetic Screening

The populism of the Party's sickle cell education was mirrored in the most practical facet of the campaign—the free screening it offered for the genetic disease. When in 1974 members of the Houston chapter's health cadre trained students at Texas Southern University to administer sickle cell anemia screening tests, they were seeking to transform lay people into community health workers.[98] With this process of knowledge transmission, repeated by Party chapters nationally, the activists aimed to cultivate "revolutionary medicine" by demystifying the "bourgeois" medical professions.[99]

A signal feature of the Party's sickle cell anemia initiative, the democratization and deprofessionalization of sickling diagnosis, was made possible by recent technological developments and began on the recommendation of a member of the Party's Seattle chapter. In 1969 Ortho Diagnostics released the Sickledex kit, a simple screening test for sickle cell anemia.[100] Requiring only a finger prick of blood, Sickledex was not as invasive as the electrophoretic analysis, which necessitated a larger volume, usually drawn with a syringe. Screening with Sickledex, which detects hemoglobin S, the abnormal form of the blood molecule

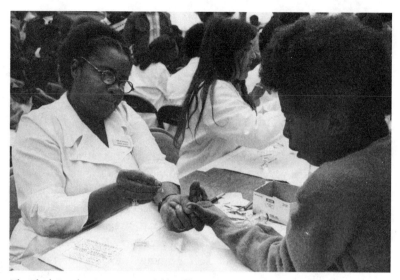

The Black Panther Party's mass sickle cell screenings were facilitated by volunteer as-sistance and a rapid, widely available, and easy-to-use test. Courtesy of Steven Shames and Department of Special Collections and University Archives, Stanford University Libraries.

that results in sickling, involved the following: using a lancet, a health worker made a small puncture on a patient's fingertip to obtain a small sample of blood. The blood was drawn up into a glass pipette and com-bined with a reagent powder that had been dissolved in a chemical solu-tion. After approximately five minutes, the density of the blood-reagent liquid was visually assessed by placing the glass tube in front of a sheet of paper printed with black lines. If the liquid was opaque—that is, if the black lines were not visible through the tube—the presence of hemo-globin S (and thus either sickle trait or sickle cell anemia disease) was indicated. If the sample became translucent, such that the black lines in the background could be seen, neither sickle trait nor disease was pres-ent in the sample.

Prior to using Sickledex technology, Black Panther chapters that con-ducted sickle cell screening used a traditional method. Small stressed that at Berkeley's George Jackson PFMC the activists used an electrophoresis machine solely to analyze blood samples. For remote events, such as large-scale screening at parks, the organization used the Sickledex test that was introduced by Valentine Hobbs, the Seattle Panther who had launched the Sydney Miller PFMC in that city.[101]

Still widely employed today, Sickledex test kits were used extensively in the 1970s by the Panthers, community clinics, public health agencies, and hospitals. Because, as a pharmaceutical newsletter explained, "no special skills [were] required in performing or interpreting the . . . test,"[102] the introduction of Sickledex accommodated the Party's objective of transferring expertise from physicians, nurses, medical technicians, and other professionals "to the masses."[103] In addition to its accessibility, this test was significantly less expensive than the electrophoresis technique popularized by Pauling beginning in 1949.[104] Whereas hemoglobin electrophoresis cost between ten and twenty dollars per use in the 1970s, the new tests were about fifty cents per use on average.[105] Sickledex kits were even less expensive when purchased in the large quantities required by the Party and were often sold to the activists at a reduced price or donated outright. Small's responsibilities as director of the Panther's sickle cell foundation included meeting the management of Bay Area medical supply companies to make such arrangements.

After Sickledex's introduction, sickle cell screening became a portable enterprise because the analysis did not have to be undertaken in a medical lab or a hospital (as was the case with large electrophoresis apparatuses). Genetic screening, as a result, now could be carried out by the Party and others in untraditional settings, ranging from the private sphere to the grand public occasion. In New York City, Oakland, Chicago, and a few other cities, the Panthers embarked on local "outreach programs" in which "trained teams of community workers" comprising health cadre and volunteers traveled door-to-door administering free genetic screening tests to blacks, "in their very homes."[106] Free sickle cell screening was also available at nine clinics: Houston, Chicago, Berkeley/Oakland, Los Angeles, Portland, Seattle, Boston, Philadelphia, and New Orleans.[107] Staff from Chicago's Spurgeon "Jake" Winters PFMC additionally implemented an extensive school-based screening program with the express consent of the local board of education.[108] The Seattle chapter even screened inmates at Walla Walla State Prison for the sickling trait and disease.[109]

By 1972 the Chicago Party purported to have tested more than 2,500 students in five public elementary schools. Of these, 169 students were identified as carriers of the recessive trait and 2 were diagnosed with sickle cell anemia disease. All of the students were given referrals for genetic counseling sessions, during which the implications of the sickling trait were discussed and, in cases of an anemia diagnosis, treatment options recommended.[110] By February 1972 the chapter claimed to have screened, all told, more than 7,000 Chicagoans for sickle cell anemia, identifying more than 600 with the trait or disease. Former Party member JoNina Abron recalls that the Chicago Party chapter tested close to "600 children" in one instance. This chapter subsequently administered Sickledex tests to students at additional elementary schools, a high school, and a junior college in the greater Chicago metropolitan area.[111]

In addition to the testing it offered at residences and chapter clinics, the Party's adoption of Sickledex also facilitated free, on-the-spot genetic screening at large gatherings such as protests, rallies, and conventions. In these settings, the cause of sickling assumed deeper political resonance because the testing was often discharged alongside electoral advocacy and organizing. In June 1972 the Party sponsored the "Anti-War, African Liberation, Voter Registration Survival Conference" at Oakland Auditorium. Befitting the Party's multiagenda strategy at this time, advertisements for the event announced that genetic screening ("10,000 Free Sickle Cell Anemia Tests") would take place alongside the political mobilization planned for the day.[112] By their own accounting, Party chapters regularly administered thousands of free screening tests at public gatherings such as this.[113] The Portland chapter, for example, gave sickle cell anemia tests to more than two thousand people. Of these, one hundred tested positive for the trait and four for sickle cell anemia. These large-scale and, at times, theatrical events fostered awareness of the disease (and the activists' sickle cell anemia campaign) as well as support for the Party's broader spectrum of "serve the people" initiatives, to the consternation of state police and federal authorities that sought to discredit the Panthers by dampening the public's enthusiasm for its battery of community service programs.

For the Party, Sickledex technology was paradoxically both an efficacious vehicle of its health politics *and* the source of some of the most vehement criticism of its sickle cell anemia campaign. Although people tested for sickle cell by the Party received almost immediate confirmation of their positive or negative result, the test did not distinguish between a positive result for the typically asymptomatic trait and a positive result for the lethal sickle cell anemia disease. (Drawing this distinction

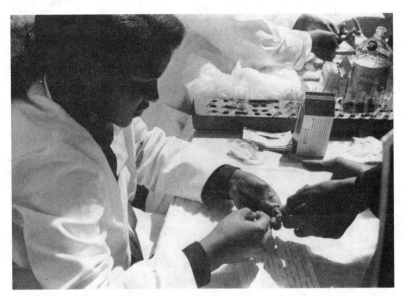

Although critics described the Black Panther Party's screening program as disorderly and confusing, the health activists used both Sickledex and follow-up electrophoresis technology and kept records of the testing program. Courtesy of Steven Shames and Department of Special Collections and University Archives, Stanford University Libraries.

required subsequent hemoglobin electrophoresis analysis.)[114] In retrospect, some have charged that the Party's reliance on this test produced confusion and anxiety among blacks; yet others, from interested observers to former Party members and their allies, maintain that the health activists brought needed attention to sickle cell sufferers.

The Panthers devised the sickle cell anemia campaign to counteract the neglect of the disease by mainstream medicine and to address the substandard and at times insensitive care its constituencies usually received. Accordingly, the Party was deeply invested in ensuring that it provided accurate testing (although its plans for reducing or eradicating sickle cell anemia were less clear).[115] To this end, the instruction of Party rank and file in the proper use of screening kits and the necessity of electrophoretic follow-up in positive cases was a primary intent of Small and Henry "Smitty" Smith's tour of Party chapters' clinics.[116] Several Party clinics owned or had access to electrophoresis equipment for conducting supplementary analyses of Sickledex results. After mass testing events in Oakland and Berkeley, Party health cadre transported positive tests "back to the [George Jackson People's Free] Clinic" where "Smitty" made finer-grained analysis with the chapter's "own electrophoresis machine."[117] Smitty was also the Oakland chapter's genetic counselor.[118] In a recent interview, Seattle's Hobbs stressed that the Panthers took their role as genetic counselors quite seriously: "Genetic counseling was in [sic] important component of the clinic. We advised patients and relatives at risk of an inherited disorder of the consequences and nature of the disorder, the probability of developing or transmitting it, and the options available to them in terms of managing and preventing it."[119]

The Chicago chapter owned two electrophoresis machines, and the People's Free Clinic in Seattle had one device on its premises.[120] Portland's "tiny, but well-stocked backroom laboratory" was capable of extensive chemical analysis.[121] Davis, laboratory director of nearby Emmanuel Hospital, helped Ford establish health services in Portland, with "a special emphasis on sickle cell anemia," and arranged for the clinic to have both Sickledex and electrophoresis testing capabilities.[122]

In Chicago the Party was lauded for being more attuned to the nuances of the genetic screening, more rigorous in the notification of screening results, and more diligent in the provision of genetic counseling than local public health authorities. In 1972 a story by the journalist Edwin Black in the *Chicago Guide* (now *Chicago Magazine*) suggested that the Party's sickle cell anemia campaign was a model for the city's board of health to follow. The health agency had come under fire for not informing the individuals it screened that they carried the sickle cell trait; authorities reasoned that there was no need to pass on information about a recessive trait that seldom caused discomfort or illness.[123] A "prominent Chicago research physician" quoted in the article compared the health agency's practice of "non-notification" to the Tuskegee syphilis experiment that had come to light in a July 1972 exposé in the *New York Times* two months prior. He stated, "A large body of . . . expert public opinion within the healthcare profession . . . is persuaded, as I am, that it is no accident that these people were used for the syphilis thing, or that race is unrelated to the lack of sickle-cell programs."[124] The agency eventually reversed its "non-notification" policy because, in the words of one board executive, "the Black Panther program ha[d] forced the city into it" by embarrassing them with its success.[125] "I don't know how complete the Panther program was," he continued, "but they were sincere and apparently doing a job well enough to make an impact upon people."[126]

Evidence of at least some due diligence and success on the part of the Party notwithstanding, critics have charged that genetic screening programs did more harm than good. The sociologist Troy Duster singled out the Bay Area Panther screening programs as guilty of disseminating inaccurate information about sickle cell.[127] Given the ad hoc nature of the Party's genetic screening program, errors were certainly made in the interpretation of results and with post-test follow-up. However, as the social and legal theorist Dorothy Roberts has clarified, it was the large public health screening programs that generated inaccurate information and subsequent distrust during this period.[128] Roberts writes that public health clinics "often provided no [genetic] counseling, there was rampant confusion between carriers of the trait and those who had the disease. Many people who had only sickle-cell trait were mistakenly convinced that their health was in jeopardy."[129] Inaccuracies were characteristic of many sickle cell screening programs of the time, including the community clinics, philanthropies, hospitals, and public health systems that relied on Sickledex for sickle cell screening.[130] The physician and medical historian Howard Markel significantly attributes the misinterpretation of results to the technical limitations of Sickledex and notes that such errors of interpretation were pervasive in this period.[131] Thus the Party's genetic screening program was neither the only one to suffer from inaccuracies nor the most egregious case. Yet in the context of other worrisome events in the 1970s lying at the nexus of race, class, gender, and the body, including incidents of workplace discrimination against sicklers, the revelation of the Tuskegee study, and reports of the forced sterilization of black women, the errors and misjudgments committed by many of the organizations and agencies that ran genetic screening programs were a legitimate and real cause of concern for some African Americans.

The Party nevertheless was a key player in creating critically needed public discourse about the disease, as former Party members attest.[132] Observers and former allies concur. The pioneering physician Bert Lubin, a longtime Bay Area resident, who is presently director of Children's Hospital and Research Institute in Oakland, where many recent advances in treatment for sickle cell anemia have been made, asserts unequivocally that "the Panther's sickle cell program was a good thing. It opened people's eyes."[133] Davis, reflecting on his collaboration with the Portland Party, sums up that the screening initiative was a "very positive thing" for the black community.[134] On balance, the Party's sickle cell anemia campaign of educational outreach paired with genetic screening was constructive.

Sickle Cell "Crisis"

It was also contested. Both the praise and the criticism the Party faced suggests how controversial and also how powerful the issue of sickle cell anemia had become in many quarters. In the early 1970s philanthropists, African American cultural outlets, legislators, and the Nixon administration competed with the Party in the scramble to design a strategy to eradicate sickle cell anemia and, by association, to show support for black communities. The historian of medicine Keith Wailoo writes that the sickling crisis "came to represent the failures of medicine to address suffering, particularly in the black community . . . the crisis would become a key feature of the clinical and social portrait of sickle cell anemia."[135]

Not coincidentally, what might be expressed as the diminishing of the Party's ideological monopoly over public sickling discourse coincided with its evisceration at the hands of the Federal Bureau of Investigation's counterintelligence program, or COINTELPRO. With this concerted program of political repression, the FBI marshaled electronic surveillance, harassment, and a climate of paranoia to cripple the efforts of organizations that had been identified as "black hate groups."[136] COINTELPRO began in the mid-1950s as a "new phase" of an existing program devoted to the surveillance of radicals. From August 1967 onward, it focused specifically on black radical activists and black nationalist organizations, including the Party.[137] By 1968 the Party was such a cause of concern to FBI director J. Edgar Hoover that he used a public forum—the front page of the *New York Times*—to denounce the Party as "the greatest threat to the internal security of the country."[138] A 1969 FBI directive revealed that Hoover even instructed Chicago and San Francisco Bay Area agents to "'eradicate [the Panthers'] "serve the people" programs'" that he believed shed a positive light on the group.[139]

The FBI worked with local police and bureaucracies in its campaign to discredit the Party. Party health clinics came under the scrutiny of local public health authorities allegedly concerned with unsanitary conditions and inadequate medical facilities. The Spurgeon "Jake" Winters PFMC in Chicago, for example, received a visit shortly after it opened in December 1969 from local health officials who threatened to close the clinic, "charging numerous building and Board of Health violations."[140] Former Party chief of staff David Hilliard recalled that the Party's free sickle cell anemia screening was "crippled [when] the FBI urged Oakland police to arrest Party members for making unlawful solicitations and planted news stories trying to discredit the program."[141] Police harassment and raids frequently resulted in ransacking of the Party chapters' health facilities, during which supplies were damaged or destroyed and medical equipment was broken, as was the case at the Chicago and Los Angeles clinics.[142]

Funds for the Party's social programs were acquired partly through direct solicitation or through the sale of the group's newspaper.[143] The FBI stifled the Party's funding sources for its health programs. The *Black Panther* was especially targeted because of its extensive national circulation, because it served as an undiluted vehicle for disseminating the Party's political positions, and because it was a principal source of the Party's operating budget.[144] In August 1972 four members of the

The Black Panthers partly supported their sickle cell anemia program through donations solicited in public spaces, such as the parking lot of this Oakland grocery store in 1971. Courtesy of Steven Shames.

Southern California chapter were arrested for allegedly soliciting donations for the sickle cell anemia campaign. According to the Party newspaper, television news in Los Angeles reporting on the incident failed to identify those arrested as Party members. Instead, they were described as "fraud operators," a depiction that in effect criminalized the Party's health activist work.[145] There is evidence to suggest that the FBI was behind this crackdown. The FBI "urged local police in Oakland and surrounding communities to arrest for unlawful solicitation Black Panther Party [members] who sought donations for the [sickle cell anemia] program in public places."[146] In the Bay Area, Party members continued to be arrested for solicitation "even after a San Francisco solicitation ordinance . . . was declared unconstitutional by a California court."[147] Moreover, the FBI instructed members of the television and press media "to publish articles and broadcasts falsely attacking the legitimacy" of the sickle cell campaign to "reduce contributions to the program."[148] In such a climate, the People's Sickle Cell Anemia campaign was easily undermined.

The political value of the sickle cell crisis was not lost on the administration of President Richard Nixon.[149] In February 1971, in a health address to Congress, Nixon declared it "a sad and shameful fact" that investigations into the causes of "a most serious disease which occurs in the black population . . . have been largely neglected throughout our history."[150] He also proposed that this oversight be rectified with a "fivefold" increase in the budget for the research and treatment of sickle cell anemia.[151]

Having previously identified the dismantling of the Office of Economic Opportunity (a driver in the War on Poverty) as a major feature of his presidency, and with the full intention of asking for reductions in federal funding to the National Institutes of Health in his next budget, President Nixon's newfound concern for the disease amounted to a calculated political strategy to demonstrate his administration's attention to the needs of black communities while maintaining manufactured fiscal scarcity. Nixon offered narrow biological citizenship instead of economic access or equality. Donna Spiegler, a staffer for Merlin DuVal, Nixon's assistant secretary of health and scientific affairs, frankly asserted that the president's support for sickle cell anemia "was a gimmick for Nixon to get the black vote" for a second term in office.[152] As

Wailoo elaborates, in "championing both the war on cancer and (surprising both his supporters and opponents) new research on sickle cell anemia in his February 1971 health message, [Nixon] gained positive political attention for these bold initiatives while remaining true to his conservative ideals."[153]

Considering the bill that would become the 1972 National Sickle Cell Anemia Control Act, Congress held hearings during which black athletes, medical professionals, civil rights activists, and legislators lobbied on behalf of the new law.[154] The Black Panther Party was notably absent from these deliberations. During these hearings, many witnesses referred to the funding disparities between sickle cell anemia and other genetic diseases identified by Scott in his *JAMA* article. The bill's cosponsor, Senator Tunney, specifically referenced the Scott paper on the floor of the Senate.[155]

In May 1972 Congress passed the National Sickle Cell Anemia Control Act, which allotted $155 million in funding for sickle cell anemia over three years for the research and prevention of the disease. President Nixon signed it into law.[156] The May 27, 1972, issue of the *Black Panther* responded to the new law in this way:

> [Nixon] recently signed a bill that allocated millions of dollars toward the "eradication" of Sickle Cell Anemia. We are not fooled by "Nixon's Sickle Cell Bill," for we know that what we will see is the phoney Sickle Cell organizations getting even more money (if in fact it is given), with little change in the people's condition in regard to Sickle Cell Anemia.[157]

Scathing critiques of the numerous foundations that had sprung up to combat sickle cell anemia also ran in the *Black Panther*. Panther leader Brown complained that with the Party's efforts "being duplicated [by other organizations], our money and energy were being so drained, the impact of our Survival Programs [was] inevitably . . . diminished."[158]

Unsurprisingly, then, the Party condemned the efforts of other organizations. The National Sickle Cell Disease Research Foundation came under fire in the *Black Panther* for holding its April 1972 convention in a tony New York City hotel, "far from the reach of the masses."[159] The Party believed that successful sickle cell anemia prevention efforts should emerge from and remain within poor black communities, rather than originate in the established citadels of philanthropy and medicine. Aside from being out of touch with poor blacks, because the foundation operated with federal funds, it also represented to the Party the state's effort to co-opt both the disease and its waning inability to "spin" the disease ideologically. (However, the Party was not opposed in principle to alliance with philanthropies, such as the one created with Williams's Mid-Peninsula Sickle Cell Anemia Foundation).[160]

Also irksome to the Party were the sickle cell efforts initiated by soul music–format radio stations. The Party criticized the Boston station WILD, which sponsored an on-air fund-raising drive by "begging for research funds with cute slogans like 'It's Sickle Cell Time ya'll.'"[161] This commercial radio campaign sandwiched solicitations for sickle cell anemia research between R&B ballads and funk songs, trivializing the political stakes of the disease that the Party was at pains to emphasize.

All of the contenders in the sickle cell crisis sought to deploy the disease politically, but toward ideologically different ends. All recognized that sickle cell anemia, by virtue of being a "black disease," could be used to highlight race-based medical neglect or to mollify political differences. African American philanthropies and cultural outlets, for example, employed what might be termed a "categorical" standpoint. Sickle cell anemia was a cause of concern inasmuch as it was a "black" disease.[162] For its part, the federal government sought to address a single angle on sickle cell anemia that might be understood as a "representational" standpoint. The Nixon administration hoped that its fiscal support for sickle cell anemia research would be seen as support for the black population writ large and, moreover, might translate into improved approval ratings and votes despite the fact that the president's other policies concurrently undermined the health of African American communities in many other ways. As Tapper keenly observes, the administration "was clearly more inclined to address the government's neglect of specific segments of the population through genetic screening—a relatively inexpensive strategy—than to work to transform the social and racial hierarchies that produced the neglect in the first place."[163] Of course, the Party was concerned not merely with combating and potentially curing sickle cell anemia but also with remedying the inequalities to which Tapper alludes. Although elements of the displeasure the Party expressed in its newspaper over the encroachment of politicians and philanthropies on *its* issue might suggest territorialism or even sour grapes, something far more crucial was at stake for the organization. The categorical and representational approaches to the sickle cell anemia crisis stripped away the social health frame in which the Party contextualized the disease (and potentially also one of its primary bases of support from black communities).

Economic and racial inequities were precisely what were at stake for the Party, and neglect of sickle cell anemia was simply the tip of an iceberg of oppression. Yet, because the Party's sickle cell anemia campaign had focused so centrally on "neglect"—the failure of a capitalist system to provide for poor and oppressed communities—the campaign lost some of its political potency when this disregard was redressed by the state and philanthropies. Moreover, as sickle cell anemia was transformed into a metaphor of black American experience, both politicians and more centrist civil rights organizations like the National Urban League and the NAACP appropriated many of the Party's claims about the link between social status and health status.[164] At the same time, a growing number of prominent African American physicians began to charge that the federal government's response to the sickle cell crisis amounted to a "political ploy," one that occluded the deeper structural issues affecting black health, such as a lack of access to medical care and impoverished living conditions.[165] As a concerned physician put it, "You need to upgrade the medical care for the population from which these patients come."[166] In light of this incorporation of its rhetoric into mainstream discourse, on the one hand, and the dismantling of its social health frame, on the other, it became difficult for the Party to employ sickle cell anemia as a mobilizing medium for radical ideology.

To be sure, the Party played an important role in bringing sickle cell anemia to the attention of African American communities and likely influenced the Nixon administration's decision to allocate significant federal resources for research on the disease. But this allocation of state resources also served to neutralize the Party's larger political critique. The campaign was thus an object lesson on the challenges faced by African American health activists in deploying a social health frame by yoking their cause to larger social issues. Yet by 1974 the Party's perspective on sickle cell anemia had also become less radical.[167] Perhaps in response to criticism about the dangers of sickle cell testing, perhaps in response to the receding moral authority and clearly with an eye toward getting local, state, and federal funding for its community service programs, toward the mid-1970s the Party began to emphasize its collaboration with medical professionals from "accredited hospitals," the "mandatory" number of trained medical professionals needed to run its clinics and sickle cell anemia screening program, and its diligence in taking health background information from people tested for the disease.[168] In the Party-edited special issue of the *CoEvolution Quarterly*, under the section heading "Volunteers," the Party emphasized that those who donated their time were trained medical professionals or "have received training in Sickle Cell Anemia testing from accredited hospitals." This section also highlighted the fact that a Party sickle cell anemia program required "two doctors who consult with local foundations" and who "also provide the Foundation with liaison hospitals which conduct Sickle Cell research and which may be willing to donate some of their facilities and equipment free of charge to the Foundation."[169] The Panthers' sickle cell anemia campaign, which initially stressed the importance of lay knowledge and participation, was becoming professionalized. The organization still attempted to offer medicine for the people, but not necessarily by the people. The critique of expertise and biomedical authority, which the Party had tethered to the sickle cell anemia campaign, became disassociated from it, just as the critiques of racism and capitalism had been. By 1975, when members of the Oakland Party participated in a community health fair alongside the American Cancer Society, the Alameda County Lung Association, and the American Red Cross, its sickle cell anemia campaign was mainstream and its social health frame was fragile.[170]

5

AS AMERICAN AS CHERRY PIE

Contesting the Biologization of Violence

> Black doctors, neurosurgeons, psychiatrists, and concerned
> citizens, where are you? Please come forth to prevent this
> dangerous form of pacification! In the meantime, black
> brothers and sisters, shelter your cingulum, amygdalas
> and thalamuses from assault by a neurosurgeon who wants
> to make you a "better person."
>
> —Gloria Evans-Young, "Letter to the Editor," *Ebony*

In 1973 the Black Panthers became involved in a challenge to the formation of the Center for the Study and Reduction of Violence, a research center at the University of California at Los Angeles that would be dedicated partly to investigating the biological etiology of violence. In this instance, the Party tilted emphasis from providing healthcare to underserved communities, with attention to medical mistreatment that characterized its ongoing clinic work and sickle cell activism, to focusing on the dismantling of both the biologization of social issues and repressive medical surveillance. In other words, with this campaign, the Panthers sought to protect those who were at risk of overexposure to the power of the healthcare state. To this end, the Party's tactics also shifted as was required by the matter at hand, from the creation of alternative medical care services and institutions to a "politics of knowledge," via legal advocacy, lobbying, and the "recontextualization" of biomedical theories.[1]

Heralded by California governor Ronald Reagan in his January 1973 State of the State address, the proposed "violence center" would support research into the origins and causes of violence. The center's conceptual architect and foremost proponent was Dr. Louis Jolyon "Jolly" West, director of the UCLA Neuropsychiatric Institute that was to house it, and a psychiatrist whose colorful and controversial professional history included studies of brainwashing, hypnosis, and sleep deprivation; early clinical experiments with LSD; and research correlating the era's student activism with antisocial behavior.[2] In keeping with this trajectory, West proposed a slate of biomedical studies to address what he deemed the "veritable plague" of violence.[3]

Huey P. Newton was alarmed when he became aware of plans to establish the center. In particular, the Panther chairman objected to the fact that some of the proposed research programs specifically targeted minority groups and vulnerable populations for participation in experimental psychiatric studies—including invasive brain surgery. The Black Panthers joined forces with civil rights, feminist, prisoners' rights, and students' organizations—made up of the western region chapter of the NAACP, the National Organization for Women (NOW), the Mexican-American Political Association (MAPA), Committee Opposing Psychiatric Abuse of Prisoners (COPAP), United Farm Workers Organizing Committee (UFOC), and the California Prisoners' Union (CPU)—to attempt to block public funding to the violence center and thereby impede its formation. This Party-led coalition was allied with Fred J. Hiestand, an activist–attorney who represented its interests with regard to the center in negotiations with politicians and before state legislative bodies.[4] In April 1973 Hiestand testified before the California Senate Health and Welfare Committee on behalf of this coalition; reading from a prepared "administrative complaint"—a document more tactical than legal, but one that nonetheless bore the authoritative imprimatur of the law to the journalists and politicians among whom it was circulated—the lawyer detailed the activists' opposition to the violence center.

A centerpiece of Hiestand's presentation was a counterargument about the causes of violence that was in stark contrast with the medical and biological behavioral models advanced by the center's backers and constituent researchers and that furthermore highlighted the consequences of this research for marginalized communities. Before the California legislature, Hiestand delineated a social etiology of violence that drew on the ideological commitments of the attorney's lead client, the Black Panthers, and reflected Party leader Newton's stewardship and active participation in its crafting. Hiestand's critical assessment of the research center therefore reflected the Party's opposition to state-sanctioned police violence, exercised through its neighborhood self-defense activities as well as the group's adherence to the philosophies of Frantz Fanon, who postulated that subaltern aggression was a legitimate response to oppression. For the Party, in keeping with its social health perspective, violence was a symptom of societal dis-ease; it was, in the famous words of Party minister of justice H. Rap Brown, "as American as cherry pie."[5]

At stake for the activists was the *biologization* of violence, the reduction and attribution of what they deemed a deeply political and social phenomenon to a manifestation of the inherent pathology of individuals (black men, in particular). For the Party and its allies, the biologization of violence augured two related and worrisome outcomes. On the one hand, the Party's challenge to the violence center evidenced resistance to a process that Peter Conrad and others define as "medicalization." While health activists often seek medicalization as an outcome— for example, in the case of contemporary "contested illnesses" such as chronic fatigue syndrome or Gulf War syndrome—Newton and his allies sought to prevent the transformation of violence into a medical phenomenon.[6] Mindful perhaps of Irving Zola's suggestion that medicalization "depoliticizes" an issue by "locating both the source and treatment of social problems in an individual," thus closing off other explanations or solutions, the Party defended a social health perspective on violence that, in this instance, identified biomedical rationales as antithetical to the larger cause of black well-being.[7] On the other hand, the racial, gendered, and institutional facets of this particular course of biologization suggested that it would be carried out in such a fashion as to make already marginalized populations more vulnerable to medicine as an instrument of social control. That is, given the specific historical and institutional context in which this biologization would take place and the populations that would be subject to it, it was very unlikely that medicalization would lead to reduced culpability or greater social understanding for violence. Rather, this medicalization would effect the further criminalization of social groups—black males, the incarcerated— and in turn justify calls for increased surveillance and social control.

After months of political negotiation and two days of hearings, and in response to vehement protest from a wide spectrum of activists, the state of California denied funding to the center. Other potential backers followed suit. The center was defeated. This was somewhat of a Pyrrhic victory for Newton and his allies, as blocking resources to the center as an entity would not prevent individual researchers from pursuing other sources of support for their investigations. However, given the history of abusive biomedical experimentation to which vulnerable and marginalized groups had been subject historically because their social status

SNCC member–turned–Black Panther leader H. Rap Brown declared that violence was "American as cherry pie," a phrase that described discord as inherent to U.S. culture rather than the provenance of communities of color, as was suggested in parts of the "violence center" proposal. Photograph by Marion S. Trikosko, July 27, 1967. Library of Congress Prints and Photographs Division.

constituted them as "accessible" to researchers, the defeat of the violence center was a significant expression of the Party's promotion of black well-being, in the forms of both corporeal and social healthfulness, and indeed a notable triumph.

The Panthers' sickle cell anemia campaign had stressed that disease could emerge from the convergence of the history of racism, biology, and neglect. In its violence center activism, on the other hand, the party ceded no ground to medicalization, biological determinism, or essentialist notions of racial identity. The Party and its allies also challenged the motivations, political and otherwise, of the center's planners in selecting the types of violent behavior to be studied and asked what was at stake in choosing to focus on some expressions of violence while ignoring state-sanctioned forms like imperialist warfare and repressive policing. Though the Panther-led coalition would not be solely responsible for quashing the planned center, the breadth of this coalition and Hiestand's efforts on its behalf afforded the Party and its allies a central role in shaping the terms of the contest.

A Coalition Coalesces

After two years' incarceration, Newton was released from prison in the fall of 1970, when a conviction for the murder of an Oakland police officer was overturned on appeal. He resumed day-to-day leadership of the Party, ordering the closing of several chapters and centralizing Party cadre at the group's Oakland headquarters. Newton also shifted the organization's focus, de-emphasizing its more militant tactics. Instead he directed the Party's attention and energies toward its many "serve the people" programs, by redoubling efforts on some initiatives and developing new ones. An opportunity for the Party to extend further its health politics arose in 1972 when Newton met Hiestand.

After completing his legal studies in 1968, Hiestand began work with the Senior Citizens Project of California Rural Legal Assistance. Hiestand had several legal successes there, including one in which he won increased medical benefits on behalf of California welfare recipients and "a precedent-setting case" that mandated the accurate dating of dairy products in poor communities.[8] Hiestand joined the staff of a San Francisco public interest law firm, Public Advocates, Inc., supported by the Ford Foundation and other private funders in 1972, at the invitation of the firm's founders: J. Anthony Kline, Sidney M. Wolinsky, and Robert L. Gnaizda.[9] Hiestand's work at the firm allowed him the freedom to embark on collaborative initiatives with civil rights groups and activist organizations.[10]

The occasion for Newton and Hiestand's first meeting was the latter's interview of the Party leader for a special issue of the *Guild Practitioner*—a publication of the progressive National Lawyers Guild—on the topic of incarceration and political prisoners.[11] "I went to interview him . . . the interview took about two or three hours . . . and we hit it off sort of right away," Hiestand recalled.[12] At the conclusion of their interview, Newton announced that he had more to say on the subject. During subsequent discussions it became evident to Hiestand that this "was no longer an interview, but a dialogue . . . about how we might work together."[13] Hiestand began to represent the Party in late 1972.

For Newton, working with Hiestand and Public Advocates afforded the Party the opportunity to expand its repertoire of social change programs and its protest tactics to include "civil law suits" through which the Party sought "relief for its members and Black and poor people generally, from various injustices."[14] For his part, Hiestand, who was inspired by the charismatic Newton, viewed his representation of the Party as a chance to bolster his legal activism and to "help to rehabilitate the BPP's . . . undeserved reputation as unreasonable and violent."[15] Newton and Hiestand's collaboration resulted in the expansion of the Party's health politics on two fronts. First, there were a series of public interest lawsuits. In *Black Panther Party v. Granny Goose* (1972), they worked together to get several large Oakland employers to obey California's employment laws. Hiestand "discovered the pay-while voting" law on the books that required that employees of mid-sized or larger companies receive two hours' pay on election days so that they would not have to choose between missing work and voting. "The Panthers sent notices, signed by Huey, to all the big employers in Oakland, telling them this was the law . . . [and] that they should post this notice or an equivalent one prominently, so employees [were aware of] their rights," recounts Hiestand.[16] In another suit, *Black Panther Party v. Kehoe* (1974), the organization, represented by Hiestand, successfully sued Oakland area nursing homes and convalescent hospitals to compel them to make public certain information about health code violations.[17] This suit was consistent with the Black Panthers' outreach to black senior citizens in Oakland and its health politics.

Another initiative involving senior citizens was the formation of the

Party's Seniors Against a Fearful Environment, or S.A.F.E., program. Some elderly complained to the Panther leadership that they were often the victims of petty theft at the hands of Oakland area young people and wanted to know what the Party intended to do about the problem. Newton and Seale responded with the creation of S.A.F.E., through which the Party became the guardians of Oakland's elderly: Party members served as escorts, providing safe passage for senior citizens to financial institutions, medical and other appointments, and on shopping errands.[18]

Second, Hiestand represented the Party in its challenge to the plans to establish the project at UCLA, serving as the mouthpiece for a coalition of activist organizations that included the Party, NOW, the western region of the NAACP, UFOC, MAPA, and the CPU.[19] This coalition, most of which had worked with Hiestand or Public Advocates in the past, coalesced around the shared goal of thwarting an attempt by scientists at UCLA to establish the violence center.[20] The coalition also reflected Newton's network and the Panthers' tradition of building alliances with other activist groups. In its early days, the Party forged coalitions with several other organizations, including the Peace and Freedom Party, on whose platform Eldridge Cleaver ran for president of the United States in 1968. The evolution of its health politics owed a great deal to its collaborations with SHO, MCHR, and other radical health activists. The Party also fostered associations with other civil rights groups, forming a "rainbow coalition" with the Young Lords Party, the Young Patriots, and Students for a Democratic Society.[21]

The "Violence Center"

West drafted plans for the violence center in September 1972 after several months of discussion with Dr. Earl W. Brian, secretary of human resources for Governor Reagan; Dr. J. M. Stubblebine, director of the California Department of Mental Hygiene (later the Department of Health); and other medical advisers and state officials.[22] The center was to be funded partly by the state of California. It was anticipated that state funds would be matched by public agencies, including the federal Law Enforcement Assistance Administration (LEAA), which allocated money locally through the California Council for Criminal Justice (CCCJ). The LEAA was a new federal program that in subsequent years through its funding power and priorities shaped incarceration policy in the United States.[23] Thus the "violence center" represented not merely an effort to biologize (and medicalize) violence but to do so through resources dedicated to expanding the carceral state.[24]

From its beginnings, the violence center was explicitly linked with crime prevention and with the political and ideological aims of Governor Reagan, who was elected on a "law and order" platform.[25] This observation was echoed in the local press: in the words of a reporter for the *Los Angeles Times*, Harry Nelson, criticisms of the violence center focused a good deal on "the motives of the two principal financial backers—a state administration that is politically conservative and a federal agency whose goal is to reduce crime." This association was solidified when Reagan made the first public announcement of the center on January 11, 1973, during his annual State of the State message. In this speech, the governor praised the planned center and its mission, which he broadly described as the study of the causes of "all types of violent behavior, what causes it, how it may be detected, prevented, controlled and treated."[26] Reagan's advocacy of the center, however, was more narrowly focused than his general definition of its aims. The governor expected that the center would become a central component of his plan to "overhaul" the criminal justice system in California.[27] Reagan's support of the center included a promise of financial backing. To establish the center, the governor proposed to "redirect" funds allocated to existing planned research projects in the 1973–74 state budget to the center.[28]

Although West was elated to have the governor's support, which he had carefully cultivated in the months preceding the announcement of the center, he was dissatisfied about the possibility of the center's research findings being used for crime prevention and social control. However, securing funding would require such compromises of his vision for the center.

The center was imagined as a cutting-edge neuropsychiatric outpost to investigate violence. According to West's proposal, the center (initially dubbed the Center for Prevention of Violence) was intended to help society "gain a greater understanding of causative and contributing factors involved in all forms of pathologically violent behavior."[29] Arguing for the necessity of the center, West lamented—but did not empirically demonstrate—increases in violent incidents in the United States, including suicides, homicides, and domestic abuse, and asserted that "violence is becoming a veritable plague in this country."[30] Here

West tapped into a growing collective sense in the 1970s, in the wake of the assassinations of Martin Luther King Jr., John Kennedy, and Robert Kennedy, that violence was becoming a significant problem of American society. During this period, for instance, popular magazines and network television frequently ran stories depicting and decrying violence. The ongoing Vietnam War and instances of urban unrest also led to an impression among some that violence was becoming a serious American social problem.[31]

Pitching the center's rationale to the interests of middle-class property owners, West promised that under his tutelage the center would offer an alternative to white flight and implied that the investigations under consideration could make urban areas like Los Angeles safe again. Continuing in this vein, in the introduction to the center proposal, West justified the urgent need for the violence center by referring to "the spectre of unprovoked attack [that] haunts city-dwellers alone outdoors after dark"—those so afraid of the urban environment that they "triple-lock" their doors or, instead, "flee the cities . . . [to] avoid potentially dangerous situations."[32] In the context of the "white flight" that followed the 1960s urban uprising, the "spectre" invoked by West was clearly that of the blacks and Latinos who lived in Los Angeles and similar cities—though he would repeatedly claim that the center was to focus on varied forms of social violence, broadly defined.

According to the proposal, the study of violence would be multidisciplinary and undertaken from various perspectives, including genetic, endocrinal, psychological, neurophysical, epidemiological, and psychosocial research.[33] Among the genetic research proposals was a plan to study male adults and children with the XYY chromosome syndrome that was then believed to cause aggressive conduct. A study of the endocrine system would explore female propensity to violence at stages of the menstrual cycle, while psychological studies were to include clinical treatment of patients. The neurophysical paradigm proposed the use of psychiatric surgery.

On its surface, the proposal did not appear to contain much that was controversial. What captured the attention of Hiestand, Newton, and the Party's allies were the ideological underpinnings and theoretical assumptions of several of the research programs that would be part of the center, and the scant but worrisome particulars provided about specific research projects. The devil was in the details.

Some of the center's interdisciplinary research programs combined claims of medical pathology and biological determinism by way of explanation for the causes of violence. On the one hand, research programs hypothesized that violence was a manifestation of physiological disease or mental illness. On the other hand, these two aspects worked together to craft a narrative of black and Latino violent pathology.

In particular, one planned center project, called "Violence and the Brain," captured the dystopic imagination of the activists who made up the Party-led coalition. The study, which called for the use of psychosurgery (the removal or alteration of an area of diseased brain tissue thought to cause aggressive behavior), provoked the most vehement outrage from the Party and its allies, the UCLA community, and others. This program was to be carried out by a team of researchers that included Dr. Frank R. Ervin, a psychiatrist recently hired by the Neuropsychiatric Institute from the controversial Boston Neuro-Research Center.[34] According to Hiestand, it had been "critically evaluated by its own funding sources, the Federal Law Enforcement Assistance Administration (LEAA), for being scientifically unsound and for misusing federal monies." "The proposal submitted to LEAA by the Boston project," Hiestand explained, was "practically identical in terms of its individual research components to the UCLA" proposal submitted to the California State Health and Welfare committee for funding approval.[35]

Ervin was coauthor, with the neurosurgeon Dr. Vernon H. Mark, of *Violence and the Brain,* a provocative book published in 1970 in which the authors complained that social and environmental explanations of violent behavior mistakenly "take for granted that every individual has a normally functioning, entirely healthy brain."[36] To the contrary, they maintained that "past environment, once it is past, is no longer a sociological phenomenon. It is embedded in our brain and its use is dependent on the function or malfunction of the cerebral tissue."[37]

The book delineated the researchers' hypothesis about the etiology of violence that would inform their research at the UCLA center. The authors offered what they termed "a new and biologically oriented approach to the problem of human violence."[38] They posited that upward of fifteen million persons in the United States had some kind of brain disease and further argued that "an appreciable percentage" of repeatedly violent individuals could "be found in this 5 to 10% of the population whose brains do not function in a perfectly normal way."[39] Ervin and Mark recommended "surgical intervention" as a way for psychiatrists and neuroscientists to do their part to reduce violence by repeat offenders; specifically, they promoted a psychosurgery procedure in which "tiny electrodes are implanted in the brain and used to destroy a very small number of cells in a precisely determined area."[40] Once inserted, the electrodes could be left in the patient's brain, if necessary, "until the surgeon is sure which brain cells are firing abnormally and causing the symptoms of seizures and violence."[41]

Three years prior to the publication of *Violence and the Brain*, Ervin and Mark, with their colleague William Sweet, entered the national debate about urban violence with a September 1967 editorial in the *Journal of the American Medical Association*. They speculated that biological dysfunction might be partly to blame for incidents of violence in America's cities, writing:

> The urgent needs of underprivileged urban centers for jobs, education and better housing should not be minimized, but to believe that these factors are solely responsible for the present urban riots is to overlook some of the newer medical evidence about the personal aspects of violent behavior. . . . The lesson on urban rioting is that, besides the need to study the social fabric that creates a riot atmosphere, we need intensive research and critical studies of the *individuals* committing the violence. The goal of such studies would be to pinpoint, diagnose, and treat these people with low violence thresholds before they contribute to further tragedies.[42]

While this editorial by Ervin and his coauthors paid lip service to the social and economic factors that might contribute to social aggression, its central argument was that pathological individuals were the cause of urban violence.

If these researchers were still hedging their bets in the *JAMA* editorial, the thinking of at least one of them was already drawing closer to the theories that would be put forth in *Violence and the Brain*. In 1967 Mark submitted his hypothesis that brain dysfunction caused urban violence for consideration by the National Advisory Commission on Civil Disorders, also known as the Kerner Commission—a body convened at the behest of President Lyndon Johnson to study the origins of the numerous urban uprisings that occurred in the second half of the

1960s. Mark theorized that uprisings like those that occurred in the Los Angeles community of Watts in 1965 were carried out by unruly African Americans with diseased brains.[43]

With these arguments, Ervin and his colleagues were attempting to both biologize and medicalize violence. As defined by the sociologists Peter Conrad and Joseph W. Schneider, medicalization is the process by which social conditions or phenomena are defined or redefined as medical problems requiring medical solutions. They posit that forms of socially abnormal behavior have changed from being understood as morally deficient behavior (sin) to being perceived through the lens of law (crime) or of medicine (madness, illness). Medicalization is both organic and atomizing; a social condition is transformed into a biological pathology—in this case, violence—and is understood to be isolated within the boundaries of an individual body, rather than as emerging from the social body.[44] The damaged brain thesis amounted to an attempt by some researchers to classify violent behavior as a form of mental illness or brain dysfunction that could be controlled and monitored by psychiatrists and neuroscientists.[45]

In the years preceding the center controversy, Ervin, Mark, and Sweet had moved increasingly toward a biological determinist model of social aggression. Mark and Ervin, for example, devoted considerable space in the introductory pages of *Violence and the Brain* to arguing that societal influences alone were insufficient for explaining violence. Though West's proposal was more artful than Ervin and Mark's treatises on the biological seat of violence, it recapitulated many of the arguments they put forth. For example, West mused, "A violent act stems from the mind of a human being. What is the state of such a mind?"[46] West allowed that not "all violent persons have abnormally functioning brains," but anticipated that placing electrodes "deep within the brain" would provide a way to determine how the brain, which he referred to as the "organ of behavior," was linked to violent actions.[47] Ervin's participation in the center and West's ostensible acceptance of his theories fanned rumors that the researchers would perform psychosurgery on members of vulnerable communities. As this speculation heated up, Ervin's name that was included in early versions of the center proposal was removed from later drafts, presumably because the violence center's backers were attempting to assuage their critics and potential funders.

The Party's "Challenge to Racist Geneticists"

The Black Panthers' protestations over the center derived partly from its members' appreciation that jails and prisons were "total institutions" at which incarcerated persons had little agency and at which biomedical research could therefore be especially oppressive.[48] The Panthers' perspective also demonstrated the activists' understanding, growing out of the ideas of Fanon and "Che" Guevara, that violence was a deeply political phenomenon. For the Party, violence was neither irrational nor evidence of biological pathology; rather, it was a manifestation of social dis-ease. At the same time, the Party's response to the violence center did reflect its engagement with 1970s debates and controversies about race and biology.

In its newspaper, the Party directly addressed the biologically essentialist theories of the University of California at Berkeley psychologist Arthur Jensen. A specialist in education, Jensen came to public attention in 1969 when he published the first of many papers that claimed to link intelligence to genes.[49] In 1972, in his book *Genetics and Education*, he declared that "Negroes" were up to eight times more likely to have "mental retardation" than whites.[50] More broadly, Jensen's opus supported "genetic inferiority theory," that is, the dubious notion that some human groups are biologically inferior to others (with blacks at the bottom of the genetic hierarchy). These differences, Jensen contended, were manifest in intelligence and behavior. In September 1973 the Party "announced an unprecedented challenge" to Jensen's "theories of Black inferiority" that was timed to coincide with a meeting of the International Genetic Foundation on the Berkeley campus.[51]

As sociomedical racialism was making new inroads,[52] the Party challenged scientific claims about race as a facet of its fight against medical discrimination—and as African Americans had done previously (see chapter 1). Its first line of attack against Jensen was to expose the racial essentialism underlying the psychologist's research hypotheses. It worked to abrade the scientific patina that legitimized the conjectural linking together of "natural abilities" and "political, intellectual and moral status," to borrow W. E. B. Du Bois's words.[53]

The activists also highlighted the analytic tautology of research that proceeded from the assumption of innate, unequivocal racial differences and that consequently yielded outcomes overdetermined by race; within such a milieu of circular logic, blacks were always classed as biological "lack" or "excess" relative to some sociotechnically constructed norm. As with its framing of sickle cell anemia that combined insights from population genetics with racial health disparities discourse, the Party did not object to scientific research or to the comparative analysis of social groups per se. Rather, the activists denounced studies like Jensen's that compared *only* blacks and whites. Making this point, Seale mused that "few scientists seem interested in comparing, say Northern Italians with Southern Italians . . . . Appalachian Whites with Social Register Whites."[54] These examples drew attention to the simultaneous ideological potency *and* arbitrariness of classification and comparison in research on human variation. Continuing, Seale suggested that the intrinsic "racism" of studies like Jensen's that focused "only on Blacks[']" supposed biological inadequacies might be "eliminated" through the use of different categories of analysis.[55]

Seale surmised that such an approach would be not only antiracist but also "more scientific."[56] This latter assertion pointed to the activists' second major criticism of Jensen's research—its lack of scientific merit. The Party fashioned itself as a concerned stakeholder—united with many others—in the pursuit of better biomedicine and bioscience. To this end, the Black Panthers critically assessed Jensen's research with the same confidence that they encouraged in the "lay experts" at their clinics, who critically engaged medical authority and practice.[57] Seale and Brown established the Party's credibility through their adjudication of Jensen's assumptions, as above; their performance of its command of genetics discourse; and, related to this, their articulation of a "scientific counterdiscourse."[58]

The Party affirmed its acceptance of evolutionary theory, stating that because "groups perpetuate each other through marriage, it is reasonable to expect that over generations they have produced clearly defined genetic strengths and weakness that can be compared with other groups."[59] This claim that, with its invocation of "marriage," was surprisingly conservative coming from a group that lived communally and often took in children at its Oakland school, who were not being well cared for by their biological families, evinced some possible common ground between the Party and Jensen. Having established this point, however, the activists then sharply diverged from the spurious associations the psychologist made between inheritance and intelligence: "The Black Panther Party, the Black community, and the vast majority of geneticists and educators," its statement read, "believe that the greatest intellectual differentials are among individuals rather than races."[60] Here the activists echoed a soon-to-be-landmark assessment of human variation published one year earlier by the geneticist Richard Lewontin that established the now-axiomatic assertion that there is more genetic variation within "races" than between them.[61] Invoking its intellectual solidarity with a "vast majority" of researchers, activists, and black citizens, the Party cast Jensen as an outlier and, in doing so, endeavored to also cast doubt on his scientific bona fides.

The Party's appraisal of Jensen's claims included an alternative vision of how antiracist, socially responsible research should be conducted. Cognizant of the burden of biomedical scrutiny historically born by marginalized and vulnerable groups, the activists advised that "*all* ethnic and racial groups" should be studied equally.[62] They furthermore recommended that such studies should be "assessed" by a national committee of scientists who could determine the "significance and consequences" of research on human genetic variation.[63]

The Party then related this issue of research design to the issue of citizens' oversight of state funding: "The decision as to whether Americans wish to financially support . . . studies [such as Jensen's]," it pronounced, "should be left to the democratic process."[64] Channeling Mao, Brown proclaimed, "Let 1000 such studies bloom if that is how the nation wishes to use its scientific resources."[65] The implication of Brown's statement was that citizens should have a say in the allocation of collective resources. The Party's concurrent challenge to the UCLA violence center proceeded from this perspective of robust citizenship; indeed, its opposition to the planned research facility centrally involved an engagement with legislative deliberation.

Vulnerable Communities

In West's initial center proposal—the proposal underwent several revisions in response to public criticism—he was preoccupied by the violence allegedly perpetrated by members of minority and marginalized groups; the disproportionate risk that accordingly would be borne by these communities alarmed members of the coalition seeking to block funding to the center. More alarmingly, West's proposal made mention of a plan to enlist California prisoners as subjects in the center's experimental research projects: among the possible settings was the California Medical Facility at Vacaville, a prison north of the Bay Area where both Cleaver and David Hilliard had spent time. Researchers from the University of California system commonly used inmates at this state prison for experiments.[66] Indeed, it was revealed in February 1972—just months prior to the announcement of plans for the violence center—that three prisoners at Vacaville had been subjected to psychosurgery.[67] Thus, if implemented, the center could have potentially had a direct and deleterious impact on members of the Party.

Party members' brushes with the law stoked prisoners' rights activism within the Party, which took the form of political writing, community outreach, and assistance to the incarcerated. Much of Cleaver's notorious best seller *Soul on Ice* comprises reflections on the structural forces and personal choices that landed him in prison before joining the Party.[68] Party bard George Jackson, who was murdered while doing time at San Quentin prison, wrote eloquently before his assassination about the inhumanity of prison conditions, specifically Soledad State Prison, in the popular book *Soledad Brother*.[69] The Southern California chapter regularly ran pieces in its newsletter about the callous treatment of jailed Party members. Many of these writings focused on the paucity of adequate medical treatment for the incarcerated and the often-coercive nature of what treatment was available.[70]

Therefore, Party members, many of whom had encountered abominable prison conditions firsthand, recognized that it was extremely difficult for the incarcerated to grant true "informed consent." Drawing on personal experience, Newton knew that a prisoner would submit to almost anything, including risky medical procedures, when financial incentives or other inducements that marginally enhanced prison life were offered;[71] under such conditions, biomedical research among prisoners was inherently coercive. Newton's concerns were confirmed by a Vacaville prison official who observed that "the main benefit [of experiments on human subjects at the facility was] . . . that research programs cut down on disciplinary problems. A man had to have a relatively infraction-free record to qualify as a volunteer subject. And the Department figures if he has thirty dollars a month to spend on canteen, he'll be a lot cooler."[72] Newton's recent experience of incarceration, of being a member of a "vulnerable population" into today's bioethics parlance, conditioned his reaction to some of the studies proposed by violence center researchers. He would draw on these experiences to help shape the arguments presented by Hiestand on behalf of the Party and its allies.[73]

The vulnerability of prisoners to programs such as that proposed at the violence center also captured the attention of the larger black community. The controversy over the center occurred just a few months after an article by the *New York Times* reporter Jean Heller disclosed to the public the four-decades-long Tuskegee syphilis study. In the climate of heightened suspicion of the medical establishment that followed this revelation, psychosurgery became a hot-button issue for African Americans.[74] Black physicians and neuroscientists spoke up about the dangers of experimental procedures like psychosurgery, as did members of the nascent Congressional Black Caucus.[75]

In the February 1973 issue of *Ebony* magazine, a news organ of black Middle America, one article detailed the emergence of this most recent effort to conjure biomedical answers to deeply social dilemmas. Authored by B. J. Mason, "New Threat to Blacks: Brain Surgery to Control Behavior" described efforts by Ervin, Mark, and Sweet to develop a research program to investigate the neurological basis of what Sweet termed "senseless" violence.[76] Taking a calm but cautionary tone, the article discussed the researchers' theory that violence could be caused by unidentified brain pathology and featured a series of diagrams detailing the surgical manipulation of the brain. Brain surgery advocates quoted in the article maintained that patients became more manageable after psychosurgery. But critics quoted in the same piece complained that the procedure left patients in a "blunted" and zombie-like state.[77] Mason's article also drew attention to the fact that African Americans, who increasingly made up a lopsided percentage of the incarcerated population, would be unduly subjected to prison experimentation.

Campus Controversy

The Panthers were but one of many groups involved in protesting the violence center and its proposed research. When the Party and its allies took up the cause of defeating the center, the coalition in effect amplified the scope of already vehement student opposition to it. Student protest erupted on the UCLA campus in the winter of 1973, after the discovery that a university-based research facility, the Neuropsychiatric Institute, was establishing the center. UCLA student groups, including the Coalition Against Campus Racism and the Violence Center, and the local chapters of Students for a Democratic Society and the Progressive Labor Party, protested in outrage.

To demonstrate their opposition to the center, UCLA student groups held rallies; wrote editorials in the university newspaper, the *Daily Bruin*; distributed flyers, pamphlets, and tracts; and performed guerrilla theater—public skits during which they compared the proponents of the center to mad scientists.[78] On- and off-campus press accounts likened the planned surgeries of the proposed violence center to the atrocities of mad scientists in contemporary science fiction films like Stanley Kubrick's *Clockwork Orange*.[79] Revelations that West proposed to the U.S. Department of Defense that the center assume ownership of an abandoned Nike missile base in the nearby Santa Monica Mountains as a site where "comparative studies" for the "alteration of undesirable behavior" could be conducted in a "securely fenced" and "isolated but convenient location" only served to heighten activists' Faustian suspicions.[80] While these suspicions may have been deemed far-fetched, they also found expression in the popular culture of the day; the novelist Michael Crichton, who had at one time been a student of Ervin's, extrapolated on the fine line between medical human experimentation and scientific abuse in his book *The Terminal Man*, which was described by a *New York Times* reporter as "the best-selling Frankensteinian novel . . . in which the brain of a violent epileptic is tied into and controlled by a computer."[81]

Student protests lasted for several months. At their height, a dozen protestors stormed West's office in an attempt to seize the violence center. Three members of this group of students were arrested for barricading themselves in West's office and chaining themselves to his desk.[82] The planned center aroused such concern among students that even the typically apolitical UCLA basketball star Bill Walton expressed his opposition to it during a local television appearance.[83]

The students did not stand alone on the UCLA campus in challenging the planned center; faculty were also vocal in their disapproval of it, including the UCLA Faculty Committee Against Racism and Neuropsychiatric Institute researchers Dr. Fred Abrams and Dr. Isidore Ziferstein. Abrams was a common fixture at anticenter rallies and protests and a leading faculty opponent. He was eventually terminated by the institute, supposedly for reasons not involving his activism. Ziferstein expressed his opposition to the violence center with editorials in the *Los Angeles Times* and the *Daily Bruin*. Among his complaints about the center, the issue of democratic access to scientific knowledge loomed large: Ziferstein pointed out that the center's proponents aimed to discredit the student opposition by framing the debate as one of rational experts versus uninformed extremists, rather than responding directly to criticism. Writing in the *Los Angeles Times*, Ziferstein charged that violence center supporters "attempted to minimize the opposition to the center by creating the impression that the critics are not scientists or mature citizens but a 'leftist opposition' comprised largely of students."[84] Ziferstein also directly supported the Party's campaign against the center by passing along internal information about is progress to Hiestand.[85] Ever since its founding in the shadow of the University of California at Berkeley, the Black Panther organization enjoyed significant campus support for its politics and programs. In this instance, campus cooperation took the form of allied students and faculty.

Expert Witness

While plans for the violence center aligned the political and professional aspirations of the Reagan administration, local and federal law enforcement agencies, and biomedical researchers at UCLA, its realization depended on a fiscal partnership among these interests as well. For 1973 the proposed budget for the center was $1.5 million. Two-thirds of the funding was to come from the CCCJ, via the LEAA. The remaining money was slated to come from the California Department of Health, in cooperation with the Department of Corrections and the California Youth Authority, after approval from the state legislature.[86] The projected funds required from government agencies for the following fiscal year decreased by a third, to $1 million, in anticipation of funding from private foundations and philanthropists. Yet, even with private backers waiting in the wings, the center would initially be heavily dependent on funds controlled by elected officials. West knew that his ability to shape public perception of the center was crucial to securing this public funding.[87]

Public scrutiny of the UCLA violence center took the form of two legislative hearings sponsored by the California Senate Committee on Health and Welfare. What was at stake at the hearings was not simply state money but the public profile of the violence center—its legitimacy—on which it was to rely for future funding.[88] These hearings were organized to gather information about the planned center before the state legislature decided whether to allocate funds to it. If the lobbying efforts of the Party and its allies were successful, they could place the formation of the center in jeopardy.

In holding this series of hearings, California legislators took their lead from their counterparts in Washington, D.C., where the issue of human experimental research—with psychosurgery as the most dramatic and draconian example—was embroiled in controversy on the floor of the Senate. Psychosurgery became a national subject of debate after a psychiatrist in Washington, D.C., Peter Breggin, published an article about the danger of the increasing frequency of the procedure, titled "The Return of Psychosurgery and Lobotomy," in the February 24, 1972, issue of *Congressional Record*.[89] Soon after, articles began to appear in the national press, including an exposé in the *New York Times Magazine*, which examined, and for the most part confirmed, Breggin's claims that the use of brain surgery was increasing among some psychiatrists and neurosurgeons.[90] Democratic senator Edward Kennedy, who as the chairman of the Senate Committee on Health had played an important role in securing federal funding for sickle cell anemia research and screening months prior, spearheaded the series of hearings on psychosurgery beginning in early 1973.[91] Thus, by entering the debate over the violence center, the Party also became a part of a national dialogue about health rights, human subjects, and informed consent.

The California Senate Committee on Health and Welfare held the first of two day-long hearings on the violence center in April 1973. The committee listened to three supporters of the center: Robert E. Litman, a professor of psychiatry at the University of Southern California, who would serve as the center's first director; Stubblebine, the head of the state Department of Health and Welfare; and West. Because public outcry about the center had reached a fever pitch, Litman, Stubblebine, and West faced tough questions and skepticism about the center's mission and its funding model, psychosurgery, and safeguards to protect the rights of experimental subjects.[92]

West's testimony was primarily diplomatic; he attempted to deflect critique and correct what he saw as misperceptions about the center. To this end, he emphatically denied that psychosurgery would be carried out at the center. Stubblebine's testimony was less politic; his statements aimed to legitimize the biologization of violence by persuading the legislators that aggression is a medical issue rather than a social problem. Stubblebine employed metaphors that likened violent behavior to medical epidemics. He stated that violence was on par with "other life threatening communicable disease[s]." Continuing the analogy, he elaborated:

The person who is a carrier of an infectious agent is sometimes isolated or quarantined, is sometimes *required* to go under treatment and
is, in more cases than not, cured and returned to useful life in the
general society. It is entirely possible that this is the same kind of
situation that will prevail when we have greater knowledge about the
violent person or the potentially violent person.[93]

At the hearings' close, violence center opponents in attendance, including Hiestand, demanded that the committee chairman Anthony
Beilenson give them equal time to express their opinions about the center.[94] This second unplanned hearing took place the following month. At
this meeting, the Party would have the opportunity to respond to West,
Stubblebine, and Litman.

On May 9, 1973, Hiestand, at Beilenson's invitation, testified before the California Senate Health and Welfare Committee on behalf of
the Party-led coalition, along with Dr. Lee Coleman, a child psychiatrist
and representative of the Committee Opposing Psychiatric Abuse of Prisoners, and Terry Kupers.[95] During his testimony, Hiestand read from
an "administrative complaint" that he and Newton had prepared. The
document had no legal authority, and as this was a legislative hearing
and not a trial, it had no legal purpose. However, the document had the
imprimatur of legal authority and was, according to Hiestand, therefore
compelling to the lobbyists, politicians, activists—not to mention the
general public—with whom the document was shared. In this way, the
Black Panthers, through their attorney, employed legal discourse and
symbolism as part of its rejoinder to the biologization of violence.

During his testimony, Hiestand challenged the intentions of the
center and the assumptions that undergirded several planned projects.
He testified that his clients "feared [that the center] was a public relations boondoggle for the [Reagan] Administration" or perhaps "a covert
attempt to usher in a 'Clockwork Orange.'"[96] Hiestand expressed "grave
concern about the role the Center might play in encouraging or performing future behavior modification experiments on political protestors, prisoners, inmates of mental institutions, minorities, and women,"
populations that were represented by the Party and his other client organizations and that were mentioned in the violence center proposal.[97]
Hiestand directed the senators' attention to several research programs
that his clients found particularly troubling: one project that aimed to
associate violence in women with their menstrual cycles, and a second

1   FRED J. HIESTAND, ESQ.
     J. ANTHONY KLINE, ESQ.
2   CHARLES R. LAWRENCE, ESQ.
     JO ANN CHANDLER, ESQ.
3   ALBERT F. MORENO, ESQ.
     PUBLIC ADVOCATES, INC.
4   433 Turk Street
     San Francisco, California 94102
5   Telephone: (415) 441-8850

6

7   BEFORE THE CALIFORNIA COUNCIL

8   ON CRIMINAL JUSTICE

9

10   BLACK PANTHER PARTY; NATIONAL   )
     ASSOCIATION FOR THE ADVANCEMENT   )
11   OF COLORED PEOPLE, WESTERN REGION;   )
     NATIONAL ORGANIZATION FOR WOMEN;   )   ACTION NO.
12   UNITED FARMWORKERS' ORGANIZING   )
     COMMITTEE; MEXICAN-AMERICAN   )
13   POLITICAL ASSOCIATION; COMMITTEE   )
     OPPOSED TO THE PSYCHIATRIC ABUSE   )   ADMINISTRATIVE COMPLAINT
14   OF PRISONERS; CALIFORNIA PRISONERS'   )
     UNION; and CALIFORNIA MENTAL HEALTH   )
15   COORDINATING COUNCIL,   )
)
16   Plaintiffs,   )
)
17   v.   )
)
18   CENTER FOR THE STUDY AND REDUCTION   )
     OF VIOLENCE; EARL W. BRIAN, M.D.,   )
19   as Secretary of the Health and   )
     Welfare Agency. State of Calif-   )
20   ornia; LOUIS J. WEST, M.D., as   )
     Director of the Neuropsychiatric   )
21   Institute, UCLA; J.M. STUBBLEBINE,   )
     M.D., as Director of the Department   )
22   of Health, State of California,   )
)
23   Defendants.   )
)

24

25   INTRODUCTION

26   I

27   This is an action to prevent the allocation of approx-

28 imately $1,000,000 of taxpayers' monies by the California Council

29 for Criminal Justice and the State of California to the proposed

30 Center for the Study and Reduction of Violence at UCLA (herein-

31 after "Violence Center"), unless and until it is clearly estab-

32 lished that (1) this Violence Center will operate under enforced

On May 9, 1973, Black Panther Party cofounder Huey P. Newton and his attorney Fred J. Hiestand developed and circulated an "administrative complaint"—a document that had no legal status but carried the imprimatur of the law—as a way to disseminate its arguments against state backing for the planned UCLA violence center. From the collection of Fred J. Hiestand.

project that planned experiments into violence at predominantly black and Chicano high schools in Los Angeles. These proposals, Hiestand contended, amounted to the targeting of presumably violent individuals based on the social categories of race and gender, rather than an objective attempt to seek out violence in the many contexts in which it could be found.

Hiestand articulated the Party's positions and those of its allies on another occasion when he filed a second administrative complaint on their behalf at a hearing about the center in July 1973. The administrative complaint was also submitted to the CCCJ in an effort by Hiestand to lobby the agency against approving funding for the violence center. The complaint specifically aimed "to prevent the allocation of approximately $1,000,000 of taxpayers' monies to the UCLA CSRV until adequate safeguards to protect human subjects were put in place" and "the nature and scope of each and every Violence Center project is [established as] both scientifically sound and potentially beneficial to the public interest."[98] The violence center, California Secretary of Health Brian, West, and Stubblebine were named as "defendants"; the plaintiffs included the BPP, NOW, NAACP, UFOC, MAPA, and COPAP, as well as a new coalition member, the California Mental Health Coordinating Council. As with his state Senate testimony, Hiestand complained that the center's plans did not offer "sufficient evidence to indicate that the true nature and scope of the Violence Center's proposed work is not in fact injurious to the welfare of racial and ethnic minorities, women, involuntarily incarcerated persons, and the general public" who were being "excluded from participation in the development, control, review and ultimate utilization of the so-called research results."[99]

The coalitions' concerns as expressed by Hiestand were manifold, but focused most intently on theories about the causes of violence that were the opposite of those that underpinned many of the center's projects. Indeed, in the administrative complaint, Hiestand characterized "the experimental subjects" and "the experimenters" as being of "two different worlds." The coalition challenged the contention of the center's researchers that brain dysfunction was the source of individual violent behavior. For example, the administrative complaint highlighted the fact that the proposal for the center listed "the major known correlates" of violence as "sex (male), age (youthful), ethnicity (black), and urbanicity."[100] The document also quoted a passage from the same proposal that linked violent behavior "to participation in subcultures with particular attitudes toward the value of human life, and with attitudes equating violent physical expression with 'manliness.'"[101] The intersection of these characteristics (youthfulness, "manliness," etc.) in a single individual was suggested to predict the likelihood of violent behavior. Such claims took up the charged, political language of black family and black male pathology that circulated during this time in such narratives as "The Moynihan Report," and unwittingly revealed the social embeddedness of some center researchers' biological claims. If these discourses defined the black male individual as the locus of violence—a man who was, effectively, criminal-minded—the activist's definition of black male identity was "group-minded" and socially, rather than biologically, oriented.

Hiestand's testimony and the coalition's complaint repeatedly criticized the "vagueness" of the center proposal drafts. According to Hiestand, each new center proposal grew progressively more obfuscatory; rather than respond to public demand for clarification of the details of the center's intentions, revised proposals simply removed problematic research projects, with little assurance that the omitted programs were actually off the table. In particular, activists requested that more information be released about the precise form that the center's cooperation with the criminal justice system would take, and what drugs and techniques might be used in experiments to quell violence, before the state Senate agreed to back the center.[102]

Hiestand also discussed a seemingly strategic omission made in later center draft proposals—the deletion of Ervin's name from the list of center researchers. Quoting at length from the *Ebony* article on psychosurgery, Hiestand raised the issue of Ervin's participation in the center and employment at UCLA, and thus the possibility that psychosurgery might lie in the center's future, despite what he referred to as the "sanitizing" of the center's plans. Hiestand concluded his testimony with the demand that the center receive no state funding. Should plans for the center move forward, Hiestand advised that a series of procedural safeguards be put in place, including consultation with the communities to be affected by the proposed center's research projects.

On the subject of psychosurgery, Hiestand argued that "the earlier proposals and representations made by the Defendants cannot but make the Plaintiffs and the public skeptical about the original intentions of [the] Defendants and the consequent thoughtlessness of a proposal that fluctuates in content according to public criticism." The Party coalition pointed out several other inconsistencies: though West repeatedly insisted that the center would not undertake such procedures, Stubblebine had recently mentioned in the local press that brain surgery had not been ruled out completely. In addition, the Party noted that West let slip in testimony before the state Senate that psychosurgery would not take place on the premises of the center but at other facilities; patients would then be returned to the violence center for follow-up treatment and observation. Lastly, the complaint emphasized the fact that, although many of the proposals made mention of the complex set of factors that contribute to violence, there was little "appreciation" of this in the research design.

"Our backs are getting closer to the wall."

Many events and actors precipitated the center's undoing, but its downfall finally came about when financial backing was withdrawn. The first domino fell in mid-1973, when the Senate Committee on Health and Welfare for the state of California voted to withhold funding for the center, a decision that owed much to Hiestand's testimony.[103] Although there was little public support for the violence center, the influence of the activists' interpretation of the origins of violence and their contention that the center would be used as a tool of social control was reflected in the state Senate's decision.

Within a few weeks of Hiestand's testimony, the California Senate Committee on Health and Welfare, chaired by Beilenson, voted to withhold funding for the center.[104] Furthermore, the California legislature specifically prohibited the use of state money to fund the center at UCLA or a similar research project at another state agency or university without its express permission.[105] Echoing concerns raised by the Party, Beilenson stated the committee's decision was based on five factors: the absence of a comprehensive oversight system for the center's various research programs; the vague descriptions of the specific projects in which center researchers might engage; the lack of adequate safeguards to ensure the informed and uncoerced consent of research subjects; the fact that the funds requested for the center had not been previously budgeted and therefore would require that money be shifted from other places in the state Department of Health's budget; and the lack of planned "periodic on site inspections and reports of Center activities and research" by peers and citizens.[106] This decision had an immediate impact on the center's work. In the summer of 1973, for example, West canceled all orders for lab equipment for fear that there would not be enough money in the center's budget to purchase them.[107]

The center's future was placed in further jeopardy in February 1974 when the LEAA banned the funding of any crime prevention programs that used behavioral modification or medical research.[108] The LEAA's administrator, Donald E. Santarelli, said that he found many of the proposed behavior modification programs to be "fraught with peril."[109] Santarelli explained that although "the use of experimental medical procedures on human subjects for purposes of modification and alteration of criminal and other anti-social behavior" had "come into prominence" in some research communities, the "LEAA personnel generally do not possess the technical and professional skills required to evaluate and monitor projects employing such procedures."[110]

West tried to retain financial support for the center by lobbying the CCCJ director Anthony Palumbo. West's correspondence to Palumbo contained personal assurances that none of the banned procedures would be performed at the center and pleas for the Neuropsychiatric Institute's grant application to be kept in contention for funding. In this letter, West also tried to distinguish what he termed "behavioral science" from the medical human experimentation behavior modification research that had been banned from funding by the LEAA.[111] He received a blunt response from the LEAA. Palumbo then encouraged West to withdraw the center grant application or risk having it rejected in a public and potentially embarrassing manner. In an internal memo West despaired, "Our backs are getting closer to the wall every day."[112]

In a last-ditch effort to save the center, it was placed under the umbrella of the existing Laboratory for the Study of Life Threatening Behavior, directed by Dr. Edwin Shneidman.[113] In an article about the transfer, Shneidman said that "the very concept of a 'Center for the Study and Reduction of Violence' at UCLA has been so badly damaged that it has lost its usefulness. We have decided to discard it. . . . the entire enterprise is now being revised. Some proposals are being eliminated or modified; others are being added."[114]

Not only did the Party contribute to the demise of the violence center, it also managed to repurpose some LEAA resources. In 1974 the Party's Intercommunal Youth Institute (Oakland Community School) received funding from the LEAA, one of the state criminal justice agencies that planned to underwrite the violence center initiative—to develop and support a "comprehensive juvenile crime *prevention* program" in East Oakland.[115] Such funds were typically allocated to municipal police and sheriff departments; the activists would use the monies to support youth programs.[116] One of the Party's primary grant writers, Norma Armour applied for LEAA funding with help from Elaine Brown and Joan Kelly. She recounted that this grant was solicited under the auspices of its not-for-profit entity, the Education Opportunities Service Corporation. "The clinic and all the survival programs, the school came under that umbrella," she explained. "That's how we got law enforcement money."[117] The youth programs that the Party developed with this money was based at its Oakland school and included educational and community service activities. The activists, in this way, modeled an alternative to the violence center in practice that complemented its intellectual and philosophical critiques.

The refusal of the California Senate and, consequently, also the LEAA and the CCCJ, to fund the violence center arguably manifested broader discomfort with the bio-medicalization of violence—or, at least the clumsy and draconian presentation of this process by the initiative's backers.[118] In parallel with a simultaneous national dialogue about experimental research with human subjects, state legislators' discomfort with the conversion of social problems into medical ones was conveyed in the regulatory and bureaucratic language of ethical safeguards and research protocols. The criminal justice agencies' denial of funding was inevitable given their interdependent relationship with legislators; as one administrator observed, by way of justification, these agencies furthermore lacked the infrastructure necessary for evaluating the validity of the planned courses of research.

The Party, via Hiestand, had broached these same issues during the hearings at which funding for the center was debated. As Hiestand was one of but three witnesses speaking in opposition to the research scheme (alongside the Black Panthers' PFMC clinic collaborator and MCHR member Kupers), the successful campaign against the violence center was owed in no small part to the efforts of the Party and its allies (coalition partners, student activists, and others). This important victory impeded the formation of the violence center *and* negative medicalization (medicalization as punitive social control), if not deeply entrenched racial biologization. Here was the rub: although a good deal of the Party's perspective was taken up by legislators, its revolutionary ideology, class critique, and antiracist politics were not. The Party's bid to hinder the transformation of anger, reaction, anguish, and desperation into disease was forestalled—but only for a time.

The imagined center was partly a gambit to bundle present projects at UCLA with new initiatives and, by doing so, to create a major national research institute. Although the center failed, some of this prior research persisted, supported independently through both state and federal funds. Also, as Conrad and Schneider briefly note in their seminal work on medicalization, Ervin (with his collaborator Mark) had received more than one million dollars in funding from prestigious bodies to pursue research on violence and brain pathology *before* the publication of their provocative book and *before* the UCLA debate got under way.[119] The support that Ervin would have received as a violence center researcher, therefore, amounted to a fraction of the resources already at his disposal. This record of support indicates that the medicalization of violence—and psychosurgery as an intervention—was well on its way to becoming accepted practice.

In the early 1970s, in the shadow of both nationwide urban revolts against racial oppression and the disclosure of human experimental abuse at Tuskegee and elsewhere, researchers at UCLA proposed biologically oriented studies into the causes of violence. Recognizing this proposition as one juncture in an established trajectory of scientific allegations about the innate pathology and inferiority of marginalized groups, the Party staged a challenge to the planned center that took up established tactics employed against medical discrimination; with this campaign, the activists also exploited the exercise of newly affirmed (if not fully realized) black citizenship as a vehicle of protest. The activists had successfully extended its health politics from the provision of health education and healthcare services to protection from overexposure to biomedical surveillance. Some communities in Los Angeles were given safe haven from a different kind of violence—biologization as an exercise of state power.

CONCLUSION

Race and Health in the Post–Civil Rights Era

The effects of the Black Panther Party's health activism have been multiform, registering in the evolution of individual lives, in the ebb and flow of institutions, and in the persistent struggle for healthcare access. Many former Panthers continued their work on healthcare issues, with some remaining activists and others going on to careers in the medical professions, in public health administration, and in health-related community programs. Although the Seattle chapter's break with the national group in 1972 was disheartening, Arthur Harris fully credits his time in the Party as inspiring his decision to become a nurse.[1] Cleo Silvers, who advocated for patients' rights and conducted door-to-door testing for sickle cell anemia and lead poisoning in New York City (with both the Black Panther Party and the Young Lords Party) in later years directed Build a Better Bronx, an environmental justice community organization. At present, she is a community outreach director at a leading U.S. medical center.[2]

For Tolbert Small, involvement with the Party set him on his current path, serving as a bridge from his college activism as a Friend of SNCC to his present-day efforts to make medical care accessible. Small continues to practice medicine among the poor and working-class residents of Oakland, but he does so now at the Harriet Tubman Medical Office, a sliding-scale clinic he started in the 1980s.[3] In addition to providing primary healthcare at his office, Small occasionally performs acupuncture—a skill learned when he toured China with a Black Panther Party contingent in 1972—in two treatment rooms in the lower level of the clinic dedicated to this purpose.[4] He also serves on the board of the Coalition of Concerned Medical Professionals, a health rights organization,[5] and lectures widely, advocating for universal healthcare and railing against the inadequacies of the Medicare, Medicaid, and health maintenance organization systems.

Norma Armour, who worked at the George Jackson PFMC between 1970 and 1974, remains dedicated to healthcare issues. After her time as a Panther, she studied health administration, with a focus on substance abuse issues, at a California college. Her career trajectory included a stint at the Watts Health Foundation and work as a manager for alcohol and drug abuse programs for an L.A.-area municipality. In the late 1980s she helped begin the University Muslim Medical Association clinic in Los Angeles. Armour today is a community instructor in that city's Charles Drew University of Medicine and Science, where she advises health professionals on how to improve their communication and interactions with patients from the Watts community. In her words, this work is intended to "improve outcomes for our people and eliminate health disparities." Armour notes with pride that she is "still doing the work I began over forty years ago."[6]

Participation in the Black Panthers' health politics also had a lasting effect on the future endeavors of Malik Rahim (formerly Donald Guyton). Rahim was the deputy of security for the New Orleans chapter of the Party.[7] In 2005, in the wake of the federal government's failure to ensure social welfare during Hurricane Katrina, Rahim played an essential role in helping restore services to Louisianans left abandoned in the city. Drawing on skills accumulated during his time in the Party, Rahim established, with two others, the Common Ground Health Clinic in New Orleans' Algiers neighborhood.[8] Linking his Panther past with his post-Katrina activism, Rahim has commented that "most of the things that I do now [are] based upon those experiences."[9] He explained that "to start a health clinic or a first aid station [after Katrina] wasn't anything because . . . we did [this] in the Panther Party."[10]

In describing the human-made, state-exacerbated tragedy in New Orleans, Rahim invoked the familiar Black Panther health political language of government neglect, social exclusion—and, in response, "survival programs":

Right after the hurricane, we came to the realization that the city wasn't going to provide any services. . . . there was no medical entity even operating in Algiers, and it wasn't operating especially for black folks. . . . I said to myself, "My God, these people just mean for us to die. . . . Man, it's time for you to do whatever you got to do to survive." . . . under that environment of blatant racism and total abandonment . . . we founded Common Ground.[11]

Just as the brutal facts of urban poverty, health inequality, and medical mistreatment showed the celebratory civil rights rhetoric of the late 1960s at its limits, the aftermath of Katrina confirmed that for vulnerable communities made up of lives deemed of little value, citizenship had indeed failed. The necessary building carried out by Rahim and others in New Orleans brings to light the persistent circumscription of "the right to have rights," especially for poor and black communities.

The Party's health politics reflected its similar recognition that the legal defeat of Jim Crow decades prior did not guarantee citizenship. At the same time, it exhibited the activists' shared faith that social inclusion was of paramount value. Indeed, Seattle's Elmer Dixon argued that the Black Panther Party emerged as "the struggle shifted from civil rights . . . to human rights."[12] He said further that "[it] was our duty to stand up for our God-given rights. We were not going to beg for our rights, the rights to a decent education, health care, jobs—basic human rights."[13] The Party recognized and responded to the shifting stakes of U.S. citizenship as it came to focus on life-chances and a "politics of life itself," in which rights and obligations were articulated in new domains and discourses, including that of health, well-being, medicine, and biomedical research.[14]

Medical discrimination took many forms in the second half of the twentieth century. As Jim Crow health inequality—racially segregated schools for nurses and doctors, hospital wards, and professional societies, and substandard healthcare and sociomedical racialism—began to diminish in the 1960s, different modalities of these long-standing health disparities came into focus, including issues of healthcare access and insurance coverage, physician accountability, patient empowerment, mobility in the health professions, and medical surveillance. Befitting the combination of old and new forms of health-based inequality that it faced (and faced down), the Party mobilized a wide range of responses. Principally, it created healthcare institutions via a network of community-based health clinics; it engaged in debates about the validity and merits of race-based biomedical research; and, after legal desegregation, it demanded inclusion as patient–citizens, in hospitals, in insurance plans, in community board meetings, and in legislative chambers. Consistent with an organization formed partly in contradistinction to weak notions of community control, the Party supported the right of poor blacks to shape their social welfare.

In response to the citizenship contradiction that became acute in the late 1960s when the fact that civil rights did not ensure social inclusion was brought into sharp relief, the Party envisioned a more radical form of democracy. The activists rejected capitalist liberalism and laid claim to democracy's radical potential as this potentiality was articulated in the "WHAT WE WANT" and "WHAT WE NEED" that was the Party's ten-point platform. The Party imagined and tried to engender a society in which collective goods were put above economic gain.

This was the grounding philosophy of its social health perspective. Social health included but was bigger than a single individual's well-being. The Party understood health as a scalar phenomenon; social health linked the body to society, and inextricably so. The Party's social health framing was placed in jeopardy when, for example, its accusations of neglect (and even genocide) were countered by the state through either the expansion (National Sickle Cell Anemia Act) or the contraction (UCLA violence center) of resources. The material response of the state and reformers to the issues of health inequality highlighted by the Party was, at a certain level, evidence of the activists' efficacy. From another vantage, however, these gains were made at the cost of the Party's social health perspective; marginalized communities were left with an anemic if sometimes efficacious form of biological inclusion in the place of racial equality, social justice, and economic citizenship.

It has become commonplace to describe lived intersections of state and biomedical regimes as forms of "biological citizenship." Among scholars of patient advocacy and health social movements the phrase is often used felicitously, as a way to mark the emergence and politicization of new biosocial communities. The Party's health politics prompts a return to the work of the anthropologist Adriana Petryna and, in particular, to the milieu of catastrophe and deprivation that impelled her theorization of biological citizenship. With the health politics of the Black Panthers in mind, it is worth emphasizing that biological citizenship for Petryna is a vehicle of inclusion for "increasingly poor citizens" who, if not for their "damaged biology," might be otherwise lacking in social and economic rights.[15] What happens when damaged biology or presumed biological pathology or disproportionate illness rates or disease identity come to stand in for citizenship? What are the transaction costs of biological citizenship?

Racial health disparities are a "21st Century Civil Rights Priority!"[16] So declared the phalanx of religious, political, and health industry leaders, gathered under the auspices of the National Minority Quality Forum, at a September 2007 press conference in Washington, D.C. Members of this group, which was made up of Al Sharpton and Jesse Jackson, as well as the president of the Association of Black Cardiologists, the Washington bureau chief of the NAACP, and a member of the Congressional Black Caucus, among others, spoke in turn and with urgency about the epidemic of myriad black–white health inequities. As a case in point, several speakers raised the issue of disparities in heart disease: Dr. Gerald DeVaughn, the head of the Association of Black Cardiologists, lamented that African American mortality from heart disease significantly outpaced that of whites, drawing the conclusion that "a race neutral approach . . . has not worked."[17] "By ignoring scientific evidence," added Dr. Elizabeth Ofili, a cardiologist affiliated with the Morehouse College School of Medicine, "we are placing our patients at unnecessary risk of premature death."[18]

The data to which Ofili referred were controversial clinical studies on the differential efficacy by race of BiDil, a pharmaceutical treatment for congestive heart failure. BiDil was approved by the Food and Drug Administration in 2005 for the exclusive use of "self-identified African American patients,"[19] on the logic that the genetic makeup of blacks was sufficiently distinct from other groups to warrant a "race-specific" drug. In dismissing a "race neutral approach" to cardiopathy, DeVaughn also dismissed decades of scholarship—on scientific racism, on the Tuskegee syphilis study and other forms of invidious medical experimentation, on the expropriation of black bodies for the benefit of medical science from "night riders" to Henrietta Lacks, and on racial discrimination in both healthcare facilities and the medical profession— that has rendered the perils of biological theories of race in fine detail and shown how these have been used to justify the very disparities this coalition aimed to bridge. By implication, the day's speakers suggested that *race-biased* or *race-based* medicine that began from the assumption of a shared and distinctive genetic profile was a cure for what ailed black America. Placing the issue of African Americans' access to BiDil on the front lines of "the next battleground for civil rights," the speakers at the same time represented the struggle over access to BiDil as a natural next phase in the *longue durée* of the black protest tradition.[20]

Given the history of medical discrimination in the United States, how was it that the demand for access to a race-based drug said to be efficacious for the supposed idiosyncratic physiology of black people came to be regarded as the next stage in the struggle for full citizenship? How did a civil rights tradition undergirded by claims about common humanity and shared inalienable rights become the banner under which social, political, and health industry leaders endorsed a drug predicated on African Americans' supposed essential biological difference?

The Black Panthers' activism was a critical and unwitting way station on the road to this vexed, contemporary politics of health and race that the sociologist Steven Epstein has characterized as the "inclusion-and-difference" paradigm. The Black Panther Party understood that the health inequality experienced by blacks and the poor was a dialectic of neglect and surveillance. As has been described in the preceding pages, the Black Panthers' politics of race and health accordingly had two emphases. First, the Party both advanced and rejected theories of health and human difference toward efficacious political ends. In the case of sickling and race, the Party ventured close to essentialism in its uptake of genetics theories that permitted it to make strong claims about racial oppression. Second, the Party rejected outright the suggestion that African Americans might be biologically inferior. More specifically, the activists recontextualized the assumptions of 1970s genetic science and advanced the position that socially just genetics would study *all human* groups rather than focus on blacks solely.

Today genomic science has resuscitated some debates about race, health, and biology thought to have been dormant since before the Panther era, but as the controversies over black disease predisposition and inferiority discussed in chapter 5 suggest, these debates never really went away. The dual discourse of the Party's politics of health and race suggest how we got here and where we might be headed. The Party found in health not only a new moral terrain for civil and social rights struggles but also a marker of African American inclusion and exclusion. The Black Panthers worked both within and outside mainstream medicine, critiquing its excesses, its discrimination, and its paternalism while seeking social health for poor communities. Party health activism suggests that we may be moving toward a "curious conjunction of a reliance on and a repudiation of race"—as Anthony Appiah remarked about Du Bois's early work—that will converge in new ways in the era of genetic ancestry testing for race and ethnicity and personalized medicine.[21] This is not exactly a rock and a hard place, but it is the place where marginalized communities are left after years of yearning for social inclusion on various registers. The articulation of BiDil, a pharmaceutical for African Americans, as a civil rights issue should be viewed in light of these historical dynamics that the Black Panthers demonstrate: the emergence of health as a civil rights mantle in the 1970s; postsegregationist aspirations for inclusion and social health, the repudiation of Jim Crow, and the progression of racial inequality from segregated water fountains and lunch counters to entrenched urban poverty.

Following Fanon, the Panthers also recognized how medicine could serve as a vehicle of social control; indeed, it might be said that their mission to police the police was extended onto biopolitical terrain. The Panthers' characterization of the power exercised by the medical–industrial complex as neglect resulting in genocide signaled the group's sensitivity both to how the black body had been a site of domination historically—as expressed, for example, in its analogizing of the suffering of slavery with that of sickling—and to blacks' vulnerability to the constriction of health rights, to which the activists responded with clinics and initiatives. Health was the site where these two concerns articulated. From this vantage, we can see that the Party's health politics—its provision of medical services, its health education outreach, and its social health paradigm—was also a struggle over the terms of black citizenship, a confrontation with the authority of biomedical science, and a challenge to the process of biomedical racialization. The black body came to represent the broader treatment of blacks in the United States.

ACKNOWLEDGMENTS

I t would have been impossible for me to complete this work without the encouragement, support, and guidance of a host of extraordinary and extraordinarily gracious people who, in ways small and large, collectively inspired me, prodded me along, and sustained me.

Thanks are heartily extended to the librarians of both the Special Collections Department and the University Archives at the University of California, Los Angeles Young Research Library, for their assistance, among them Dennis Bitterich, Charlotte Brown, and Jeff Rankin. The expert advice of the staffs at the Department of Special Collections and University Archives of the Green Library at Stanford University (especially Polly Armstrong and Mattie Taormina); the Beinecke Library at Yale University; the Tamiment and Fales Special Collections Libraries at New York University; the Bancroft Library at the University of California at Berkeley (in particular David Kesler, Susan Synder, and Jack von Euw); and the Special Collections department at the University of Washington is much appreciated. I was also the grateful beneficiary of the kindness and wisdom of Stephanie Spearman and the other pioneering members of the Black Heritage Society of Washington State.

For generous support of the research and writing of the book, I am grateful to the Graduate School of Arts and Sciences at New York University (Henry Mitchell MacCracken Fellowship, Dean's Fellowship and Summer Research Grant); the Ford Foundation (Postdoctoral Diversity Fellowship); and the Woodrow Wilson and Andrew W. Mellon Foundations (Career Enhancement Fellowship). I gratefully acknowledge support from the International Center for Advanced Studies (New York University), Skidmore College (Trustee Minority Dissertation Fellowship), and Trinity College (Ann E. Plato Fellowship), which helped me bring this project to fruition. In these three settings, I cherished the warm collegiality of Laurel Baldwin-Ragaven, Thomas Bender, Deb Cowen, Jordana Dym, Julia Elyachar, Wilma Hall, Andrew Lakoff, Paul Lauter, Jack Ling, Mary C. Lynn, Timothy Mitchell, Christ Otter, Margo Perkins, Greg Pfitzer, Vijay Prashad, Pushkala Prasad, Barbara Sicherman, Margaret Somers, Miriam Ticktin, Jerry Watts, Johnny Williams, and Joanna Schneider Zangrando. I owe special thanks to Amy Koteles, Gregory Morton, and Nancy Osberg-Otrembiak for fostering such welcoming spaces in which to write and think.

Opportunities to present my research on the Black Panthers' health politics in its early stages yielded generative dialogue with and useful feedback from my colleagues at Trinity College; from audiences at meetings of the Social Science History Association and the American Studies Association; from Muriel Lederman, Bernice Hausman, and attendees of the Science and Technology Studies Seminar Series at Virginia Polytechnic and State University; from Wenda Bauchspies and those in attendance at the Science and Technology Studies Program Colloquium Series at the Pennsylvania State University; from C. Brandon Ogbunugafor and attendees at my Frantz Fanon Lecture Series at the Yale School of Medicine; from participants in the Public Spheres and American Cultures Conference at the John Nicholas Brown Center for the Study of American Civilization at Brown University; and from Samuel K. Roberts, Azure Thompson, Joshua Guild, and other participants in the Robert Wood Johnson Working Group on African-American History and the Health and Social Sciences at Columbia University. At the "Science, Technology, and the Historical Influence of Race" conference at Drexel University, constructive comments and frank advice from the gatherings' organizers and participants, especially Kali Gross, Amy Slaton, Pat D'Antonio, Alison Eisenberg, Robin D. G. Kelley, and Keith Wailoo, were enormously valuable for my revision of chapter 2 and the book's larger evolution. I also benefited from spirited interactions with members of the African Americanist Colloquium at Columbia University, organized by James T. Roane, Megan French, and Victoria Phillips Geduld.

I have been fortunate to count Steve Bouscaren, Manthia Diawara, Troy Duster, Francis Smith Foster, Ed Guerrero, George Lipsitz, Tanya Luhrmann, Stephanie McCurry, Michael E. Meeker, Kobena Mercer, Toby Miller, the late and great Dorothy Nelkin, Sally Ride, Tricia Rose, Andrew Ross, Leland Saito, and Nikhil Pal Singh among my most influential teachers. Each of them has deeply shaped the course of my intellectual interests; the ruts and wrong turns are my doing solely.

Steven Epstein reviewed an early draft of the book manuscript and gave me detailed, insightful suggestions for its improvement. He is a model senior colleague, and I am deeply thankful for the many gestures of kindness and helpfulness he has shown me for many years. Adele Clarke generously served as my mentor during the period of my Wilson fellowship (and well beyond!); she read the manuscript in whole and sent me articles and book chapters on themes related to its topics (always with an accompanying note of encouragement), and I am immensely indebted to her. Julia Adams, Randall Kennedy, Delores Y. Nelson, Chris Rhomberg, Dorothy Roberts, Rachel Sherman, Thuy Linh Tu, and Ben Williams also read drafts of the book and offered valuable suggestions toward its improvement. Elizabeth Alexander, Norma Armour, Marie Branch, Alicia Schmidt Camacho, Duana Fullwiley, Alyosha Goldstein, Stephanie Greenlea, Kali Gross, Joshua Guild, Ange-Marie Hancock, Fredrick Harris, Stefan Helmreich, Fred J. Hiestand, Jonathan Holloway, Tisha Hooks, Kellie Jones, Ferentz LaFargue, Catherine Lee, Tavia N'Yongo, Jonathan Metzl, Ann Morning, Aaron Panofsky, Howard Rambsy II, Sarah Richardson, Dorothy Roberts, Wendy Roth, Cleo Silvers, Nikhil Pal Singh, Amy Slaton, Helen Tilley, Lucia Trimbur, and Michael Veal gave generously of their time, providing engaged and invaluable responses to various chapters.

An extended network of friends and colleagues deserves my thanks for intellectual interchange that fostered my thinking, for suggestions and ideas, for input on aspects of the project, and for reassurance along the way. I apologize in advance for any omissions and acknowledge, in particular, Camille Acey, Mia Bay, Derrick Bell, Emily Bernard, Helmut Breiderhoff, Daphne Brooks, Phil Brown, Jeff Chang, William Jelani Cobb, Dalton Conley, Thulani Davis, Gary Dauphin, Rick Duque, Ron Eglash, Tanya Erzen, Henry Louis Gates Jr., John Gennari, Alexander

Green, Helena Hansen, Keith Harris, Rebecca Herzig, Karla Holloway, Peter James Hudson, Adria Imada, Peter Knight, Howard Markel, Paul D. Miller, Mark Naison, Anna Neumann, Rosalind Nicholas, Anne Pollack, Hugh Raffles, Howard Rambsy II, Emmanuel Raymundo, Sal Restivo, Nikolas Rose, Jane Rhodes, Nichole Rustin, Susan Schweick, Wes Shrum, Rebecca Skloot, Julie Sze, Kali Tal, Yaro Tal, Bryant Terry, Makani Therna-Nixon, Fatimah Tuggar, Priscilla Wald, Vron Ware, Alexander Weheliye, and Eliza Williams as well as Guy Walter, Cédric Duroux, and the Villa Gillet crew.

I have benefited incalculably from the intellectual fellowship of several stimulating intellectual communities. For many years, Troy Duster and Dorothy Nelkin convened the New York Consortium on Science and Society, and I learned a great deal from these exchanges with visiting scholars and with Nadia Abu El Haj, Lennard Davis, Stefan Helmreich, Bradley Lewis, Emily Martin, Ann Morning, Alan McGowan, Rayna Rapp, and Tania Simoncelli. I was fortunate to have been brought into the fold of the Black Modernities working group and have learned a great deal from my collective reading, conversation, and debate with Herman Bennett, Tina Campt, Hazel Carby, Brent Edwards, Phillip Brian Harper, Saidiya Hartman, Jennifer Morgan, and Tavia N'Yongo. My colleagues in the Cambridge Race and Science workshop have inspired me in more ways than they could possibly know; my deep appreciation to Jon Beckwith, Catherine Bliss, Lundy Braun, Michael Carson, Ann Fausto-Sterling, Duana Fullwiley, Alan Goodman, Jennifer Hamilton, Evelynn Hammonds, Jennifer Hochschild, Everett Mendelsohn, Susan Reverby, Sarah Richardson, Alexandra Shields, and William Quivers.

Immeasurable gratitude is due Norma Armour, Marie Branch, William Bronston, Elaine Brown, William Davis, Kent Ford, Cleo Silvers, Kathleen Neal Cleaver, Arthur Harris, Fred J. Hiestand, Billy X. Jennings, Terry Kupers, Robert Levine, Fitzhugh Mullan, Azure Thompson, Bernard Thompson, Tolbert Small, and Stephanie Spearman, who lavishly shared memories and items from their storied lives. This book would not exist except for their magnanimity. My special thanks to Billy X. Jennings and the It's About Time Black Panther Party archive for permission to use its rare and valuable materials in my book.

I am especially obliged to a talented cohort of scholars of the Black Panther Party whose unique approaches to the study of the organization and the period during which it emerged both inspired and informed my own research: Johanna Fernandez, Leigh Raiford, Besenia Rodriguez,

Robyn Spencer, and Yohuru Williams. Curtis Austin was exceedingly charitable and helped me with my search for images for my book; I hope I can show to other scholars the kindness he has shown to me. My Black Panther Party fellow traveler Donna Murch passed along primary resources relevant to my manuscript that she came across while researching and writing her excellent book.

I thank photographer Steven Shames for entrusting me with his one-of-a-kind images of the Black Panther Party and Nilda Rivera at Polaris Images for facilitating the use of these images in the book.

I tried out and hashed out portions of this book with students at Yale and Columbia, both inside and outside the classroom; I am grateful for their insights and their forbearance. In particular, several former and current students were the testing ground for many of the ideas here, and I acknowledge them with pleasure and appreciation: Ifeoma Ajumwa, Cecilia Cardenas-Navia, Abigail Coplin, Cat Pitti Esquivel, Caroline Gray, Stephanie Greenlea, Sean Greene, Cassie Hays, Tisha Hooks, Nicole Ivy, Ben Karp, Warren McKinney, Manuella Meyer, Carlos Miranda, Nanlesta Pilgrim, James Roane, Joan Robinson, Besenia Rodriguez, David Scales, and Lucia Trimbur.

A big, warm gratitude shout-out to the research assistants who skillfully helped me in innumerable ways during the long generation of this project: Stephanie Alvarado, Mary Barr, Aaron Figura, Lindsey Greene-Upshaw, Talibah Newman, Elizabeth Olson, and Thalia Sutton. During the final months of the book's completion, I would have been quite literally lost without the impeccable assistance of Valerie Idehen, who helped me clear the publication finish line. Throughout early morning and late-night work sessions, on weekdays and weekends, she remained the most organized person I know and also the most gracious and even-keeled. An uncommon combination—Valstyle, indeed!

My time as assistant professor in the departments of African American studies, sociology, and the American studies program at Yale University, where I began my professional career, was seminal. I express deep appreciation to my Yale colleagues for cherished years of intellectual camaraderie, especially Julia Adams, Elizabeth Alexander, Elijah Anderson, David Blight, Hannah Brückner, Alicia Schmidt Camacho, Jill Campbell, Hazel Carby, George Chauncey, Kamari Clarke, Kathleen Neal Cleaver, Ron Eyerman, Terri Francis, Kellie Jones, Paul Gilroy, Ronald Gregg, Ezra Griffiths, Jonathan Holloway, Matthew Frye Jacobson, Gerald Jaynes, Glenda Gilmore, Uli Mayer, Marcella Nunez-Smith, Ainissa

Ramirez, Steven Pitti, Peter Stamatov, Robert Stepto, Emilie Townes, Ebonya Washington, Laura Wexler, and Michael Veal. Ann Fitzpatrick, Jon Galberth, Janet Giarratano, Nancy Hopkins, Geneva Melvin, and Jodie Stewart-Moore daily and with patience helped me navigate the ins and outs of the institution. I am appreciative to the Yale administration for variously supporting my scholarly development and, in particular, my thanks to Emily Bakemeier, Jon Butler, Richard Brodhead, Jill Cutler, Joseph Gordon, Charles Long, and Mary Miller.

Many thanks to colleagues at Columbia University for my warm welcome to the institution and especially to Nadia Abu El Haj, Lila Abu-Lughod, Rachel Adams, Karen Barkey, Peter Bearman, Marcellus Blount, Yinon Cohen, Gil Eyal, Priscilla Ferguson, Dana Fisher, Eric Foner, Katherine Franke, Herbert Gans, Lynn Garafola, Steven Gregory, Farah Jasmine Griffin, Fredrick Harris, Saidiya Hartman, Marianne Hirsch, Jean E. Howard, Shamus Khan, Alice Kessler-Harris, Kellie Jones, George Lewis, Yao Lu, Debra Minkoff, Alessandra Nicifero, Gary Okihiro, Elizabeth Povinelli, Valerie Purdie-Vaughns, Samuel K. Roberts, Saskia Sassen, Carla Shedd, Josef Sorett, Seymour Spilerman, David Stark, Neferti Tadiar, Dorian Warren, Diane Vaughn, Sudhir Venkatesh, and Joshua Whitford. Thanks to Dora Arenas, Anne Born, Sharon Harris, Nusaiba Jackson, Page Jackson, Shawn Mendoza, and Vina Tran for helping me find my way at my new home.

I am thoroughly indebted to Jason Weidemann—a truly phenomenal editor—for his commitment to this project. Brimming with keen insight and good humor, Jason guided the book's publication at the University of Minnesota Press with a rare eye for both fine details and the big picture. Indeed, colleagues were often awestruck when I conveyed examples of the skill and care with which Jason shepherded the publication process. I also extend my appreciation to Danielle Kasprzak for her assistance in bringing this project to fruition. The departments of the University of Minnesota Press work as a team on each book, so I offer my thanks to that constellation of greatly appreciated people who played a role in making this book better. I thank the members of the Press's faculty advisory board as well as several anonymous reviewers for their assiduous reading of the manuscript and thoughtful recommendations on how it could be improved. I acknowledge my former agent, the superb Dan O'Connell, for his unflagging enthusiasm for this project over many years. Additionally, I benefited from Audra Wolfe's expert editorial advice and from Jane E. Boyd's singular ability to help bring clarity and order to prose.

I have drawn again and again from the well of experience and compassion of several individuals who for more than a decade have liberally shared their accumulated wisdom and their precious time with me. Collectively, they provided much perspective, guidance, and kindhearted words of support on many occasions. From the many opportunities he has afforded me to his enthusiastic praise married with honest criticism, Troy Duster has been incredibly generous, and I can only hope to be able to pay these riches forward. Paul Gilroy is a peerless thinker; with both long, soulful dialogue and the pithiest of comments, he motivates me to think harder and better, and for these interchanges and for his friendship I am profoundly grateful. From the moment I landed on the threshold of her office door at MIT in the late 1990s to the very present moment, Evelynn Hammonds has been unfailingly encouraging and supportive: I am fortunate to have Dean Hammonds, a path-breaking scholar of race, gender, and biomedicine, as a mentor. When this project was a mere kernel of an idea, Andrew Ross encouraged me to grow and foster it. He was there at the beginning and remains an important intellectual presence in my life. Keith Wailoo somehow manages to raise the bar for young scholars and at the same time demystifies the life of the mind in ways that make it seem doable; he both inspires and energizes.

Elizabeth Alexander and Thuy Linh N. Tu are my confidantes, my intellectual sparring partners, my dear, dear friends, my sisters. I admire them for so many things but especially for their bigheartedness, integrity, and sheer brilliance. Thuy Linh has been my trusted interlocutor on matters personal and professional for more than fifteen years. I treasure her. Elizabeth personifies genius and beauty.

Many thanks to my extended family—the Nelsons, the Mundys, and the Williamses. Like family, Father Russel Raj, OCD, has been a wellspring of encouragement. My three siblings have always had more faith in me than I have in myself: by trying to see my potential through their eyes I was buoyed in rough creative waters. I am happily beholden to Andrea Nelson Saunders, Aaron Saunders, Robert Nelson Jr., Dawn Nelson, Anthony Nelson, and Vera Nelson for their love and support. I am continually awed by the boundless promise of Aidan Nelson, Austin Nelson, Anthony Nelson Jr., Alexis Nelson, Alondra Hall, Anita Hall, Ariella Nelson, Brianna Nelson, Bryce Saunders, Joseph Hall Jr.,

Mya Nelson, Reina Saunders, and Renee Nelson. My parents, Robert S. Nelson Sr. and Delores Y. Nelson, whose sole aim in life often seems to be to provide all for their children that they were not able to achieve or attain, are exemplars of dedication and unconditional love. Their many sacrifices made possible any accomplishment I ever achieved.

I thank Randall Kennedy for his loving intelligence and his constancy. His wit, wisdom, and affection make my life rich beyond measure. He makes me better.

NOTES

Preface

1. This statement is inspired by Bruno Latour's now-famous assertion, "Science . . . is politics by other means." See Bruno Latour, *The Pasteurization of France* (Cambridge, Mass.: Harvard University Press, 1993), 229.

2. "White House Remarks on Decoding of Genome," *New York Times*, June 27, 2000.

3. David Hinckley, "Health Care Bill Triggers Eruption from Rush Limbaugh, Glenn Beck, and John Gambling," *New York Daily News*, March 22, 2010, http://articles.nydailynews.com/2010-03-22/news/27059757_1_health-care-bill-glenn-beck-stupak.

4. Ezra Klein, "Rush Limbaugh: Health-Care Reform Is 'Reparations,' a 'Civil Rights Act,'" *Washington Post*, February 22, 2010, http://voices.washingtonpost.com/ezra-klein/2010/02/rush_limbaugh_health-care_refo.html.

5. Steven Smith, "Wellesley Professor Unearths a Horror: Syphilis Experiments in Guatemala," *Boston Globe*, October 2, 2010, http://www.boston.com/news/science/articles/2010/10/02/wellesley_professor_unearths_a_horror_syphilis_experiments_in_guatemala/.

6. Susan M. Reverby, "'Normal Exposure' and Inoculation Syphilis: A PHS 'Tuskegee' Doctor in Guatemala, 1946–48," *Journal of Policy History* 23, no. 1 (2011): 6–28.

7. Harriet Washington, *Medical Apartheid: The Dark History of Medical Experimentation on Black Americans from Colonial Times to the Present* (New York: Random House, 2007).

8. Brian D. Smedley, Adrienne Y. Stith, and Alan R. Nelson, eds., *Unequal Treatment: Confronting Racial and Ethnic Disparities in Health Care* (Washington, D.C.: National Academies Press, 2003).

9. On the effect of historical abuse on the health-seeking behavior of African Americans, both before and after the revelation of the Tuskegee study, see Vanessa Northington Gamble, "Under the Shadow of Tuskegee: African Americans and Health Care," *American Journal of Public Health* 87, no. 11 (1997): 1773–78. On how past medical mistreatment influences blacks' willingness to participate in clinical research studies, see Giselle Corbie-Smith, Stephen B. Thomas, and Diane Marie M. St. George, "Distrust, Race, and Research," *Archives of Internal Medicine*, November 25, 2002, 2458–63.

10. Washington, *Medical Apartheid*, 15.

11. For example, as recently as February 2010, the campaign of Los Angeles County public health officials to have African Americans vaccinated for the H1N1 flu was unsuccessful. Blacks make up 32.4 percent of the residents of the South Central community, but received only 7.73 percent of the flu vaccinations at county clinics. Some in the media attributed this low participation rate to the dissemination via social media of warnings that invoked past medical abuse (Molly Hennessy-Fiske, "Few African Americans Vaccinated at L.A. County H1N1 Flu Clinics," *Los Angeles Times*, February 9, 2010, http://latimesblogs.latimes.com/lanow/2010/02/few-africanamericans-vaccinated-at-la-county-h1n1-flu-clinics.html; and Linda Villarosa, "The Guatemala Syphilis Experiment's Tuskegee Roots, theroot.com, October 2, 2010, http://www.theroot.com/views/tuskegee-study-s-guatemalan-roots).

12. Lee D. Baker, *From Savage to Negro: Anthropology and the Construction of Race, 1896–1954* (Berkeley: University of California Press, 1998); Troy Duster, *Backdoor to Eugenics*, 2nd ed. (New York: Routledge, 1990); Stephen Jay Gould, *The Mismeasure of Man*, rev. ed. (New York: Norton, 1996); Evelynn Hammonds and Rebecca Herzig, eds., *The Nature of Difference: Sciences of Race in the United States from Jefferson to Genomics* (Cambridge, Mass.: MIT Press, 2009); Dorothy Roberts, *Killing the Black Body: Race, Reproduction, and the Meaning of Liberty* (New York: Vintage, 1998); Audrey Smedley, *Race in North America: Origin and Evolution of a World View* (Boulder, Colo.: Westview, 1998); William Stanton, *The Leopard's Spots: Scientific Attitudes towards Race in America, 1815–1859* (Chicago: University of Chicago Press, 1982); and Keith Wailoo, *Drawing Blood: Technology and Disease Identity in Twentieth-Century America* (Baltimore, Md.: Johns Hopkins University Press, 1999).

13. Jane Rhodes, *Framing the Black Panthers: The Spectacular Rise of a Black Power Icon* (New York: New Press, 2007), 5–6, emphasis added. On media bias as a component of state repression of the Party, see Christian Davenport, *Media Bias, Perspective, and State Repression: The Black Panther Party* (New York: Cambridge University Press, 2009).

14. Many of the articles in the *Black Panther* were unsigned, making it difficult to attribute authorship to them. The editors, however, are known: Eldridge Cleaver, the Party's minister of information, first edited the paper. Elaine Brown took over as editor in 1971; she had been the deputy minister of information for the Party's Southern California chapter from 1969 to 1971. Ericka Hug-

gins edited the paper in 1971 and 1972, when Brown campaigned for a slot on Oakland's city council. The paper was also edited by David Du Bois—stepson of W. E. B. Du Bois—from 1972 to 1975, and subsequently by Michael Fultz, a former member of the Boston chapter. JoNina Abron was the paper's last editor (1978–80). Cleaver, Brown, and Du Bois were the paper's editors during the period covered in this book. In addition, other Party members and its leadership, including Huey P. Newton and Bobby Seale, contributed writing to the paper. See also Philip Foner, ed., *The Black Panthers Speak* (New York: Lippincott, 1970), 8–14; Bobby Seale, *Seize the Time: The Story of the Black Panther Party and Huey P. Newton* (New York: Random House, 1970), 177–81; David Hilliard and Lewis Cole, *This Side of Glory: The Autobiography of David Hilliard and the Story of the Black Panther Party* (New York: Little, Brown, 1993), 338; and Elaine Brown, *A Taste of Power: A Black Woman's Story* (New York: Anchor Books, 1992), 207, 271, 273–75, 343, 410.

15. "The Law: Sterilized: Why?" *Time,* July 23, 1973, http://www.time.com/time/magazine/article/0,9171,878602,00.html. Prior to the deceptive sterilization procedures, the Relf sisters had for months been given injections of Depo-Provera, a then experimental contraceptive with severely unpleasant side effects. Both incidents were documented and politicized in the Party's newspaper.

16. Charles Tilly, "Retrieving European Lives," in *Reliving the Past: The Worlds of Social History,* ed. Olivier Zunz (Chapel Hill: University of North Carolina Press, 1985, 15).

Introduction

1. Several other similar events took place in the spring and summer of 1972, including a "Black Survival Conference" on May 13, 1972, and an "Anti-War, African Liberation, Voter Registration, Survival Conference" on June 24, 1972. On the survival conferences, see Bobby Seale, *Lonely Rage: The Autobiography of Bobby Seale* (New York: Times Books, 1978), 224; Bobby Seale to Eve Kenley, April 5, 1972, series 1, box 4, folder 9, Dr. Huey P. Newton Archives, Special Collections, Green Library, Stanford University; Dick Hallgren, "Black Panthers Draw Big Crowd," *San Francisco Chronicle,* March 30, 1972; "Chairman Bobby Seale for Mayor!" *Black Panther Intercommunal News Service,* May 20, 1972; and "The Black Panther Party's Anti-War, African Liberation, Voter Registration, Survival Conference," *Black Panther,* June 10, 1972.

2. "This Will Tide Us Over to Liberation," *Black Panther,* April 8, 1972.

3. Hugh Pearson, *Shadow of the Panther: Huey Newton and the Price of Black Power in America* (Cambridge, Mass.: Da Capo, 1995), 247; *Black Panther,* April 16, 1972; and Seale, *Lonely Rage,* 224.

4. On May 13, 1972, Seale announced that he would run as a candidate for mayor of Oakland. Moments before doing so, in a dramatic gesture, Seale drew back the curtain on the stage of the Oakland Auditorium to reveal ten thousand

bags of free groceries—including the now-iconic "chicken in every bag"—that had been gathered by the Party to distribute to attendees of the event. On this same occasion, Brown announced her candidacy for an Oakland city council seat. See Seale, *Lonely Rage*, 224–27; Brown, *Taste of Power*, 276–77, 321–23; Pearson, *Shadow of the Panther*, 247–48; and "Chairman Bobby Seale for Mayor!" See also "Bobby Seale to Run for Mayor of Oakland," *Los Angeles Times*, January 19, 1974; and "Tame Panthers?" *Time*, December 25, 1972, 13–14. This turn to electoral politics was somewhat of a renewed focus for the Party because Cleaver, Seale, and Newton had run as candidates on the Peace and Freedom Party ticket in 1968 for the offices of president of the United States, California State assemblyman, and U.S. congressman, respectively. See Seale, *Seize the Time*, 237–40; and Gene Marine, *The Black Panthers* (San Francisco: Ramparts Books, 1969), chap. 10.

5. See, for example, Curtis J. Austin, *Up against the Wall: Violence in the Making and Unmaking of the Black Panther Party* (Fayetteville: University of Arkansas Press, 2006), esp. chap. 7; and Charles William Hopkins, "The Deradicalization of the Black Panther Party" (PhD diss., University of North Carolina, Chapel Hill, 1978). Newton argued that the service programs were organizing tools toward revolution, not reformist politics. See Art Goldberg, "The Panthers after the Trial," *Ramparts*, March 1972, 24–25.

6. Even Seale and Brown's campaign platform broached the issue of health. The candidates recommended the creation of tax-funded "preventative medical health care programs" that would provide services, as well as training and jobs in the health sector, as one solution to Oakland's burgeoning unemployment rates ("Bobby Seale and Elaine Brown on Un-Employment in Oakland," Community Committee to Elect Bobby Seale and Elaine Brown to City Office of Oakland, African Americans in California collection, Bancroft Library, University of California, Berkeley).

7. Black Panther Party (guest editors), "The Black Panther Party Program, March 29, 1972 Platform," *CoEvolution Quarterly* 3 (Fall 1974): 48; Elaine Brown, interview with author, December 6, 2008, Savannah, Georgia.

8. The neoconservative David Horowitz's writing is the most extreme example of this position on the Party. See his coauthored work with Peter Collier, *Deconstructing the Left: From Vietnam to the Clinton Era* (Lanham, Md.: University Press of America, 1991); and Horowitz's memoir, *Radical Son: A Generational Odyssey* (New York: Free Press, 1998). Similar criticisms are made in Pearson, *Shadow of the Panther*.

9. See, for example, Huey P. Newton, *The War against the Panthers: A Study of Repression in America* (1980; repr. New York: Harlem River, 2000).

10. Jeanne F. Theoharis and Komozi Woodard, eds., *Freedom North: Black Freedom Struggles outside the South, 1940–1980* (New York: Palgrave, 2003).

11. National media coverage of the civil rights struggles of the 1950s and 1960s contributed to the construction of hard distinctions between northern

and southern activism and the "civil rights" and "black power" movements. See Jeanne Theoharis, introduction to *Freedom North*, 12–13.

12. King argued that nonviolent, civil disobedience was intended partly to "awaken a sense of moral shame" among those who opposed racial equality. See Martin Luther King Jr., "Nonviolence and Racial Justice," *Christian Century Magazine*, February 6, 1957, 165–67.

13. I borrow the term "un-civil" from Theoharis, introduction, 12.

14. King, quoted in John Dittmer, *The Good Doctors: The Medical Committee for Human Rights and the Struggle for Social Justice in Health Care* (New York: Bloomsbury, 2009), ix.

15. Norma Armour, interview with author, March 19, 2009, Los Angeles; "Winston-Salem Free Ambulance Service Opens, *Black Panther,* June 26, 1971, 7.

16. Paul Starr, *The Social Transformation of American Medicine* (New York: Basic Books, 1982), 388–89.

17. Van Gosse, "A Movement of Movements: The Definition and Periodization of the New Left," in *A Companion to Post-1945 America*, ed. Jean-Christophe Agnew and Roy Rosenzweig (Hoboken, N.J.: Wiley-Blackwell, 2006), 277–302. See also Jacquelyn Dowd Hall, "The Long Civil Rights Movement and the Political Uses of the Past," *Journal of American History* 91 (March 2005): 1233–63; Larry Isaac, "Movement of Movements: Culture Moves in the Long Civil Rights Struggle," *Social Forces* 87 (2008): 33–63; and Nikhil Pal Singh, *Black Is a Country: Race and the Unfinished Struggle for Democracy* (Cambridge, Mass.: Harvard University Press, 2004).

18. Patricia Sullivan's *Days of Hope* and Mary Dudziak's *Cold War Civil Rights*, for example, show that the civil rights movement began decades prior to the 1955 Montgomery, Alabama, bus boycott that conventionally marks its start; similarly, Timothy Tyson's examination of the life of Robert F. Williams pushes back the time line of the black power movement into the 1950s. Works by William Chafe, Dittmer, and Yohuru Williams situate civil rights struggles in local politics of specific communities, while recent books by Martha Biondi, Theoharis, and Woodard, among others, remind us that racial terror and social inequality were characteristic qualities of American society on both sides of the Mason-Dixon Line. The range of experiences and motivations of participants in civil rights struggles are given expression in Doug McAdam's *Freedom Summer*. See Martha Biondi, *To Stand and Fight: The Struggle for Civil Rights in Postwar New York City* (Cambridge, Mass.: Harvard University Press, 2003); William Chafe, *Civilities and Civil Rights: Greensboro, North Carolina, and the Black Struggle for Freedom* (New York: Oxford University Press, 1981); John Dittmer, *Local People: The Struggle for Civil Rights in Mississippi* (Champaign: University of Illinois Press, 1995); Mary L. Dudziak, *Cold War Civil Rights: Race and the Image of American Democracy* (Princeton, N.J.: Princeton University Press, 2002); Doug McAdam, *Freedom Summer* (New York: Oxford University Press, 1988); Patricia Sullivan, *Days of Hope: Race and Democracy in the New Deal Era* (Chapel Hill:

University of North Carolina Press, 1996); Theoharis and Woodard, *Freedom North*; Timothy B. Tyson, *Radio Free Dixie: Robert F. Williams and the Roots of Black Power* (Chapel Hill: University of North Carolina Press, 1999); and Yohuru Williams, *Black Politics/White Power: Civil Rights, Black Power, and Black Panthers in New Haven* (St. James, N.Y.: Brandywine, 2000).

19. Evelynn Brooks Higginbotham, "African-American Women's History and the Metalanguage of Race," *Signs: Journal of Women in Culture and Society* 17 (Winter 1992): 251–74.

20. Paula Pfeffer, *A. Philip Randolph, Pioneer of the Civil Rights Movement* (Baton Rouge: Louisiana State University Press, 1996), esp. chaps. 1, 6; and Joanne Grant, *Ella Baker: Freedom Bound* (New York: Wiley and Sons, 1998), chap. 2. A considerable portion of writings by Party members is dedicated to examining the interlocking oppressions of racism and economic inequality. See, for example, Huey P. Newton, "On Pan-Africanism or Communism: December 1, 1972," in *The Huey P. Newton Reader*, ed. David Hilliard and Donald Weise (New York: Seven Stories, 2002), 248–55.

21. Stewart Burns, *To the Mountaintop: Martin Luther King's Mission to Save America, 1955–1968* (New York: Harper Collins, 2004), 404. For an account of the evolution of the SCLC Poor People's Campaign and the Nixon administration's resistance to it, see Gerald D. McKnight, *The Last Crusade: Martin Luther King, Jr., the FBI, and the Poor People's Campaign* (Boulder, Colo.: Westview, 1998), 21.

22. On Fannie Lou Hamer's life and her experiences with health inequality and surreptitious medical procedures, see Kay Mills, *This Little Light of Mine: The Life of Fannie Lou Hamer* (New York: Plume, 1993), 20–22; Jennifer Nelson, *Women of Color and the Reproductive Rights Movement* (New York: New York University Press, 2003), 68; and Roberts, *Killing the Black Body*, 90–91.

23. Also, as Jonathan Metzl demonstrates, references to illness—mental illness in particular—were used against King and others in this period to characterize racism as a form of social disease. See Jonathan Metzl, *The Protest Psychosis: How Schizophrenia Became a Black Disease* (New York: Beacon, 2009), 119–25.

24. On black health activism in the Progressive Era, see Vanessa Northington Gamble, *Germs Have No Color Line: Blacks and American Medicine, 1900–1940* (New York: Taylor and Francis, 1989); and Northington Gamble, *Making a Place for Ourselves: The Black Hospital Movement, 1920–1945* (New York: Oxford University Press, 1995). See also Susan Smith, *Sick and Tired of Being Sick and Tired: Black Women's Health Activism in America, 1890–1950* (Philadelphia: University of Pennsylvania Press, 1995), esp. chap. 1. On the medical civil rights movement, see Herbert Morais, *The History of the Negro in Medicine* (New York: Publishers Company, 1967), chap. 9.

25. Northington Gamble, *Making a Place for Ourselves*.

26. Elaine Brown, interview with author, December 7, 2008, Savannah, Georgia.

27. "Health Care—Pig Style," *Black Panther*, February 7, 1970.

28. Alice Kessler-Harris, "In Pursuit of Economic Citizenship," *Social Politics: International Studies in Gender, State, and Society* 10, no. 2 (2003): 157–75; and Margaret R. Somers, *Genealogies of Citizenship: Markets, Statelessness, and the Right to Have Rights* (Cambridge: Cambridge University Press, 2008).

29. Kessler-Harris, "In Pursuit of Economic Citizenship," 159; Somers, *Genealogies of Citizenship*, 25.

30. Kessler-Harris, "In Pursuit of Economic Citizenship," 164.

31. Ibid., 164–65; Somers, *Genealogies of Citizenship*.

32. Armour, interview.

33. Constitution of the World Health Organization (1948), http://www.who .int/about/definition/en/print.html (accessed May 2, 2007).

34. Ibid.

35. *Black Panther*, June 1971.

36. Ibid.

37. I am aware of one other use of the term *social health*. The health education scholar Robert Russell used the phrase to describe "that dimension of an individual's well-being that concerns how he gets along with other people, how other people react to him, and how he interacts with social institutions and societal mores" ("Social Health: An Attempt to Clarify This Dimension of Well-Being," *International Journal of Health Education* 16 [1973]: 75). He also noted that well-being derives from a person's orientation in society (74–82).

38. Similar conceptualizations can be found in Rudolph Virchow, *Cellular Pathology as Based upon Physiological and Pathological Histology* (1860; repr. Birmingham, Ala.: Classics of Medicine Library, 1978); Sharla Fett, *Working Cures: Healing, Health, and Power on Southern Slave Plantations* (Chapel Hill: University of North Carolina Press, 2002); and David McBride, *From TB to AIDS: Epidemics among Urban Blacks since 1900* (Albany: State University of New York Press, 1991).

39. John Ehrenreich and Barbara Ehrenreich (for Health/PAC), *The American Health Empire: Power, Profits, and Politics* (New York: Random House, 1970). At the Party-sponsored People's Revolutionary Constitutional Convention of September 1970, the activists resolved: "We are opposed to the medical industrial complex of medicine. We believe in socialized medicine. Inherent in this concept is prevention and free comprehensive, community-controlled medicine. The only way to socialize medicine is through revolution." See "Appendices," in *Liberation, Imagination, and the Black Panther Party*, ed. Kathleen Cleaver and George Kastiaficas (New York: Routledge, 2001), 300.

40. David A. Snow and Robert D. Benford, "Ideology, Frame Resonance, and Participant Mobilization," *International Social Movement Research* 1 (1988): 197–217. On framing, see also Erving Goffman, *Frame Analysis: An Essay on the Organization of Experience* (Boston: Northeastern University Press, 1986); and Goffman, *Presentation of Self in Everyday Life* (New York: Doubleday, 1959). The concept of framing describes the symbolic strategies employed by activists to

convey political positions and persuade others of their legitimacy. As elaborated by the sociologists Snow and Benford, efficacious framing is accomplished through several steps: a social problem is diagnosed; blame for the problem is assigned; and a prescription for social action is offered.

41. Starr, *Social Transformation of American Medicine,* chap. 4.

42. Juan Williams, *Eyes on the Prize: America's Civil Rights Years, 1954–1965* (New York: Penguin, 1988), 232–33, 236; McAdam, *Freedom Summer.*

43. Lillian Rubin, "Maximum Feasible Participation: The Origins, Implications, and Present Status," *Annals of the American Academy of Political and Social Science* 385 (1969): 14–29.

44. "Special Message to Congress Proposing a National Health Strategy," February 18, 1971, American Presidency Project, http://www.presidency.ucsb.edu/ws/index.php?pid=3311 (accessed October 12, 2009).

45. Ehrenreich and Ehrenreich, *American Health Empire,* 4–6.

46. *Black Panther,* October 18, 1969.

47. Black Panther Party (guest editors), "People's Free Medical Research Health Clinics," *CoEvolution Quarterly: Supplement to the Whole Earth Catalog* 3 (1974): 21.

48. Allen M. Hornblum, *Acres of Skin: Human Experiments at Holmesburg Prison* (New York: Routledge, 1998). For a synthetic history of medical experimentation with African Americans, see Washington, *Medical Apartheid.* For a compelling account of one black woman's questionable interaction with biomedical researchers, see Rebecca Skloot, *The Immortal Life of Henrietta Lacks* (New York: Crown, 2010).

49. Ehrenreich and Ehrenreich, *American Health Empire,* 14.

50. Fitzhugh Mullan, *White Coat, Clenched Fist: The Political Education of an American Physician* (1976; repr. Ann Arbor: University of Michigan Press, 2006), chap. 6.

51. "Bunchy Carter Free Clinic," *Black Panther Community News Service* (Southern California chapter), January 19, 1970.

52. For example, the historian Spencie Love has demonstrated that the rumors that the death of noted African American surgeon Charles Drew was caused by the fact that he was denied care in a segregated Southern hospital were inaccurate. Nevertheless, Love concludes that this apocryphal account, while not based in fact, suggested a social truth—blacks' apprehensions about the healthcare system. See Spencie Love, *One Blood: The Death and Resurrection of Charles R. Drew* (Chapel Hill: University of North Carolina Press, 1996).

53. "Medical Genocide," *People's News Service* (Southern California chapter), June 12, 1970.

54. James H. Jones, *Bad Blood: The Tuskegee Syphilis Experiment* (1981; repr. New York: Free Press, 1993); Susan M. Reverby, *Examining Tuskegee: The Infamous Syphilis Study and Its Legacy* (Chapel Hill: University of North Carolina Press, 2009).

55. Gisele Corbie-Smith, "The Continuing Legacy of the Tuskegee Syphilis

Study: Considerations for Clinical Investigation," *American Journal of the Medical Sciences* 317 (1999): 5–8; Northington Gamble, "Under the Shadow of Tuskegee." For examples from the popular media of the time of how the July 1972 revelation of the Tuskegee study stoked mistrust of medicine in black communities, see William Rice, "Why Being Black Can Be Bad for Your Health," *Daily News* (New York), January 26, 1973; and "Expose, Punish Heads of Syphilis Study—NAACP," *Los Angeles Sentinel*, August 31, 1972.

56. McBride, *From TB to AIDS*, 126.

57. Ibid.

58. Lily M. Hoffman, *The Politics of Knowledge: Activist Movements in Medicine and Planning* (Albany: State University of New York Press, 1989). See also Steven Epstein, *Impure Science: AIDS, Activism, and the Politics of Knowledge* (Berkeley: University of California Press, 1996).

59. Kenneth Reich, "National Pattern Followed in Raid on Panthers Here," *Los Angeles Times*, December 9, 2009.

60. Austin, *Up against the Wall*, 335.

61. HIV/AIDS activists in the 1980s shared similar aims. See Steven Epstein, "The Construction of Lay Expertise: AIDS Activism and the Forging of Credibility in the Reform of Clinical Trials," *Science, Technology, and Human Values* 20 (1995): 408–37.

62. JoNina M. Abron, "'Serving the People,'" in *The Black Panther Party (Reconsidered)*, ed. Charles E. Jones (Baltimore, Md.: Black Classic, 1998), 178, 184. See also "Rules of the Black Panther Party." Rule number 21 read: "All branches must implement First Aid and/or Medical Cadres" (in "Political Education Kit for Black Panther Party Members," Palmer Smith Papers, University of Washington Special Collections). Party Minister of Justice Ray "Masai" Hewitt announced the Party's plan to extend the PFMC network in November 1969, several weeks prior to the January 1970 directive that Seale sent to all chapters.

63. For a theoretical overview of health social movements, see Phil Brown and Stephen Zavestoski, eds., *Social Movements in Health* (Malden, Mass.: Blackwell, 2005).

64. A fine discussion of the women's health movement is offered in Sandra Morgen, *Into Our Hands: The Women's Health Movement in the United States, 1969–1990* (New Brunswick, N.J.: Rutgers University Press, 2002). See also Sheryl Burt Ruzek, *The Women's Health Movement: Feminist Alternatives to Medical Control* (New York: Praeger, 1978). On the history and significance of the SHO, see Naomi Rogers, "'Caution: The AMA May Be Dangerous to Your Health': The Student Health Organizations (SHO) and American Medicine, 1965–1970," *Radical History Review* 80 (2001): 5–34; and William Bronston, interview with author, August 19, 2007, New York. On the MCHR, see Dittmer, *Good Doctors*. On the "rainbow coalition," see Lincoln Webster Sheffield, "People's Medical Care Center," in Foner, *Black Panthers Speak*, 175; Miguel "Mickey" Melendez, *We Took to the Streets: Fighting for Latino Rights with the Young Lords* (New York: Macmillan, 2003), 85.

65. This is the motto of the Berkeley Free Clinic, which was an institutional collaborator with the Party.

66. H. Jack Geiger, "Community Health Centers: Health Care as an Instrument of Social Change," in *Reforming Medicine: Lessons of the Last Quarter Century*, ed. Ruth Sidel and Victor Sidel (New York: Pantheon, 1984), 11–32.

67. Washington, *Medical Apartheid*.

68. Ibid.; Skloot, *Immortal Life of Henrietta Lacks*.

69. Steven Epstein, *Inclusion: The Politics of Difference in Biomedical Research* (Chicago: University of Chicago Press, 2007), 17.

70. David S. Meyer and Nancy Whittier, "Social Movement Spillover," *Social Problems* 41 (1994): 277–98.

1. African American Responses to Medical Discrimination before 1966

1. See Morais, *History of the Negro in Medicine*, chap. 9.

2. Lewis E. Weeks, ed., "Montague Cobb," in *In First Person: An Oral History* (Ann Arbor, Mich.: Lewis E. Weeks and American Hospital Association and Hospital Research and Educational Trust, 1983); and Lesley M. Rankin-Hill and Michael Blakely, "W. Montague Cobb (1904–1990): Physical Anthropologist, Anatomist, and Activist," *American Anthropologist* 96 (1994): 74–96. See also Morais, *History of the Negro in Medicine*, chaps. 8–9; and Smith, *Sick and Tired*, 76, 169.

3. Edward H. Beardsley, *A History of Neglect: Health Care for Blacks and Mill Workers in the Twentieth-Century South* (Knoxville: University of Tennessee Press, 1987), 264–66.

4. Ibid. More specifically, the U.S. Supreme Court refused to hear the *Simkins v. Cone* case and let the lower court decision stand; see Morais, *History of the Negro in Medicine*, 240–41, app. L. See also W. Michael Byrd and Linda A. Clayton, *An American Health Dilemma: Race, Medicine, and Health Care in the United States, 1900–2000* (New York: Routledge, 2002), 267.

5. For a few notable exceptions, see Smith, *Sick and Tired*; McBride, *From TB to AIDS*; Nancy Leys Stepan and Sander L. Gilman, "Appropriating the Idioms of Science: The Rejection of Scientific Racism," in *The Racial Economy of Science: Towards a Democratic Future*, ed. Sandra Harding (Bloomington: University of Indiana Press, 1993), 170–93; Morais, *History of the Negro in Medicine*; and Northington Gamble, *Making a Place for Ourselves*.

6. Beardsley, *History of Neglect*, 245–56.

7. Hoffman, *Politics of Knowledge*. See also Epstein, *Impure Science*.

8. McBride, *From TB to AIDS*. See also Kenneth F. Kiple and Virginia Himmelsteib King, *Another Dimension to the Black Diaspora: Diet, Disease, and Racism* (New York: Cambridge University Press, 1981); Jones, *Bad Blood*; and Samuel Kelton Roberts Jr., *Infectious Fear: Politics, Disease, and the Health Effects of Segregation* (Chapel Hill: University of North Carolina Press, 2009).

9. Smith, *Sick and Tired*, 80; Beardsley, *History of Neglect*, 114–19; and

McBride, *From TB to AIDS*, 75–82. For background information on the activities of the Julius Rosenwald Fund, see Edwin R. Embree and Julia Waxman, *Investment in People: The Story of the Julius Rosenwald Fund* (New York: Harper, 1949).

10. David McBride, *Integrating the City of Medicine: Blacks in Philadelphia Health Care, 1910–1965* (Philadelphia: Temple University Press, 1989); and Northington Gamble, *Making a Place for Ourselves*.

11. Hoffman, *Politics of Knowledge*.

12. For example, in his essay "The Conservation of Races," Du Bois famously deconstructed and reinterpreted data that claimed African Americans had smaller brains (and, by implication, were less intelligent) than whites. See W. E. B. Du Bois, "The Conservation of Races," in *W. E. B. Du Bois Speaks: Speeches and Addresses, 1890–1919*, ed. Philip S. Foner (New York: Pathfinders, 1970), 72–85.

13. McBride, *From TB to AIDS*, 126. For the gendering of caretaking in the black community, see Darlene Clark Hine, *Black Women in White: Racial Conflict and Cooperation in the Nursing Profession, 1890–1950* (Bloomington: Indiana University Press, 1989), chaps. 1–2.

14. McBride, *From TB to AIDS*, 86.

15. Beardsley, *History of Neglect*, 11.

16. McBride, *From TB to AIDS*, 2. See also Beardsley, *History of Neglect*, chap. 1.

17. Smith, *Sick and Tired*, 1–2, 51–57.

18. Charles Payne, "'Men Led but Women Organized': Movement Participation of Women in the Mississippi Delta," in *Women in the Civil Rights Movement: Trailblazers and Torchbearers, 1941–1965*, ed. Vicki L. Crawford, Jacqueline Anne Rouse, and Barbara Woods (Bloomington: Indiana University Press, 1990).

19. In early-twentieth-century health social movements, Susan Smith argues, men "held most of the formal leadership positions and [lay and professional] women did most of the grassroots organizing" (*Sick and Tired*, 1).

20. Hazel V. Carby, "Policing the Black Woman's Body in an Urban Context," *Critical Inquiry* 18 (Summer 1992): 738–57.

21. Williams is credited with performing the first open-heart surgery in the United States in 1897. See Kelly Miller, "Eminent Negroes," in *Race Adjustment: Essays on the Negro in America* (New York: Neale, 1908), 195–96; and Helen Buckler, *Daniel Hale Williams: Negro Surgeon* (New York: Pitman Publishing, 1954), 77, 85–96.

22. Buckler, *Daniel Hale Williams*, chap. 6; Lewis H. Fenderson, *Daniel Hale Williams: Open Heart Doctor* (New York: McGraw-Hill, 1971), 53–54; Smith, *Sick and Tired*, 23.

23. Buckler, *Daniel Hale Williams*, 70–75.

24. Louis Harlan, *Booker T. Washington: The Wizard of Tuskegee, 1901–1915* (New York: Oxford University Press, 1983); Meier, *Negro Thought in America*; and Smith, *Sick and Tired*, chap. 2.

25. Washington, *Up from Slavery*, 31–32.

26. Ibid., 36–38.

27. Ibid., 54, 126.

28. Kevin Gaines, *Uplifting the Race: Black Leadership, Politics, and Culture in the Twentieth Century* (Chapel Hill: University of North Carolina Press, 1996), esp. chaps. 3–4.

29. William Hardin Hughes and Frederick D. Patterson, eds., *Robert Russa Moton of Hampton and Tuskegee* (Chapel Hill: University of North Carolina Press, 1956), 60–62.

30. Booker T. Washington, "An Address before the Negro Organization Society of Virginia: What Cooperation Can Accomplish," November 12, 1914, in *The Booker T. Washington Papers*, ed. Louis R. Harlan and Raymond W. Smock, vol. 13 (Urbana: University of Illinois Press, 1989), 167.

31. Harlan, *Booker T. Washington*, 187–88; 233; Smith, *Sick and Tired*, 34.

32. Washington, "Address before the Negro Organization Society of Virginia," 169.

33. Louis R. Harlan, *Booker T. Washington: The Making of a Black Leader, 1856–1901* (New York: Oxford University Press, 1972), 68.

34. Harlan and Smock, *Booker T. Washington Papers*, 167–68, 218.

35. The unfortunate consequence of this argument was that it sacrificed African American women's honor on the altar of racial politics. It cast black women—cooks, wet nurses, and washerwomen—as bearers of disease and vectors of contagion. For more on the black woman laborer as a source of contagion, see Tera Hunter, *To 'Joy My Freedom': Southern Black Women's Lives and Labors after the Civil War* (Cambridge, Mass.: Harvard University Press, 1997), chap. 5.

36. Anson Phelps Stokes to Booker T. Washington, November 24, 1914, in Harlan and Smock, *Booker T. Washington Papers*, 13:182–83; Smith, *Sick and Tired*, 39.

37. "The Principal's Report to the Board of Trustees of Tuskegee Institute," May 31, 1915, in Harlan and Smock, *Booker T. Washington Papers*, 13:303–4.

38. Monroe Work, "The Economic Waste of Sickness." Paper presented at the Health Conference, Gulfside, Mississippi, June 5, 1929; quoted in Smith, *Sick and Tired*, 56.

39. Smith, *Sick and Tired*, 69.

40. Ibid., 33. The National Negro Health Movement and the Office of Negro Health Work were closed in 1950 when prominent blacks and state and federal administrators who supported integration efforts concluded that a separate public health office and health education campaign for African Americans was anathema to such progress.

41. Tony Martin, *Race First: The Ideological and Organizational Struggles of Marcus Garvey and the Universal Negro Improvement Association* (Westport, Conn.: Greenwood, 1976), 7–8, chap. 2.

42. Ibid., 14.

43. Ibid., chap. 3.

44. Lawrence W. Levine, "Marcus Garvey and the Politics of Revitalization," in *Black Leaders in the Twentieth Century*, ed. John Hope Franklin and August Meier (Chicago: University of Illinois Press, 1982), 105–38; and Robert A. Hill, ed., *Marcus Garvey: Life and Lessons* (Berkeley: University of California Press, 1987). See also Michelle Mitchell, *Righteous Propagation: African Americans and the Politics of Racial Destiny after Reconstruction* (Chapel Hill: University of North Carolina Press, 2004), chap. 8.

45. "Essays by Marcus Garvey," in Hill, *Marcus Garvey*, 48, 50.

46. Ibid.

47. "Chronology," in *The Marcus Garvey Papers*, ed. Robert A. Hill, vol. 2 (Berkeley: University of California Press, 1987), 619.

48. Hill, *Marcus Garvey*, 402. The BCN was advised by the UNIA's surgeon general, the Montreal physician D. D. Lewis.

49. A unit of the Black Cross Nurses still exists in Belize (Dr. Julius Garvey, conversation with author, September 25, 2010, Atlanta, Georgia). For the history of this chapter, see Anne Macpherson, "Colonial Matriarchs: Garveyism, Maternalism, and Belize's Black Cross Nurses, 1920–1952," *Gender and History* 15 (2003): 507–27.

50. Hill, *Marcus Garvey Papers*, 3:383. The BCN was also likely inspired by the Blue Circle Nurses. In response to their exclusion from the Red Cross during World War I, frustrated members of the National Association of Colored Graduate Nurses (NACGN) established the Blue Circle Nurses in 1917. These nurses served the same function as the Red Cross nurses, but for black soldiers solely. See Hine, *Black Women in White*, 104.

51. Hine, *Black Women in White*, 134–36.

52. Martin, *Race First*, 32.

53. "Report by Bureau Agents A. A. Hopkins and E. J. Kosterlitzky, December 6, 1920," in Hill, *Marcus Garvey Papers*, 3:99.

54. Edmund David Cronon, *Black Moses: The Story of Marcus Garvey and the Universal Negro Improvement Association* (Madison: University of Wisconsin Press, 1968), 64. Although the U.S. Navy refused the assistance of African American women seeking to be Red Cross nurses, the army employed their services with only a month of the war remaining. When African American nurses were finally permitted to join the Red Cross, the icons of their service, the red cross-shaped pins, were marked with the letter "A" to indicate the wearer's special racial status.

55. "Rules and Regulations Governing the Universal African Black Cross Nurses," in Hill, *Marcus Garvey Papers*, 3:766–67; "Universal Negro Catechism," in Hill, *Marcus Garvey Papers*, 3:315; and Hill, *Marcus Garvey*, 362.

56. Hine, *Black Women in White*, esp. 89–107.

57. Cronon, *Black Moses*, 64. Garvey suffered from respiratory problems including pneumonia and bronchitis. In the month-long UNIA convention of August 1920, Surgeon General Lewis implored the auxiliary of BCN to "see that

he [Garvey] keeps healthy." Lewis continued, "There is no subject that interests me more than that of health. It is the keynote to success" ("Report of the Convention," in Hill, *Marcus Garvey Papers*, 2:619).

58. Martin, *Race First*, 32.

59. See, for example, William L. Van Deburg, *Modern Black Nationalism: From Marcus Garvey to Louis Farrakhan* (New York: New York University Press, 1997), 1–19.

60. Malcolm X and Alex Haley, *The Autobiography of Malcolm X* (New York: Ballantine, 1965), chap. 1.

61. McAdam has shown that the parents of summer project volunteers included prominent intellectuals and politicians. See *Freedom Summer*, 157–60.

62. Aaron O. Wells (MCHR chairman and physician), quoted in Morais, *History of the Negro in Medicine*, 166.

63. Dittmer, *Good Doctors*; Morais, *History of the Negro in Medicine*, 116, chap. 9, app. O; and Len Holt, *The Summer That Didn't End* (New York: William Morrow, 1965), 78.

64. Holt, *Summer That Didn't End*, 81.

65. David French (former MCHR chairman), quoted in Morais, *History of the Negro in Medicine*, 256.

66. Morais, *History of the Negro in Medicine*, 168.

67. Ibid., 261.

68. Holt, *Summer That Didn't End*, 81; Morais, *History of the Negro in Medicine*, 168; Ruzek, *Women's Health Movement*; and McAdam, *Freedom Summer*, 105–15.

69. McAdam, *Freedom Summer*, chaps. 4–5.

70. Morais, *History of the Negro in Medicine*, 167, 256; Dittmer, *Good Doctors*, chap. 8.

71. McAdam, *Freedom Summer*, chaps. 4–5, esp. 102–5, 114–15.

72. Morais, *History of the Negro in Medicine*, 168.

73. Smith, *Health Care Divided*, 116–17; Morais, *History of the Negro in Medicine*, 164–68, 198–99; and Hoffman, *Politics of Knowledge*, 70–79. The MCHR agenda also included the promotion of universal health coverage and agitating for the full integration of the American Medical Association, which remained off-limits to black medical professionals in the South.

74. Beardsley, *History of Neglect*, chap. 11; and Morais, *History of the Negro in Medicine*, chaps. 8–9.

75. Dr. Charles V. Roman, quoted in Morais, *History of the Negro in Medicine*, 68.

76. Smith, *Sick and Tired*, 76.

77. Ibid. Notably, the NAACP spurned National Negro Health week activities in the 1920s and 1930s; however, the NMA was an active participant in them. See Smith, *Sick and Tired*, 44, 62.

78. Cobb, a Howard University Medical School faculty member and physician, was president of the NMA from 1964 to 1965.

79. W. Montague Cobb, cited in Smith, *Sick and Tired*, 79.

80. Reprinted as W. Montague Cobb, "The National Health Program of the N.A.A.C.P.," *Journal of the National Medical Association* 45 (July 1953): 333–34.

81. Hospital Survey and Construction Act, 79th Congr., 2d sess. (August 13, 1946), CH 958.

82. Cobb, "National Health Program," *Journal of the National Medical Association* 45 (July 1953): 335.

83. Imhotep was a physician in ancient Egypt.

84. Morais, *History of the Negro in Medicine*, 144. See also Smith, *Health Care Divided*, 54.

85. Morais, *History of the Negro in Medicine*, 144–45.

86. Smith, *Health Care Divided*, 62–63. Morais concurs. He argues that the Imhotep movement inspired other organizations to take the issue of desegregation seriously. For example, in the early 1960s, the American Hospital Association began to investigate remedies to hospital segregation. In addition, in 1964, the Department of Health, Education, and Welfare convened "an Imhotep-like" conference on hospital desegregation in Washington, D.C., which was attended by members of the AMA, the NMA, the American Dental Association, and the American Nurses Association, among others. See Morais, *History of the Negro in Medicine*, 181–83.

87. Morais, *History of the Negro in Medicine*, 82; Smith, *Health Care Divided*, 107.

88. Other earlier and important yet failed legal cases in the medical civil rights movement were *Eaton et al. v. James Walker Memorial Hospital,* an unsuccessful 1956 challenge to medical discrimination initiated by the African American physician Dr. Hubert Eaton against a Wilmington, North Carolina, hospital that refused staff privileges to black doctors. *Hawkins v. North Carolina Dental Society* in 1960 was an unsuccessful attempt to use the courts to compel integration in medical societies. Though these early cases were unsuccessful, they were key moments that contributed to eventual litigation success (much like the lower court cases that preceded *Brown v. Board*). See Smith, *Health Care Divided*, chap. 3.

89. Morais, *History of the Negro in Medicine*, 52–58, 162–73, 179–80.

90. Hine, *Black Women in White*, 109, 115, 129–30.

91. Brent Staples, "Rooting Out Racism in Medicine," *New York Times*, August 14, 2008, http://theboard.blogs.nytimes.com/2008/08/14/rooting-out-racism-in-medicine/.

92. Hine, *Black Women in White*, 89.

93. Ibid., 162. Cosponsors of the MCCR/MCHR request included CORE, NAACP, SNCC, and the American Jewish Congress. See also Dittmer, *Good Doctors*, chap. 5.

94. Ibid.

95. Morais, *History of the Negro in Medicine*, 204; Staples, "Rooting Out Racism in Medicine"; and Robert B. Baker, Harriet Washington, Ololade Olakanmi

et al., "African American Physicians and Organized Medicine, 1846–1968," *JAMA* 300 (July 2008): 306–13.

96. Hine, *Black Women in White*, 92.

97. Ibid., 94.

98. Ibid.

99. Ibid., 121.

100. Ibid., 151–53.

101. Ibid., 183–86.

102. Ibid.

103. Ibid., 192.

104. See, for example, McBride, *From TB to AIDS*; Natalia Molina, *Fit to Be Citizens? Public Health and Race in Los Angeles, 1879–1939* (Berkeley: University of California Press, 2006); Nayan Shah, *Contagious Divides: Epidemics and Race in San Francisco's Chinatown* (Berkeley: University of California Press, 2001); and Paul Farmer, *AIDS and Accusation: Haiti and the Geography of Blame* (Berkeley: University of California Press, 1992).

105. According to McBride, these ideas began to wane after World War II. Yet others have argued that sociomedical racialism was but one phase in the longer history of racial formation in biomedicine. For instance, using the example of sickle cell anemia, the anthropologist Melbourne Tapper argues that forms of medical racialism persist. See Melbourne Tapper, *In the Blood: Sickle Cell Anemia and the Politics of Race* (Philadelphia: University of Pennsylvania Press, 1999), chap. 1. Duster makes a similar suggestion about the persistence of social stratification amid the most recent developments in genomics. See, for example, Troy Duster, "Race and Reification in Science," *Science*, February 18, 2005, 1050–51; and Duster, *Backdoor to Eugenics*.

106. McBride, *From TB to AIDS*, 15. See also Jones, *Bad Blood*, esp. chap. 2; and Beardsley, *History of Neglect*, 12–14. See also Hunter, *To 'Joy My Freedom,'* chap. 8.

107. McBride, *From TB to AIDS*, 10, 12.

108. McBride, *From TB to AIDS*, 22–23. McBride suggests that in addition to different priorities, many black physicians were ill-equipped to counter the more research-oriented racialist claims because they had received minimal training owing to segregated medical schools and postgraduate and specialist training programs (23).

109. McBride, *From TB to AIDS*, 65.

110. Ibid.

111. Stepan and Gilman, "Appropriating the Idioms of Science," 172.

112. Ibid., 183.

113. Frederick L. Hoffman, *Race Traits and Tendencies of the American Negro*, http://www.archive.org/details/racetraitstendenoohoffrich (accessed December 14, 2008); and Beatrix Hoffman, "Scientific Racism, Insurance, and Opposition to the Welfare State: Frederick L. Hoffman's Transatlantic Journey," *Journal of the Gilded Age and the Progressive Era* 2, no. 2 (2003): 151. Hoffman's

claims still reverberate in the U.S. insurance industry and have been cited as the one reason why African Americans historically have been charged higher insurance premiums than whites. See Scot J. Paltrow, "Old Notion of Black Mortality May Have Influenced Insurers," *Wall Street Journal*, December 26, 2000.

114. Hoffman, "Scientific Racism, Insurance, and Opposition to the Welfare State," 152.

115. Stepan and Gilman, "Appropriating the Idioms of Science," 184–85.

116. W. E. B. Du Bois, "Review of Frederick Hoffman's Race Traits and Tendencies of the American Negro, http://www.webdubois.org/dbReviewOfHoffman.html (accessed October 27, 2008).

117. Montague Cobb called *Health and Physique* the "first significant scientific approach to the health problems and biological study of the Negro," quoted in *Atlanta University Publications* (Nos. 1, 2, 4, 8, 9, 11, 13, 14, 15, 16, 17, 18), ed. Ernest Kaiser (New York: Arno, 1968), vi. However, Du Bois's monumental work, *The Philadelphia Negro: A Social Study*, completed after his training in sociology at the University of Berlin, is credited by many as the first. For discussion of Du Bois's training in Berlin, see Paul Gilroy, *The Black Atlantic: Modernity and Double-Consciousness* (Cambridge, Mass.: Harvard University Press, 1995), chap. 4; and David Levering Lewis, *W. E. B. Du Bois: Biography of a Race, 1868–1919* (New York: Henry Holt, 1993), chap. 6.

118. W. E. B. Du Bois, ed., *The Health and Physique of the Negro American: Report of a Social Study Made under the Direction of Atlanta University: Together with the Proceedings of the Eleventh Conference for the Study of the Negro Problems, Held at Atlanta University, on May the 29th, 1906. Atlanta University Publications, Number Eleven* (Atlanta: Atlanta University Press, 1906), 5, emphasis added. This remains an important distinction because, to this day, longevity rates are still accepted as the normative and exclusive gauge of African American health.

119. Notably, Du Bois made no criticisms of the method itself; his critique was not of scientific research per se but of racially biased research.

120. Du Bois, *Health and Physique*, 24. See also Byrd and Clayton, *American Health Dilemma*, 78–80.

121. Ibid.

122. Ibid., 89.

123. Ibid., 88. See also Roberts, *Infectious Fear*, 19–40.

124. Ibid., 89.

125. Ibid. See also Stepan and Gilman's discussion of Du Bois's intervention in "Appropriating the Idioms of Science," 184.

2. Origins of Black Panther Party Health Activism

1. Black Panther Party, "Black Panther Party Program," 48–49.

2. Mark Brody, "Panthers Map a People's Health Plan," *Daily World*, June 25, 1969, 9.

3. Office of Economic Opportunity, *Community Action Program Guide* (Washington, D.C.: Government Printing Office, 1965). A comprehensive analysis and critique of CAP is offered in Kenneth B. Clark and Jeanne Hopkins, *A Relevant War against Poverty: A Study of Community Action Programs and Observable Social Change* (New York: Harper and Row, 1968).

4. Brown, *Taste of Power,* 276, emphasis added. See also Brown, interview, December 6, 2008.

5. Komozi Woodard, *A Nation within a Nation: Amiri Baraka (LeRoi Jones) and Black Power Politics* (Chapel Hill: University of North Carolina Press, 1999), 6. See also Robert O. Self, *American Babylon: Race and the Struggle for Postwar Oakland* (Princeton, N.J.: Princeton University Press, 2003); Robert Self, "'To Plan Our Liberation': Black Power and the Politics of Place in Oakland, California, 1965–1977," *Journal of Urban History* 26, no. 6 (2000): 759–92. In interviews with Sol Stern, a writer for *Ramparts* magazine who wrote an article on the Party for the *New York Times Magazine,* Newton and Seale define their goals against what they deemed the moderation of the southern-centered civil rights movements and the wasted energies of the urban uprisings of the late 1960s ("The Call of the Black Panthers," August 6, 1967, 68). Newton expresses a similar sentiment in Wallace Turner, "A Gun Is Power, Black Panther Says," *New York Times,* May 21, 1967.

6. Seale, *Lonely Rage*; Seale, *Seize the Time*; Foner, introduction, xv; and Marine, *Black Panthers,* 12–13.

7. See Shirley Ann Moore, "Getting There, Being There: African-American Migration to Richmond, California, 1910–1945," in *The Great Migration in Historical Perspective: New Dimensions of Race, Class, and Gender,* ed. Joe William Trotter Jr. (Bloomington: Indiana University Press, 1991), 106–26. On general migration patterns in the San Francisco Bay Area, see Marilynn Johnson, *The Second Gold Rush: Oakland and the East Bay in World War II* (Berkeley: University of California, 1993). For an exhaustive account of blacks in the West, see Quintard Taylor, *In Search of the Racial Frontier: African Americans in the American West, 1528–1990* (New York: Norton, 1998).

8. For general discussion of African American migration patterns up to the immediate post–World War II period, see Nicholas Lemann, *The Promised Land: The Great Black Migration and How It Changed America* (New York: Vintage, 1992); Carole Marks, *Farewell—We're Good and Gone: The Great Black Migration* (Bloomington: Indiana University Press, 1989); Trotter, *Great Migration in Historical Perspective*; and Isabel Wilkerson, *The Warmth of Other Suns: The Epic Story of America's Great Migration* (New York: Random House, 2010). For discussion of cultural representations of this historic movement of black Americans, see Farah Jasmine Griffin, *"Who Set You Flowin'"? The African-American Migration Narrative* (New York: Oxford University Press, 1995).

9. Self, "'To Plan Our Liberation,'" 765.

10. Donna Murch, "The Campus and the Street: Race, Migration, and the Origins of the Black Panther Party in Oakland, CA," *Souls* 9 (2007): 334.

11. Self, *American Babylon*, 135–44, 159–76. Also instructive for illuminating the political economy of race and cities is Thomas J. Sugrue's seminal work *Origins of the Urban Crisis: Race and Inequality in Postwar Detroit* (Princeton, N.J.: Princeton University Press, 1996).

12. William Julius Wilson, *More Than Just Race: Being Black and Poor in the Inner City* (New York: Norton, 2009), 40.

13. Donna Jean Murch, *Living for the City: Migration, Education, and the Rise of the Black Panther Party in Oakland, California* (Chapel Hill: University of North Carolina Press, 2010).

14. See Fabio Rojas, *From Black Power to Black Studies: How a Radical Social Movement Became an Academic Discipline* (Baltimore, Md.: Johns Hopkins University Press, 2007).

15. Murch, "Campus and the Street," 334.

16. Ibid., 341.

17. E. Frances White, "Africa on My Mind: Gender, Counter Discourse, and African-American Nationalism," *Journal of Women's History* 2 (1990): 73–97. In this essay, White directs our attention to how "African-Americans in the late twentieth century construct and reconstruct collective political memories of African culture to build a cohesive group that can shield them from racist ideology and oppression"(74). These collective political memories of cultural nationalism, she argues, "set up standards of social relations that can be both liberating and confining" for women's freedoms (75).

18. "Huey Newton Talks to the Movement about the Black Panther Party, Cultural Nationalism, SNCC, Liberals and White Revolutionaries," in Foner, *Black Panthers Speak*, 50.

19. Seale, *Seize the Time*, 12–13; Seale, *Lonely Rage*, 125–26; Marine, *Black Panthers*, 24–34; Newton, *Revolutionary Suicide*, 104; Stern, "Call of the Black Panthers," 67; Foner, *Black Panthers Speak*, xv.

20. This ideological difference resulted in grave consequences in January 1969 when members of the Party were involved in a confrontation with the black cultural nationalist US Organization at the University of California at Los Angeles that resulted in the deaths of Panthers John Huggins and Alprentice "Bunchy" Carter. For more on this fatal infighting, see Scot Brown, *Fighting for Us: Maulana Karenga, the US Organization, and Black Cultural Nationalism* (New York: New York University Press, 2003), chap. 5. Brown, like Murch, stresses the importance of the California college and university system to the emergence of black radicalism in the late 1960s. Members of the Party and US were students in UCLA's "High Potential Program"—a college entrance program for black and Latino nontraditional students—during the 1968–69 academic year (95). It later came to light that the FBI stoked and exaggerated these ideological differences as part of its COINTELPRO campaign to destroy black radicals.

21. Maulana Ron Karenga, quoted in Brown, *Fighting for Us*, 108.

22. See "OEO Gives Grant for Health Care," *Los Angeles Sentinel*, June 1,

1972. See also Bonnie Lefkowitz, *Community Health Centers: A Movement and the People Who Made It Happen* (New Brunswick, N.J.: Rutgers University Press, 2007).

23. See Seale, "Using the Poverty Programs," in *Seize the Time*, 35, 44. See also Seale, *Lonely Rage*, 152; Foner, *Black Panthers Speak*, xv; and Henry Hampton and Steve Fayer, *Voices of Freedom: An Oral History of the Civil Rights Movement from the 1950s through the 1980s* (New York: Bantam Books, 1990), 350–52, 517; Marine, *Black Panthers*, 39, 137; and Daniel Crowe, *Prophets of Rage: The Black Freedom Struggle in San Francisco, 1945–1969* (New York: Garland, 2000), 168.

24. The organization's name was inspired by the independent Lowndes County Political Party (LCPP) that had been organized with the assistance of SNCC in Alabama and which used an image of the black panther as its symbol (Heath, *Off the Pigs!* 14). Indeed, in a September 22, 1966, essay published in the *New York Review of Books* titled "What We Want," SNCC chairman Stokely Carmichael reflected on his experiences with community organizations like the LCPP. In this essay, he proclaimed, "The creation of a national 'black panther party' must come about; it will take time to build, and it is much too early to predict its success." In addition, Party members Kathleen Cleaver, H. Rap Brown, and, for a time, Carmichael were former members of SNCC (Carson, *In Struggle*). Brown writes that the voter registration drive organized by the Party in Oakland in 1975 was inspired by SNCC drives during the civil rights movement (*Taste of Power*, 417).

25. The platform detailed the Party's goals and demands, among them self-determination for black communities; an end to police brutality; food, clothing, and shelter; education; full employment; military service exemptions for black men; trials for black people by truly representative juries; and the release of all black inmates from U.S. jails and prisons.

26. Seale, *Seize the Time*, 59; and Huey P. Newton, *To Die for the People: The Writings of Huey P. Newton* (1972; repr. New York: Writers and Readers Publishing, 1995), 46, emphasis added.

27. Newton, *To Die for the People*, 25.

28. Kessler-Harris, "In Pursuit of Economic Citizenship."

29. See Seale, "Using the Poverty Programs," 35, 44.

30. See ibid.

31. Brown, *Taste of Power*, 148.

32. "Panthers on Antipoverty Board," *Los Angeles Sentinel*, June 22, 1972; "'The Black Panther Party Is Not a Separatist Party': An Interview with Huey Newton," *Washington Post*, August 16, 1972; "Tame Panthers?" 13–14. Not all observers viewed the Party's inroads into local politics as radical politics. The *Time* article contended that the Party's victories in local electoral politics indicated the activists' "shift toward moderation" (13). The alternative publication *Grassroots* was skeptical that the Panthers' involvement in mainstream politics could result in more than perpetuating the status quo; while the Party is ap-

plauded for adding "20,000 new voters on the registration list," it is criticized for adding these voters to the ranks of traditional partisan politics, as Democrats, rather than "independents, Peace & Freedom, or even Panthers." See Anton Wood, "The New Bobby Seale's Old Politics," *Grassroots*, July 1973, 14.

33. Former Panther JoNina Abron has argued that the self-determination philosophy expressed by former SNCC leader Carmichael and Charles Hamilton in their *Black Power: The Politics of Liberation in America,* published in 1967, "urged Black communities to develop experimental programs 'out of day-to-day work out of the interaction between organizers and the communities in which they work'" ("'Serving the People'").

34. "Huey Newton Talks to the Movement," in Foner, *Black Panthers Speak,* 64.

35. Daniel Patrick Moynihan, *Maximum Feasible Misunderstanding: Community Action in the War on Poverty* (New York: Free Press, 1969), xi.

36. Office of Economic Opportunity, *Community Action Program Guide* (Washington, D.C.: Government Printing Office, October 1965). A comprehensive analysis and critique of CAP is offered in Kenneth B. Clark and Jeanne Hopkins, *A Relevant War against Poverty: A Study of Community Action Programs and Observable Social Change* (New York: Harper and Row, 1968).

37. Moynihan, *Maximum Feasible Misunderstanding.*

38. Brown, *Taste of Power,* 149–50.

39. Clark and Hopkins, *Relevant War against Poverty,* especially chaps. 3, 4. In a postmortem of the CAP, Clark and Hopkins concluded that the programs may have helped more to create and sustain a class of black managers and professionals than to alleviate urban poverty. See also Self, "'To Plan Our Liberation.'" For how this debate over community control played out with the federally backed medical clinics, see Lefkowitz, *Community Health Centers,* 11–13.

40. Quoted in Hilliard and Cole, *This Side of Glory,* 227.

41. Hilliard and Cole, *This Side of Glory,* 158.

42. Quoted in Brown, *Taste of Power,* 248–49.

43. Crowe, *Prophets of Rage,* 185. See also Self, "'To Plan Our Liberation,'" 773. This association with federal programs continued. In 1972 Party members Erika Huggins, William Roberts, Andrea Jones, and Herman Smith were elected as board members of a Berkeley antipoverty program ("Panthers on Antipoverty Board," *Los Angeles Sentinel,* June 22, 1972).

44. Crowe, *Prophets of Rage,* 179–81; Duster, *Backdoor to Eugenics,* 46–50. According to Smith, a similar situation occurred in Mississippi in the early twentieth century with black midwives, who "reshaped" government intervention "to the benefit of black community health" (*Sick and Tired,* 118).

45. Moynihan, *Maximum Feasible Misunderstanding,* xvii.

46. Lefkowitz, *Community Health Centers,* 11.

47. Kenneth M. Ludmerer, *Time to Heal: American Medical Education from the Turn of the Century to the Era of Managed Care* (New York: Oxford University Press, 1999), chap. 1. See also Starr, *Social Transformation of American Medicine,* 112–23.

48. Ludmerer, *Time to Heal*, xxii.

49. Byrd and Clayton, *American Health Dilemma*, 101.

50. Skloot, *Immortal Life of Henrietta Lacks*.

51. Ludmerer, *Time to Heal*, 120.

52. Ibid.

53. Roberts, *Killing the Black Body*, 90–91; Byrd and Clayton, *American Health Dilemma*, 452–59.

54. See, for example, "Sterilize Welfare Mothers?" *Black Panther*, May 1, 1971, 4.

55. Interview with author, March 18, 2009, Los Angeles.

56. Crowe, *Prophets of Rage*, 166; Self, "'To Plan Our Liberation,'" 773.

57. Seale, *Seize the Time*, 412.

58. Bobby Seale, interview with Ronald Jemal Stephens and Clyde Robertson, 1989, cited in Crowe, *Prophets of Rage*, 219; see also page 223.

59. Seale, *Seize the Time*, 71–72. Brown recalls that Newton was also inspired by revolutionary struggles in Africa in which activists created "alternative institutions" including schools and hospitals" (*Taste of Power*, 303–4). See also Black Panther Party (guest editors), "Survival Programs of the Black Panther Party," *CoEvolution Quarterly* 3 (Fall 1974).

60. Heath, *Off the Pigs!* 40.

61. Seale, *Seize the Time*, 62, 73, 99–106, 226; Marine, *Black Panthers*, 73; Foner, *Black Panthers Speak*, xix; Seale, *Lonely Rage*, 153, 157–58.

62. "Armed Negroes Protest Gun Bill," *New York Times*, May 3, 1967; Wallace Turner, "Gun Is Power"; Stern, "Call of the Black Panthers," 10; Seale, *Seize the Time*, 148–66. See also Seale, *Lonely Rage*, 166–74; and Terry Cannon, *All Power to the People: The Story of the Black Panther Party* (San Francisco: Peoples Press, 1970), 21.

63. Stern, "Call of the Black Panthers," 11; Hampton and Fayer, *Voices of Freedom*, 372.

64. Seale, *Seize the Time*, 187.

65. Stern, "Call of the Black Panthers," 11; Seale, *Seize the Time*, 228. Seale explained that local police sought to weaken the Party by harassing its leaders including Newton, Hilliard, and himself.

66. Hilliard and Cole, *This Side of Glory*, 141. Clayborne Carson writes, "As Newton awaited trial, the BPP concentrated its efforts on building mass support for his successful legal defense, and Eldridge Cleaver emerged as the Party's major spokesman and the central figure in its relations with SNCC" (*In Struggle: SNCC and the Black Awakening of the 1960s* [Cambridge, Mass.: Harvard University Press, 1981], 279).

67. Heath, *Off the Pigs!* 3; Hilliard and Cole, *This Side of Glory*, 192–99.

68. Hilliard and Cole, *This Side of Glory*, 192–99; see also Heath, *Off the Pigs!* 67.

69. Seale, quoted in Hampton and Fayer, *Voices of Freedom*, 354; see also Foner, *Black Panthers Speak*, xix.

70. Hampton and Fayer, *Voices of Freedom*, 517.

71. "Panthers to Put Down Guns, Newton Says," *Los Angeles Times*, January 31, 1972.

72. Terry Kupers, telephone interview with author, October 16, 2007.

73. Ibid.

74. The Portland chapter's dental clinic was named for revered black leader Malcolm X.

75. "Panthers to Put Down Guns"; Heath, "New Strategies for the Period, 1969–1971," in *Off the Pigs!* 82–115; Hampton and Fayer, *Voices of Freedom*, 517; Marine, *Black Panthers*, chap. 9.

76. Carol Rucker, "Interview of Carol Rucker by Lewis Cole," Columbia University Black Panther Project (Alexandria, Va.: Alexander Street, 2005), 55.

77. Ibid.

78. "Panthers to Put Down Guns"; and Brown, *Taste of Power*, 220–23.

79. Eldridge Cleaver, "On Meeting the Needs of the People," *Black Panther*, August 16, 1969, quoted in Foner, *Black Panthers Speak*, 167. See also Brown, *Taste of Power*, 233, 248–49; and Abron, "'Serving the People,'" 179.

80. Hampton and Fayer, *Voices of Freedom*, 518; *Black Panther*, November 16, 1968; Heath, *Off the Pigs!* 84–85; Brown, *Taste of Power*, 248, 276; Abron, "'Serving the People,'" 182. The name for this campaign of community service programs was borrowed from a phrase frequently used by Mao Zedong—"serving the people." The influence of Mao on the philosophies of the Party is elaborated below.

81. Roy Wilkins, "The 'New' Panthers," *New York Post*, February 26, 1972; Brown, *Taste of Power*, 247–49; and "Panthers to Put Down Guns." The Party's extensive "survival kit" of community programs was detailed in the *CoEvolution Quarterly* supplement to the *Whole Earth Catalog* in the fall of 1974. Newton required that new chapters of the Black Panther Party establish at least two of these four survival programs—Free Breakfast Program, Free Clothing Program, Free Health Clinic, Free Bussing Program (Huey P. Newton to Sastreo Yemanja, July 22, 1971, series 2, box 1, folder 21, Dr. Huey P. Newton Archives, Special Collections, Green Library, Stanford University).

82. Martha Gies, "A Father's Story," *Portland Monthly*, March 2005, 154. Ford is now president of a labor union in Portland, Oregon.

83. Rucker, "Interview."

84. Austin, *Up against the Wall*, 140–42.

85. In a recent essay on the Black Panther Party titled "Global Solidarity," Michael L. Clemons and Charles Jones situate the Party in an international context and show that the organization inspired radical imitators from as far away as India and the United Kingdom—the authors call them "global emulators"— who attached the Panther name to their local struggles. In turn, the Party was motivated, Clemons and Jones argue, by "a wide array of revolutionary theorists from Africa, Europe, Asia and Latin America," including Mao, Guevara, and Fanon. See Clemons and Jones, "Global Solidarity: The Black Panther Party

in an International Arena," in Cleaver and Kastiaficas, *Liberation, Imagination, and the Black Panther Party*, 27. See also C. Guevara, "The Revolutionary War," in *Venceremos! The Speeches and Writings of Che Guevara*, ed. J. Gerassi (New York: Macmillan, 1968), 27–88; and C. Guevara, "On Revolutionary Medicine," in Gerassi, *Venceremos!* 112–19.

86. Newton, *Revolutionary Suicide*, 111.

87. Hilliard and Cole, *This Side of Glory*, 119–21, 140, 152, 163, 180, 183, 247, 267. Hilliard writes, "Fanon—and the Algerian Revolution—has provided our most important theoretical model" (247). In *Seize the Time* Seale claimed to have read *The Wretched of the Earth* on six occasions (25–26). For more on the role that Fanon's, Mao's, and Guevara's writing played in the political theory of the Party, see Seale, *Seize the Time*, 26, 30–31, 34; and Brown, *Taste of Power*, 109, 112, 135–38, 245, 248, 251, 255, 285.

88. Members of the Party recall that Malcolm X was also an important source of inspiration. See, for example, Eldridge Cleaver, *Eldridge Cleaver: Post-Prison Writings and Speeches*, ed. Robert Scheer (New York: Random House, 1967), 36. As a member of the Nation of Islam (NOI), Malcolm X encouraged black communities to develop their own institutions. See *Malcolm X Speaks: Selected Speeches and Statements*, ed. George Breitman (New York: Grove, 1966), 5–7, 37–40. In his autobiography, Malcolm X distinguishes racial segregation "forced" on blacks by powerful whites from freely chosen separation in which blacks would supply their own "jobs, food, clothing and housing" (*The Autobiography of Malcolm X* [New York, Grove, 1965], 201–4). According to Manning Marable, Malcolm X's post-NOI agenda was "reformist" and included "the election of independent black candidates for public office, voter registration drives, rent strikes to promote better housing conditions for blacks, the building of all-black community schools, the creation of cultural centers, and initiating black community and neighborhood self-defense" (*Race, Reform, and Rebellion: The Second Reconstruction in Black America, 1945–1990*, 2nd ed. [Jackson: University of Mississippi Press, 1991], 90).

89. Guevara, "On Revolutionary Medicine," 112.

90. Ernesto Che Guevara, *Guerrilla Warfare*, ed. Brian Loveman and Thomas M. Davies (Lincoln: University of Nebraska Press, 1985), 79; Clemons and Jones, "Global Solidarity," 28, 31.

91. Ernesto Che Guevara, *Episodes of the Cuban Revolutionary War, 1956–1958*, ed. Mary-Alice Waters (New York: Pathfinder, 1996), 88–91. See also Ernesto Che Guevara, "The Duty of Revolutionary Medical Workers," in *Che Guevara and the Cuban Revolution: Writings and Speeches of Ernesto Che Guevara* (Sydney: Pathfinder, 1987), 124–32.

92. Guevara, "On Revolutionary Medicine," 115.

93. Ibid.

94. Ibid., 114.

95. See Fanon, "Colonial War and Mental Disorders," in *Wretched of the Earth*, 249–310.

96. Eldridge Cleaver, "Psychology: The Black Bible," in *Post-Prison Writings and Speeches* (New York: Vintage/Ramparts Books, 1967), 18–20. For the influence of Fanon on Cleaver's thinking, see also Robert Scheer, introduction to *Post-Prison Writings and Speeches*, xi–xii. Seale recalls introducing Newton to the work of Fanon (*Seize the Time*, 25; see also Marine, *Black Panthers*, 31–32, 36). Seale writes, "Some brothers would come into the Party, and see us with guns, and they related *only* to the gun. But one of the things that the Party did from the very beginning was to sit brothers down and politically educate them. We assigned books and materials like *The Autobiography of Malcolm X*, *The Wretched of the Earth*, and helped them to understand their constitutional rights and some basic points of law" (*Seize the Time*, 365).

97. Hilliard and Cole, *This Side of Glory*, 247.

98. Cleo Silvers, interview with author, August 4, 2007, New York. Brown recounts that in framing the Party "survival programs," Newton was also inspired by "third world" revolutionary struggles, including the struggle in Mozambique where activists created "alternative institutions" including schools and hospitals (*Taste of Power*, 303–4).

99. Jock McCulloch, *Black Soul, White Artifact: Fanon's Clinical Psychology and Social Theory* (Cambridge: Cambridge University Press, 1983), 85.

100. Frantz Fanon, *The Wretched of the Earth*, trans. Constance Farrington (New York: Grove, 1963), 296.

101. Ibid., 301.

102. Ibid., 284; and McCulloch, *Black Soul, White Artifact*, 107.

103. Fanon, *Wretched of the Earth*, 251. On the politicization and racialization of mental health issues in the mid-twentieth century, see Metzl, *Protest Psychosis*.

104. The name of the newsletter often varied from issue to issue: a March 25, 1970, issue was called *Community News Bulletin*; a March 11, 1970, issue was called the *Black Panther Community News Bulletin*; and a May 25, 1970, issue was called *People's News Service*. Because most of the newsletters that I have access to were printed with the latter title, I have opted to use that one.

105. "Free Medical Clinic," *Community People's News Service*, March 25, 1970. Notably, this skepticism about whether African Americans could hope to receive adequate health care was voiced two years before the atrocities of the Tuskegee syphilis experiment were brought to public attention in a *New York Times* news article in July 1972. See also "Bunchy Carter Free Clinic," January 19, 1970; "Medical Genocide," *People's News Service*, June 12, 1970.

106. *People's News Service*, July 28, 1970.

107. Ibid.

108. McCulloch, *Black Soul, White Artifact*, 83.

109. Ibid., 82–85.

110. In their important work *Black Power*, Hamilton and Carmichael assert that although "Black people are legal citizens of the United States . . . they stand as colonial subjects in relation to white society. Thus institutional racism has

another name: colonialism" (Stokely Carmichael and Charles V. Hamilton, *Black Power: The Politics of Liberation in America* [New York: Random House, 1967], 5). Cleaver used a colonial analogy to describe the status of black communities in the United States: "You have a black colony and you have a white mother country and . . . two different sets of political dynamics" (Eldridge Cleaver, "The Land Question and Black Liberation," in *Eldridge Cleaver: Post-Prison Writings and Speeches,* 57). See also "Huey P. Newton Speaks," in Foner, *Black Panthers Speak,* 54–55.

111. *Quotations from Chairman Mao,* ed. Stuart Schram (New York: Praeger, 1967), 33.

112. Seale, *Seize the Time,* 82; Seale, *Lonely Rage,* 158; Foner, introduction, xv; and Newton, "Correct Handling of a Revolution," in *Black Panthers Speak,* 44; Hilliard and Cole, *This Side of Glory,* 118–21, 247; Earl Anthony, *Picking Up the Gun: A Report on the Black Panthers* (New York: Dial, 1970), 1–3; Heath, 28, 148; and Seale, quoted in Hampton and Fayer, *Voices of Freedom,* 352. "The Red Book" or "The Little Red Book" was published in the United States in 1965 as *Quotations from Chairman Mao Tse-Tung.* For an account of the use and significance of Mao's ideas to the Party, see Seale, *Seize the Time,* 79–85; Seale, *Lonely Rage,* 158–59.

113. "Medicine and Fascism," *Black Panther,* June 14, 1969.

114. Robin D. G. Kelley and Betsy Esch, "Black Like Mao: Red China and Black Revolution," *Souls* 1 (Fall 1999): 8.

115. Schram, introduction to *The Political Thought of Mao Tse-Tung* (New York: Praeger, 1969), 15–149.

116. Mao Tse-Tung, "Serving the People," in Schram, *Quotations from Chairman Mao,* 95–97; and Clemons and Jones, "Global Solidarity," 28.

117. Schram, *Quotations from Chairman Mao,* 25; and Stuart Schram, *The Political Thought of Mao Tse-Tung* (New York: Praeger, 1969), 108–9. Throughout *Quotations,* the category of "the people" was used to signal Mao's interpretation of Marxist-Leninism, which held that the masses were rightly composed of the rural peasantry.

118. See Brown, *Taste of Power,* 231–32; Newton, *Revolutionary Suicide,* 109–11; Small, interview with author, October 18, 2005, Oakland, California. See also "The *RW* Interview: Dr. Tolbert Small: Journey of a People's Doctor," *Revolutionary Worker,* February 17, 2002, http://www.rwor.org/a/v23/1130-39/1139/drsmall.htm.

119. "The Barefoot Doctors of Rural China" (dir. Diane Li; 1975). According to Party collaborator Dr. Tolbert Small, China's "barefoot doctors" program was a model for the Panthers' health politics (interview).

120. Norma Armour wrote a grant to purchase a van for the George Jackson PFMC. "I heard that the city had some money. I wrote a proposal to get money to buy a van for the clinic, so that we could do some local services. . . . So, I wrote it. And it was the first grant; I didn't know anything about grant writing. I put

something together and it got accepted. We started doing [healthcare] in the community in addition to being about to pick up patients and bring them to see the doctor" (interview).

121. Maurice J. Meisner, *Mao's China and After: A History of the People's Republic,* 3rd ed. (New York: Free Press, 1999).

122. Kelley and Esch, "Black Like Mao," 39.

123. According to Hilliard, other Party members' travels to Cuba and China and their study of collectivist healthcare practices in these countries also shaped the direction of the organization's health politics. See Brody, "Panthers Map a People's Medical Plan," 9.

124. Ibid.

125. Black Panther Party, "Black Panther Party Program," 48–49.

3. The People's Free Medical Clinics

1. "Death of a 4 Month Old Baby," *Black Panther,* February 7, 1970.

2. Ibid.

3. Ibid.

4. "Health Care—Pig Style," *Black Panther,* February 7, 1970.

5. Ibid.

6. Ibid.

7. Ibid.

8. Ibid., 15.

9. "The Opening of the Bobby Seale People's Free Health Clinic," *Black Panther,* May 15, 1971.

10. Abron, "'Serving the People,'" 178, 184. Party minister of justice Ray "Masai" Hewitt announced the Party's plan to extend the PFMC network in November 1969, several weeks prior to Seale's mandate.

11. Black Panther Party, "People's Free Medical Research Health Clinics," 21. For more on the philosophy of community-based free clinics during this period, see "People's Medicine: The Free Clinic Movement," *Grassroots,* February 1973. See also Abron, "'Serving the People,'" 149.

12. Interview, March 19, 2009.

13. Sheffield, "People's Medical Care Center," 174; "The Opening of the Bobby Seale People's Free Medical Clinic," *Black Panther,* May 15, 1971; "Racism and Red Blood Cells," *Black Panther,* October 7, 1972, 5; and Assata Shakur, *Assata: An Autobiography* (Westport, Conn.: Lawrence Hill, 1987), 217.

14. An unnamed medical student volunteer at Winters People's Free Medical Care Center in Chicago, quoted in "The Free Clinics; Ghetto Care Centers Struggle to Survive," *American Medical News,* February 21, 1972, 12.

15. Epstein, *Impure Science,* 9–10.

16. Bazell, "Health Radicals," 506–9; Beckwith, "The Radical Science Movement in the United States," *Monthly Review,* July 1986, 118–19.

17. Irene R. Turner, "Free Health Clinics: A New Concept?" *American Journal of Public Health* 62 (October 1972): 1348. Turner was a leader of MCHR; see Mullan, *White Coat, Clenched Fist,* 53.

18. Cleo Silvers, interview with author, February 22, 2007, New York. See also Fitzhugh Mullan, telephone interview with the author, October 29, 2007.

19. Interview, February 22, 2007.

20. Lefkowitz, *Community Health Centers.* See also Constance Bloomfield and Howard Levy, "Underground Medicine: Ups and Downs of Free Clinics," *Ramparts,* March 1972, 35–36.

21. A fine discussion of the women's health movement is offered in Morgen, *Into Our Own Hands.* See also Ruzek, *Women's Health Movement.* On the history and significance of the SHO, see Rogers, "'Caution'"; and Bronston, interview. On the MCHR, see Dittmer, *Good Doctors.* On the "rainbow coalition," see Sheffield, "People's Medical Care Center," 175; Miguel "Mickey" Melendez, *We Took to the Streets: Fighting for Latino Rights with the Young Lords* (New York: Macmillan, 2003), 85.

22. Or, as Armour put it, "We firmly believed that health care is a right and not a privilege" (interview).

23. "Health Radicals: Crusade to Shift Medical Power to the People," *Science* 173 (1971): 508–9.

24. "The Free Clinics: Ghetto Care Centers Struggle to Survive," *American Medical News,* February 21, 1972, 14.

25. Ibid., 13; "The Free Clinics Put It Together," *Medical World News,* February 4, 1972, 15.

26. It also evolved in critical response to the community health center program initiated by the federal government in 1965 as I suggest in chapter 3. For a history of the federal neighborhood clinic program, see Lefkowitz, *Community Health Centers,* 36. On the "free clinic" movement that grew out of 1967's Summer of Love, see Gregory L. Weiss, *Grassroots Medicine: The Story of America's Free Health Clinics* (Lanham, Md.: Rowman and Littlefield, 2006), 38–40. In his *Good Doctors,* Dittmer discusses how the experiences of MCHR members during Freedom Summer and afterward influenced the clinic movement in subsequent years.

27. "People's Medicine: The Free Clinic Movement," *Grassroots,* February 1973, 12.

28. McAdam, *Freedom Summer*; Morris, *Origins of the Civil Rights Movement: Black Communities Organizing for Change.* New York: Free Press, 1984.

29. Dittmer, *Good Doctors,* 31; Mullan, *White Coat, Clenched Fist,* 11–16.

30. Ibid.

31. Geiger became an important collaborator with the OEO on its federal community clinic program, as did the SHO, to sponsor medical summer projects in 1966 in California and in California, New York City, and Chicago, the following year (Mullan, *White Coat, Clenched Fist,* 57; Bronston, interview).

32. Dittmer, *Good Doctors,* chap. 8.

33. William Bronston, "Student Health Summer Project," *Health Rights: A Publication of the Medical Committee for Human Rights*, Spring 1966, 12. See also Bronston, interview. The MCHR also came to work closely with the SHO, which for several years, beginning in 1966, contributed to the radical health movement stream of medical services and facilities. (Independent of the MCHR, SHO organized the Summer Health Projects (SHPs), short-term initiatives funded by the OEO, in which nursing, medical, and dental students worked in poor urban and rural communities, at clinics, public hospitals, and in migrant worker camps, to provide healthcare services for the poor.)

34. Interview with author, March 18, 2009, Los Angeles.

35. Weiss, *Grassroots Medicine*, 38–40.

36. "The Free Clinics: Ghetto Care Centers Struggle to Survive," *American Medical News*, February 21, 1972, 13.

37. Armour, interview.

38. In the Party newspaper, for example, the organization was described as "the Vanguard of the American Revolution." See Connie Matthews Tabor, "Intercommunal Solidarity Day for Chairman Bobby Seale," *Black Panther*, January 23, 1971, 4.

39. The concept of the biocultural broker is introduced in Alondra Nelson, "The Inclusion and Difference *Paradox*: A Review of *Inclusion: The Politics of Difference in Medical Research* by Steven Epstein," *Social Identities* 15, no. 5 (2009): 741–43.

40. Elizabeth H. Harding, Charlene Harrington, and Gloria Jean Manor, "The Berkeley Free Clinic," *Nursing Outlook* 21 (January 1973): 42.

41. Ibid.

42. Valerie A. Jones, "The White Coat: Why Not Follow Suit?" *Journal of the American Association* 281 (January 1999): 478.

43. Sheffield, "People's Medical Care Center," 84–85.

44. Frantz Fanon, *A Dying Colonialism*, trans. Haakon Chevalier (New York: Grove, 1988); Fanon, *Wretched of the Earth*; Joshua S. Horn, *Away with All Pests: An English Surgeon in People's China, 1954–1969* (New York: Monthly Review Press, 1970); and Schram, *Quotations from Chairman Mao*.

45. Mullan, interview.

46. Silvers, interview.

47. "Employed Persons by Occupation and Race: 1957–1969," in *Labor Force, Employment and Earnings* (Washington, D.C.: Department of Labor, Bureau of Labor Statistics, December 1969), 226–28. On the shortage of African American nurses and other nurses of color in the 1970s, see Marie F. Branch, "Catch Up or Keep Up? Ethnic Minorities in Nursing," *Urban Health* (August 1977): 49–52. Courtesy of personal archive of Marie Branch, R.N., D.C.

48. The Revolutionary People's Constitutional Convention of 1970 that was organized by the Party and attended by feminist groups, New Left groups, health radicals, and members of the "rainbow coalition," as well as gay and lesbian rights activists, was indicative of the cross-fertilization I am highlighting

(Church League of America, "The Black Panthers in Action," 1969, Collection of Underground, Alternative, and Extremist Literature, 1900–1990, UCLA Special Collections). This report of the Party's activities describes its collaborations with SDS and the MCHR among other groups.

49. Sheffield, "People's Medical Care Center," 174.

50. Ibid.

51. Harding, Harrington, and Manor, "Berkeley Free Clinic," 42.

52. Ibid.

53. Interview.

54. Ehrenreich and Ehrenreich, *American Health Empire*, 13.

55. Morgen, *Into Our Hands*, 4.

56. Epstein, *Impure Science*, 8–17.

57. Morgen, *Into Our Own Hands*. See also Ruzek, *Women's Health Movement*.

58. Morgen, *Into Our Own Hands*, 22; see also chaps. 1, 2.

59. Armour, interview. See also "Free Pap Smear for Women," *People's New Service* (Black Panther Party Southern California Chapter), June 30, 1970.

60. Armour, interview.

61. Mullan, *White Coat, Clenched Fist*.

62. William Bronston, "Medical Committee for Human Rights Preliminary Position Paper on National Health Care, September 1971," William Bronston, M.D., papers, Bancroft Library, University of California, Berkeley.

63. Goldberg, "Panthers after the Trial," 26–27.

64. "Black Panther Party Plans Health Clinics," *Los Angeles Times*, November 25, 1969, 24; "Black Panthers Set Up Clinics," *Washington Post*, November 26, 1969.

65. Hilliard and Cole, *This Side of Glory*, 339; "The Sickle Cell 'Game': Phoney Foundations Try to Sabotage Black Panther Party's Sickle Cell Program," *Black Panther*, May 27, 1972; Abron, "'Serving the People,'" 184; Daniel Joseph Willis, "A Critical Analysis of Mass Political Education and Community Organization as Utilized by the Black Panther Party as a Means for Effecting Social Change" (PhD diss., University of Massachusetts, 1976), 77–80; Williams, *Black Politics/White Power*, chap. 7; Marine, *Black Panthers*, chap. 5, 180–83. Details about the formation of the Chicago Party are provided in Hampton and Fayer, *Voices of Freedom*, 519–38. The Berkeley PFMC opened in May 1971; see "The Opening of the Bobby Seale People's Free Health Clinic," *Black Panther*, May 15, 1971. The Portland PFMC opened in 1969. For details on this clinic, see Martha Gies, "Radical Treatment," *Reed Magazine*, Winter 2009, http://www.reed.edu/reed_magazine/winter2009/features/radical_treatment/index.html. The Seattle clinic opened in December of that same year: "A doctor helped to found and operate the clinic, which was open two days per week, a former Seattle Panther said, but lack of privacy and the presence of Panthers with guns tended to discourage community use of the facility. Services offered involved 'referrals' more often than treatment" (98–99). Heath noted that there was also a clinic in the Brooklyn branch of the New York City branch of the Party

(*Off the Pigs!* 98–99). On the Kansas City clinic, see *Black Panther,* August 16, 1969; and *Black Panther,* September 13, 1969; Testimony of Reverend Phillip C. Lawson, Committee on Internal Security, Public Hearing on the Black Panther Party, March 4, 1970, 2638, 2672, U.S. House of Representatives; Testimony of Walter Parker, Committee on Internal Security, Public Hearing on the Black Panther Party, March 5, 1970, 2699, U.S. House of Representatives; Testimony of Everett P. O'Neal, Committee on Internal Security, Public Hearing on the Black Panther Party, March 7, 1970, 2752–2753, U.S. House of Representatives; and Testimony of Richard A. Shaw, Committee on Internal Security, Public Hearing on the Black Panther Party, March 10, 1970, 2780, U.S. House of Representatives.

66. Dennis Levitt, "Panthers Open Free Clinic," *Los Angeles Free Press,* January 2, 1970, 3; Kupers, interview. "Bunchy" Carter was deputy minister of defense of the Southern California chapter of the Party who was shot to death at the University of California, Los Angeles, in January 1969 during a dispute with the US Organization led by Ron Karenga (Hilliard and Cole, *This Side of Glory,* 237–41; Brown, *Taste of Power,* chap. 8).

67. On the formation of the PFMCs, see "Bunchy Carter Free Clinic"; People's Health Center Vandalized," *Black Panther,* April 3, 1971, 3; Brown, *Taste of Power,* 181; Ward Churchill and Jim Vander Wall, *Agents of Repression: The FBI's Secret War against the Black Panther Party and the American Indian Movement* (Boston: South End, 1988), 69; G. Louis Heath, ed., "Activities and Programs," in *The Black Panther Leaders Speak* (New York: Scarecrow, 1976), 127. On New Haven, see Williams, "No Haven," 272.

68. "The Black Panther Party Announces . . . The Grand Opening of the Bobby Seale People's Free Health Clinic Saturday April 24th, 1971" (flyer). Courtesy of Billy X Jennings and It's About Time Black Panther Party.

69. "Dr. Tolbert Small: Journey of a People's Doctor."

70. John Saar, "Health Clinic Is Opened by Panthers," *Washington Post,* May 21, 1974.

71. Goldberg, "Panthers after the Trial," 27.

72. Andrew Witt, *The Black Panthers in the Midwest: The Community Programs and Services of the Black Panther Party in Milwaukee, 1966–1977* (New York: Routledge, 2007), 62–63. Several ex-Panthers went on to found another free health center—not affiliated with the Party—in that city in 1970.

73. "Black Panther Party Plans Health Clinics," *Los Angeles Times,* November 25, 1969.

74. Turner, "Free Health Clinics," 1349.

75. Brody, "Panthers Map a People's Health Plan," 9.

76. Taressa Stone, "The Sidney Miller Clinic—Breakfast and More," *University of Washington Daily,* April 27, 1978; Judith Black, "Panthers' Progress," *Seattle Times,* October 24, 1986.

77. In this way, the Party shared the challenges faced by all free clinics. See Bloomfield and Levy, "Underground Medicine," 35–42.

78. Interview with author, March 19, 2009, Los Angeles.

79. Brody, "Panthers Map a People's Medical Plan," 9.

80. Ibid.

81. Cox, quoted in Brody, "Panthers Map a People's Medical Plan," 9.

82. Ibid.

83. Interview with author, December 6, 2008, Savannah, Georgia.

84. At the school, children also had their sight and hearing screened and received glasses and auditory aids, if necessary. Armour, interview; also Brown, interview, December 6, 2008.

85. Brown, interview with author, December 6, 2008; also Armour, interview; and Small, interview with author, May 12, 2006, Oakland, California.

86. Interview with author, December 6, 2008.

87. Saar, "Health Clinic Is Opened by Panthers."

88. Sheffield, "People's Medical Care Center," 174.

89. "Interview of Dr. Tolbert Small by Lewis Cole," *Columbia University Black Panther Project* (1990; repr. Alexandria, Va.: Alexander Street Press, 2005), 23. See also Heike Kleffner, "The Black Panthers: Interviews with Geronimo Ji-Jaga Pratt and Mumia Abu-Jamal," *Race and Class* 35 (1993): 9–26.

90. Untitled police report on the arrest of Nelson Malloy in Nevada in October 1977, Department of Special Collections and University Archives, Stanford University.

91. Seale, *Lonely Rage*, 177.

92. Brown elevated many women to positions of power in the Party after becoming chairwoman in 1974. Her staffing decisions were met with complaints from male Party members. See Brown, *Taste of Power*, 362.

93. Jules Boykoff and Martha Gies, "'We're going to defend ourselves': The Portland Chapter of the Black Panther Party and Local Media Response," *Oregon Historical Quarterly* (Fall 2010): 290.

94. Levitt, "Panthers Open Free Clinic"; Kupers, interview; Brown, *Taste of Power*, 215, emphasis added; and Shakur, *Assata*, 198, 216–17. Joan Bird was a student at Bronx Community College (Angela D. LeBlanc-Ernest, "'The Most Qualified Person to Handle the Job': Black Panther Party Women, 1966–1982," in Jones, *Black Panther Party*, 311, 313). Shakur and Bird were part of the group of Panthers known as the New York 21, who were arrested in April 1969, on charges of conspiring to bomb several locations in the city.

95. Saar, "Health Clinic Is Opened by Panthers."

96. Williams, "No Haven," 272–73.

97. Tracye Matthews, "'No One Ever Asks, What a Man's Place in the Revolution Is': Gender and the Politics of the Black Panther Party, 1966–1971," in Jones, *Black Panther Party*, 267–304. On gender in black health advocacy, see also Smith, *Sick and Tired*.

98. Smith, *Sick and Tired*.

99. For the most part, the gender dynamics of the Party's health activism fits with Smith's assessment of women's roles and gender in black health ad-

vocacy more generally. Though Smith's focus is on six decades preceding the Party's medical advocacy, several characterizations of black women's health activism were consistent with the Party. For example, Smith notes that women were often leaders of black health programs and also "formed the backbone of the black health movement" as grassroots organizers. Black women's centrality to health initiatives owed partly to "their influence on the physical and moral health of their families." See Smith, *Sick and Tired*, 1.

100. Elichi Tsuchida to Huey P. Newton, February 21, 1972, and Huey P. Newton to Elichi Tsuchida, February 23, 1972, Dr. Huey P. Newton Papers, Department of Special Collections and University Archives, Stanford University.

101. Abron, "'Serving the People,'" 184.

102. Small, interview with author, February 26, 2006, Oakland, California.

103. Small, interview with author, October 8, 2007, Oakland, California.

104. Small, interview with author, February 26, 2006, Oakland, California.

105. Gies, "Radical Treatment."

106. Hilliard and Cole, *This Side of Glory*, 259, Seale, *Seize the Time*, 414; "Racism and Red Blood Cells," *Black Panther*, October 7, 1972; and "The Opening of the Bobby Seale People's Free Health Clinic," *Black Panther*, May 15, 1971. Black medical students from Stanford University were inspired by the Party's efforts to begin their own screening program led by Don Williams (Anonymous and Don Williams, "Combatting Genocide, Part III/Origin of Sickle Cell Anemia and G6PD Deficiency," *Black Panther*, December 4, 1971). In 1970 the medical staff of the Chicago chapter's clinic consisted of "10 doctors, twelve nurses, and two registered technicians" as well as interns "from medical schools around the city" (Sheffield, "People's Medical Care Center," 174). Volunteers—physicians and community members—were also critical to the operation of the Berkeley and Oakland clinics. See "Dr. Tolbert Small: Journey of a People's Doctor," 6.

107. Brody, "Panthers Map a People's Medical Plan," 9.

108. The Willowbrook State School was an infamous New York State institution for mentally disabled children. Mike Wilkins and several other doctors were fired in 1971 protesting and exposing the decrepit conditions at the school. Public outrage over the conditions at Willowbrook spurred legislators to pass the Civil Rights of Institutionalized Persons Act of 1980.

109. McClanahan was well known for exposing the atrocity of the war with photographs of Vietnamese children who had been burned by U.S. troops with the chemical weapon napalm that were published in *Ramparts* magazine.

110. Michael Wilkins, interview with author, August 19, 2007, New York.

111. Richard Fine and Phillip Shapiro to Mr. Henry W. Kerr, Chairman, Adult Authority, June 29, 1973, Huey P. Newton Collection, Department of Special Collections and University Archives, Stanford University. On incarcerated Party members in need of medical attention, see also William J. Drummond, "Panthers in Jail Fight Need Medical Aid, Doctor Reports," *Los Angeles Times*, February 8, 1970.

112. Small, interview with author, October 8, 2007.

113. Sheffield, "People's Medical Care Center," 174.

114. "Interview of Dr. Tolbert Small by Lewis Cole," 21.

115. Ibid.

116. "Fred Hampton Memorial Clinic Offers Free Health Services," *TK Press*, April 29, 1970; "People's Clinic from Panthers and HEALTH-RAP," *Williamette Bridge* 11 (October 1970): 7.

117. "Fred Hampton Memorial Clinic Offers Free Health Services."

118. Sheffield, "People's Medical Care Center," 174; Bronston, interview.

119. Sheffield, "People's Medical Care Center," 174; "The Opening of the Bobby Seale People's Free Medical Clinic," *Black Panther*, May 15, 1971; "Racism and Red Blood Cells," *Black Panther*, October 7, 1972; and Shakur, *Assata*, 217.

120. "Bunchy Carter Free Clinic." This was the case in New Haven, Connecticut, where the community clinic established by the Party in 1971 continued after the Party dissolved there in 1983. See Williams, "No Haven," 274, 279.

121. "People's Clinic from Panthers and HEALTH-RAP," 1.

122. "Fred Hampton Memorial Clinic Offers Free Health Services"; "The Black Panther Party Free Health Clinic" (flyer), Seattle Black Heritage Society.

123. Levitt, "Panthers Open Free Clinic."

124. Turner, "Free Health Clinics," 1350. The Chicago PFMC reopened in January 1970 as the Spurgeon "Jake" Winters People's Free Medical Care Center; it was named in honor of a chapter member who had been spearheading the work of the clinic before he was killed during an altercation with police in November 1969. See "Illinois Panthers Rebuild Office," *Second City* 2, no. 2 (August 1969): 5, Special Collections, University of California, Los Angeles.

125. Quoted in Gies, "Radical Treatment."

126. Interview with author, February 26, 2006, Oakland, California.

127. Interview.

128. Ibid.

129. Interview with author, March 18, 2009, Los Angeles.

130. "Black Panther Party Plans Health Clinics," *Los Angeles Times*, November 25, 1969.

131. See *Black Panther*, August 16, 1969, and September 13, 1969; Reynaldo Anderson, "The Kansas City Black Panther Party and the Repression of the Black Revolution," in *On the Ground: The Black Panther Party in Communities across America*, ed. Judson L. Jeffries (Jackson: University Press of Mississippi), 101–2. See also Testimony of Reverend Phillip C. Lawson; Testimony of Walter Parker; Testimony of Everett P. O'Neal; and Testimony of Richard A. Shaw.

132. Michael Wilkins, interview with author, August 19, 2007, New York.

133. Charles E. Jones, "Arm Yourself or Harm Yourself: People's Party II and the Black Panther Party in Houston, Texas," in Jeffries, *On the Ground*, 25–26.

134. Stone, "Sidney Miller Clinic," 4.

135. Ibid.

136. Mullan, *White Coat, Clenched Fist*, 44; "Black Panthers Set Up Clinics."

137. "Fred Hampton Memorial Clinic Offers Free Health Services"; William C. Davis, telephone interview with the author, October 10, 2007.

138. Jeffrey Zane and Judson L. Jeffries, "A Panther Sighting in the Pacific Northwest: The Seattle Chapter of the Black Panther Party," in Jeffries, *On the Ground*, 73.

139. "Work Ledger (1971)," courtesy of Tolbert Small; see also Small, interview with author, May 12, 2006, Oakland, California.

140. Simon Anekwe, "St. Matthew's Host to Panther Show," *Afro-American Journal*, April 16, 1970, 7.

141. Williams, "No Haven," 272.

142. Saar, "Health Clinic Is Opened by Panthers."

143. "Illinois Panthers Rebuild Office," *Second City* 2, no. 2 (August 1969): 5, Special Collections, University of California, Los Angeles. The Chicago PFMC reopened in January 1970 as the Spurgeon "Jake" Winters People's Free Medical Care Center.

144. Saar, "Health Clinic Is Opened by Panthers."

145. Black Panther Party, "People's Free Medical Research Health Clinics," 21; Stone, "Sidney Miller Clinic—Breakfast and More," 5.

146. Kupers, interview.

147. Interview with author, March 19, 2009.

148. "Interview of Dr. Tolbert Small by Lewis Cole," 25.

149. Ibid.

150. Stone, "Sidney Miller Clinic—Breakfast and More"; Judith Black, "Panthers' Progress," *Seattle Times*, October 24, 1986.

151. Branch, interview with author, March 18, 2009, Los Angeles.

152. Roz Payne, interview with the author, August 4, 2007, New York.

153. Ibid.

154. "Black Panthers Set Up Clinics."

155. "'Bunchy Carter Free Clinic," *Community News Service*.

156. Ibid.

157. Davis, telephone interview; "New Medical Clinic Opens in Albina to Provide Neighborhood Health Care," *Oregonian*, January 13, 1970 (courtesy of Dr. William C. Davis). One article suggests that the activists did not initially intend to use state and federal funding. See "People's Clinic from Panthers and HEALTH-RAP," 1.

158. Interview with author, March 19, 2009.

159. "People's Clinic from Panthers and HEALTH-RAP."

160. Zane and Jeffries, "Panther Sighting," 79.

161. Gies, "Father's Story," 156.

162. Ibid., 191.

163. Cannon, *All Power to the People*, 35; Williams, "No Haven," 272; "Black Panther Party to Provide Free Sickle Cell Anemia Test to Blacks," *Medium* (Seattle), December 17, 1970; and Abron, "'Serving the People,'" 184. Similarly,

Bay Area medical clinics were staffed by local doctors and medical students who volunteered their services (Seale, *Seize the Time*, 414). Heath writes that the Oakland medical clinic "depended upon community donations of money, medical supplies, and professional services" (*Off the Pigs!* 98); "Fred Hampton Memorial Clinic Offers Free Health Services."

164. On the Seattle chapter's well-baby clinic, see Zane and Jeffries, "Panther Sighting," 74.

165. Kupers, interview.

166. Ibid.

167. Ibid.

168. From the *Bridge*, quoted in Gies, "Radical Treatment."

169. Kupers, interview.

170. Ibid.

171. Heath, *Off the Pigs!* 98–99.

172. Patient advocates were common in community clinics in this period. See Rogers, "'Caution,'" 18; and Turner, "Free Health Clinics," 1349.

173. Turner, "Free Health Clinics," 1349.

174. Telephone interview with author, October 16, 2007.

175. Davis, telephone interview.

176. Levitt, "Panthers Open Free Clinic."

177. Benjamin R. Friedman, "Picking Up Where Robert F. Williams Left Off," in *Comrades: The Local History of the Black Panther Party*, ed. Judson L. Jeffries (Bloomington: Indiana University Press, 2007), 47–88.

178. "Free Ambulance Service," *Black Panther*, June 26, 1971, 7; and J. Smithe, comments, Black Panther Party Fortieth Anniversary conference, October 14, 2006, Oakland, California.

179. Larry Little, quoted in Friedman, "Picking Up Where Robert F. Williams Left Off," 74.

180. Friedman, "Picking Up Where Robert F. Williams Left Off," 74.

181. Ibid., 76.

182. "The Legacy of the Black Panther Party," *It's About Time* 5 (Fall–Winter 2001): 20; Friedman, "Picking Up Where Robert F. Williams Left Off," 75.

183. Leigh Somerville McMillan, "Exhibit Tells Story of Winston-Salem's Black Panther Party," *Winston-Salem Journal*, September 11, 2007; and "Legacy of the Black Panther Party," 20.

184. Davis, telephone interview; Willa Bee Holmes, "Fred Hampton Memorial Clinic Offers Free Health Services."

185. "Fred Hampton Memorial Clinic Offers Free Health Services."

186. Gies, "Father's Story," 156.

187. Ibid., 191.

188. Boykoff and Gies, "'We're going to defend ourselves,'" 290.

189. Turner, "Free Health Clinics."

190. Ronald Kozoil, "Move against Panther Clinic," *Chicago Tribune*, January 21, 1970; also see Turner, "Free Health Clinics," 1351.

191. "2 Panther Clinic Medics Oppose Licensing by City," *Chicago Tribune*, February 20, 1970.

192. Ibid.

193. Ibid.

194. Boykoff and Gies, "'We're going to defend ourselves,'" 303.

195. Williams, "No Haven," 272.

196. Marie Branch, "Prisoners Are Denied Health Rights" (pamphlet/flyer), December 30, 1969.

197. Marie Branch, Black Panther Party Clinic Meeting Notes, December 7, 1969, personal papers of Marie Branch, Ph.D., in author's possession.

198. Levitt, "Panthers Open Free Clinic."

199. Davis, telephone interview.

4. Spin Doctors

1. Seale, *Lonely Rage*, 224; Bobby Seale to Eve Kenley, April 5, 1972, series 1, box 4, folder 9, Dr. Huey P. Newton Archives, Special Collections, Green Library, Stanford University; Dick Hallgren, "Black Panthers Draw Big Crowd," *San Francisco Chronicle*, March 30, 1972. The second day of the conference took place at Oakland's Greenman Field and the third at San Pablo Park. See also Brown, *Taste of Power*, 185–86. See also Hilliard and Cole, *This Side of Glory*, 298. Bobby Hutton was the first Party member, besides Seale and Newton; he was killed in a shooting incident with Oakland police on April 6, 1968.

2. *Black Panther*, April 1, 1972; and Seale to Kenley. The mainstream press confirmed that the conference had significant attendance; on March 27 Oakland Auditorium was at "near capacity" of just over five thousand. See "Black Panthers Draw Big Crowd," *San Francisco Chronicle*, March 30, 1972. In the United States, on average, one in twelve persons carry the recessive genetic trait for sickling.

3. Seale, *Lonely Rage*, 224. On mobile medical units, see Seale's appearance on *The Mike Douglas Show*, February 12, 1972. A mobile unit was used by the Chicago Party to conduct sickle cell anemia testing. See "Will the Real Sickle Cell Program Please Come Forward," *Black Panther*, February 2, 1972.

4. Michael G. Michaelson, "Sickle Cell Anaemia: 'An Interesting Pathology,'" in *Anti-Racist Science Teaching*, ed. Dawn Gill and Les Levidow (London: Free Association Books, 1987), 62–69.

5. The word "crisis" in reference to sickling was coined by the physician V. P. Sydenstricker.

6. C. Lockard Conley, "Sickle Cell Anemia: The First Molecular Disease," in *Blood, Pure and Eloquent*, ed. Maxwell M. Wintrobe (New York: McGraw Hill, 1980), 325. In 1972 the noted geneticist, sickle cell anemia researcher, and activist James E. Bowman characterized the many factors involved in establishing screening programs as a "sickle cell crisis" ("Sickle Cell Screening—Medical-Legal, Ethical, Psychological, and Social Problems: A Sickle Cell Crisis,"

First International Conference on the Mental Health Aspects of Sickle Cell Anemia [Rockville, Md.: National Institutes of Mental Health, 1974]). See also Michaelson, "Sickle Cell Anaemia," 64.

7. For example, "Neglect of Black Disease Sickle Cell Anemia," *Medium*, December 3, 1970.

8. Brown, *Taste of Power*, 223; and Williams, "No Haven," 271–74.

9. This act, Public Law 92-294, which was unanimously approved by both the U.S Senate and House of Representatives, was passed on May 16, 1972.

10. Petryna defines "biological citizenship" as a special status or practice that arises from a "subsystem of the state's public health and welfare infrastructure where increasingly poor citizens . . . mobilize around their claims . . . of injury." See Adriana Petryna, *Life Exposed: Biological Citizens after Chernobyl* (Princeton, N.J.: Princeton University Press, 2002), 5. Kessler-Harris, "In Pursuit of Economic Citizenship."

11. On the various epistemologies of sickling, see Tapper, *In the Blood.*

12. Todd Savitt, "The Invisible Malady: Sickle Cell Anemia in America, 1910–1970," *Journal of the National Medical Association* 73 (1981): 739. See also B. J. Culliton, "Sickle Cell Anemia: The Route from Obscurity to Prominence," *Science* 178, no. 4057 (1972): 138–42.

13. Savitt, "Invisible Malady," 744. Although, in 1959 a popular African American issues magazine ran the college student Marclan A. Walker's first-person account of her life with sickle cell anemia. See "I'm Living on Borrowed Time," *Ebony* 14 (January 1959): 41–42, 44–46.

14. Savitt, "Invisible Malady," 745.

15. See, for example, "The People's Fight against Sickle Cell Anemia Begins," *Black Panther*, May 22, 1971; and "Black Genocide: Sickle Cell Anemia," *Black Panther*, April 10, 1971.

16. "Medicine and Fascism," *Black Panther*, June 14, 1969; and Brody, "Panthers Map a People's Medical Plan."

17. Robert B. Scott, "Health Care Priority and Sickle Cell Anemia," *Journal of the American Medical Association* 214 (1970): 731.

18. Ibid.

19. Ibid., 733.

20. Ibid.

21. The foundation was also referred to as the People's Sickle Cell Anemia Fund.

22. For example, Small and Williams met at Stanford on November 6, 1971 ("Work Ledger").

23. A short item requesting donation for the foundation stated "the Party is initiating a program to help research really begin that can eventually discover the cure" (*Black Panther*, May 1, 1971; see also "Fight against Sickle Cell Anemia, *Black Panther*, June 26, 1971).

24. For example, one solicitation for donations to support the sickle cell anemia campaign sought support to initiate "a program to help research really

begin that can eventually discover the cure . . . a fund has been established for this purpose" (*Black Panther,* May 1, 1971).

25. Tolbert S. Small, interview with author, October 18, 2005, Oakland, California; see also Black Panther Party, "Sickle Cell Anemia Research Foundation," *CoEvolution Quarterly* 3 (Fall 1974): 23.

26. Small, interview.

27. For example, "Combatting Genocide"; Williams, *Black Panther,* December 4, 1971.

28. One such solicitation carried the heading, "You Can Help Destroy One of the Attempts to Commit Black Genocide"(*Black Panther,* May 1, 1971). I was unable to locate any information to suggest that the Party's planned research foundation ever initiated research projects, although in an issue of the *CoEvolution Quarterly* edited by the Party, it claimed to "maintain a national advisory committee of doctors to research" the disease ("Sickle Cell Anemia Research Foundation," 23).

29. Black Panther Party, "Sickle Cell Anemia Research Foundation," 23; *Black Panther Intercommunal News Service,* November 15, 1975.

30. Gies, "Father's Story," 190.

31. L. Pauling, H. Itano, S. Singer, and I. Wells, "Sickle Cell Anemia, a Molecular Disease," *Science* 110 (1949): 543–48. For accounts of the meeting with the physician William Castle, which led Pauling to investigate sickle cell anemia, see Linus Pauling, *In His Own Words: Selected Writings, Speeches, and Interviews,* ed. Barbara Marinacci (New York: Simon and Schuster, 1995), 116–18; and Conley, "Sickle Cell Anemia," 338–46. On electrophoresis, see Stuart J. Edelstein, *The Sickled Cell: From Myths to Molecules* (Cambridge, Mass.: Harvard University Press, 1986), 92–93; Conley, "Sickle Cell Anemia," 338–42. See also Wailoo, *Drawing Blood,* 155.

32. On electrophoresis, see Edelstein, *Sickled Cell,* 92–93; Conley, "Sickle Cell Anemia," 338–42. See also Wailoo, *Drawing Blood,* 155.

33. Davis, telephone interview.

34. Ibid. Elaine Ayala, "Black Inventor Busts Stereotypes," *San Antonio Express-News,* February 26, 2006, http://mysanantonio.com/default/article/ Black-Inventor-busts-Stereotypes.php.

35. Davis, telephone interview.

36. "Interview of Dr. Tolbert Small by Lewis Cole," 8; Adam Bernstein, "Roland B. Scott Dies; Sickle Cell Researcher," *Washington Post,* December 12, 2002.

37. "Interview of Dr. Tolbert Small by Lewis Cole," 22; Kimberly Hayes Taylor, "Remembering a Pioneer: Dr. Charles Whitten," *Detroit News,* September 5, 2008, http://www.detnews.com/apps/pbcs.dll/article?AID=/20080905/ OBITUARIES/809050405/1263/OBITUARIES.

38. Bert Small, e-mail correspondence with author, March 10, 2009; Kupers, interview; Davis, telephone interview.

39. Quoted in Hilliard and Cole, *This Side of Glory,* 383.

40. Scott, "Health Care Priority and Sickle Cell Anemia," 733.

41. Ibid.

42. Wailoo, *Drawing Blood*.

43. *Hearings before the Subcommittee on Health of the Committee on Labor and Public Welfare of the United States, Ninety-Second Congress, S.676, To Provide for the Prevention of Sickle Cell Anemia,* November 11, 12 (Washington, D.C.: U.S. Government Printing Office, 1971), 20.

44. "People's Fight against Sickle Cell Anemia Begins." Similar sentiment appears in an earlier article as well: see "Black Genocide."

45. Small, interview with author, May 12, 2006; Tolbert Small, personal notes from SCA campaign tour (copy in author's possession); "Dr. Tolbert Small: Journey of a People's Doctor," 6. Satchel, who had been minister of health (sometimes referred to as deputy minister of medicine) for the Chicago Party, came to the Bay Area shortly after the Panthers Mark Clark and Fred Hampton were murdered as they slept during a raid by the Chicago police department in December 1969; Satchel was shot and seriously injured in this incident.

46. "People's Fight against Sickle Cell Anemia Begins."

47. "Sickle Cell Anemia: From Despair to Hope," *Black Panther,* April 1, 1972.

48. Stepan and Gilman, "Appropriating the Idioms of Science." I return to this discussion below.

49. Black Panther Party, "Sickle Cell Anemia Research Foundation," 23; Michael G. Michaelson, "Sickle Cell Anemia: An 'Interesting Pathology,'" in *Anti-Racist Science Teaching,* ed. Dawn Gill and Les Levidow (London: Free Association Books, 1987), 62–63.

50. Including Health and Community Action Committee, "People's Health Center Vandalized," April 3, 1971, 3; "Black Genocide"; "You Can Help Destroy One of the Attempts to Commit Black Genocide—Fight Sickle Cell Anemia," May 1, 1971, 12; "Free Sickle Cell Anemia Tests," June 5, 1971, 6; "Twenty-Five Doctors Have Not Helped Sickle Cell Victim," August 14, 1971, 4; "'So, He Has Sickle Cell Anemia,'" September 25, 1971; Williams, "Combatting Genocide," 3–4, 17–18; "Sickle Cell Anemia: From Despair to Hope," April 1, 1972; "Sickle Cell 'Game'"; "Phoney Sickle Cell Group Conspires with Police in Panther Arrests! Bobby Seale Exposes Los Angeles Sickle Cell Foundation's Treachery," *Black Panther,*" August 19, 1972, 3, 9–10; "Racism and Red Blood Cells," October 7, 1972, 5, 13; and "BPP Trains Houstonians for Free Medical Testing Program," June 22, 1974, 5.

51. For example, the Party served as guest editors of the West Coast alternative press magazine the *CoEvolution Quarterly,* and used this publication as a platform to detail all of its community service programs, including its ambulance service, sickle cell anemia campaign, and health clinics. The Boston chapter of the Party broadcast a half-hour show on sickle cell anemia in 1971 on the local Public Broadcasting Service affiliate, WGBH (to the consternation of some) during which it "charge[d] that the medical profession has ignored the disease because it almost exclusively afflicts blacks." See "A TV Channel Gives

Prime Time to Anyone with a Cause or Gripe," *Wall Street Journal,* December 16, 1971.

52. Sickle cell anemia disease results from the presence of recessive traits in both parents. When this is the case, there is a 50 percent chance of a child being a carrier of the sickle cell trait (heterozygous), a 25 percent chance that the child will contract the disease (homozygous), and a 25 percent chance that the child will be completely unaffected. Recent figures indicate that one in five hundred (or 0.2 percent) persons of African descent have sickle cell anemia disease and that one in twelve (or approximately 8 percent) carry the genetic trait (U.S. Department of Health and Human Services, Public Health Service, National Institutes of Health, National Heart, Lung and Blood Institute, "Sickle Cell Anemia," 1996, http://www.nlm.nih.gov/medlineplus/sicklecellanemia .html). Individuals who are carriers of the sickle cell trait typically show no symptoms of the disease or experience no ill effects from their carrier status.

53. "Sickle Cell Anemia: From Despair to Hope," *Black Panther,* April 1, 1972; and Williams, "Combatting Genocide."

54. Despite the decidedly middle-brow nature of his show, Douglas was no stranger to the concerns of African American communities, having hosted both Martin Luther Jr. and Malcolm X a few years prior.

55. By "authentic expertise" I refer to the legitimacy vested in medical professionals and scientific researchers by lay communities based on shared cultural experiences or histories *and* scientific authority. See Alondra Nelson, "The Factness of Diaspora: The Social Sources of Genetic Genealogy," in *Revisiting Race in a Genomics Era,* ed. Barbara Koenig, Sandra Soo-Jin Lee, and Sarah Richardson (New Brunswick, N.J.: Rutgers University Press, 2009), 253–70.

56. Williams's work with the Party included writing articles, including some of the very few bylined in its newspaper. See, for example, Williams, "Combatting Genocide." This article encapsulated the substance of Williams's presentation on *The Mike Douglas Show.*

57. Tapper, *Drawing Blood,* 3–4. He writes, "Throughout the twentieth century, sickling has emerged and reemerged at the intersection of a variety of medical, genetic, serological, anthropological, personal, and administrative discourses on whiteness, hybridity, tribes and citizenship."

58. Brown, interview, December 6, 2008.

59. Black Panther Party, "Sickle Cell Anemia Research Foundation," 7.

60. Ibid., 24.

61. Michael Tabor, *The Plague: Capitalism Plus Dope Equals Genocide* (Party pamphlet); "The Sterilization Bill," *Black Panther,* March 13, 1971; "Sterilize Welfare Mothers?" *Black Panther,* May 1, 1971; and "'They Told Me I Had to Be Sterilized or Die': Racist Doctors Try to Give Black Panther Party Comrade Genocidal Hysterectomy," *Black Panther,* July 15, 1972.

62. Jonathan Spivak, "Boon or Bane for Blacks? The Battle against Sickle-Cell Anemia Progresses, But It Brings Some Problems Along with Results," *Wall Street Journal,* January 4, 2008; Howard Markel, "Appendix 6: Scientific

Advances and Social Risks: Historical Perspectives on Genetic Screening Programs for Sickle Cell Disease, Tay-Sachs Disease, Neural Tube Defects, and Down Syndrome, 1970–1997," in *Promoting Safe and Effective Genetic Testing in the United States: Final Report of the Task Force on Genetic Testing*, ed. Neil A. Holtzman and Michael Watson (Washington, D.C.: Human Genome Research Institute, 1997), 165; Bowman, "Sickle Cell Screening," 40–54. However, the October 7, 1972, issue of the *Black Panther* included a reprint of an article from the alternative paper the *Chicago Guide* by now-renowned journalist Edwin Black about its sickle cell anemia campaign that was critical of the city's board of health for failing to provide genetic counseling to those to whom it had administered genetic tests. The article stated that "obviously, if both parents have the trait, they could have been counseled against further contraception and on how to care for their offspring, should the children be diseased. Although the article was not authored by the Party, its reprinting suggested the Party's endorsement and undercut its accusations of state genocide. See "Racism and Red Blood Cells," *Black Panther*, October 7, 1972.

63. On the concept of "life itself," see Nikolas Rose, *The Politics of Life Itself* (Princeton, N.J.: Princeton University Press, 2007). For Foucault, the state's ability "to make live and to let die" are expressions of "biopower" in the modernity.

64. "People's Fight against Sickle Cell Anemia Begins."

65. William L. Patterson, ed., *We Charge Genocide: The Crime of Government against the Negro People* (1951; repr. New York: International Publishers, 1970), xiv. Although the UN did not respond to the report, owing to pressure from the American delegation, it received widespread attention in the domestic and international press. Two similar petitions, edited by W. E. B. Du Bois, were submitted to the UN in the 1940s.

66. Patterson, *We Charge Genocide*, xiv.

67. Spivak, "Boon or Bane for Blacks?" 22.

68. "Black Genocide."

69. Tolbert Small, "Address to Li'l *[sic]* Bobby Hutton Day Celebration," *Commemorator*, May 2005, 4.

70. "Black Genocide." Slavery and sickling were frequently associated in the organization's written media. One item, for example, stated that the "disease originated primarily as the body's own protection from malaria—before black people were carted here from Africa to become slaves." See "So, He Has Sickle Cell Anemia." This article, moreover, frames sickle cell anemia as a problem of the black "nation" in its totality, though it affects relatively small numbers of people of African descent. In the United States, one in twelve blacks have the sickle cell anemia trait, and one in four hundred to five hundred persons have the disease. As such, sickle cell anemia was depicted as a disease of the African American body politics, with the individual body in "crisis" standing in for the all blacks. For more on sickling as an ill of the "black social body," see Tapper, *In the Blood*, 104.

71. Anthony C. Allison, "Protection Afforded by Sickle-Cell Trait against

Subtertian Malarial Infection," *British Medical Journal*, February 6, 1954, 290–94. The sickling of red blood cells in those with the sickle cell anemia trait inhibits the growth of the malaria parasite. See also Anthony Allison, "The Distribution of the Sickle-Cell Anemia Trait in East Africa and Elsewhere, and Its Apparent Relationship to the Incidence of Subtertian Malaria," *Transactions of the Royal Society of Tropical Medicine and Hygiene* 48 (1954): 312–18; and Conley, "Sickle Cell Anemia," 331. Tapper notes that Allison's observation was a product of the project of colonial medicine. He writes, "The natural selection approach owed much to colonial medicine, as did the migration-miscegenation discourse. . . . Traveling throughout the British colonies, he [Allison] had long been involved in the colonial medical project of drawing blood and establishing racial and tribal affinities. Privy to the malaria association's findings over the years, he eventually marshaled the available evidence to advance the hypothesis that carriers of the sickle-cell trait were immune to malaria" (*In the Blood*, 87). For a biographical sketch of Allison, see Conley, "Sickle Cell Anemia," 350–53. See also Wailoo, *Drawing Blood*, 180–81.

72. Self, "'To Plan Our Liberation,'" 767–68. In addition, Shakur's biography notes that Afrocentricity was one point on which the New York chapter of the Party diverged ideologically from the Oakland-based national headquarters (*Assata*, 190).

73. On sickling, African history, and appeal of Allison's findings for African American cultural politics, see Wailoo, *Drawing Blood*, 180.

74. Wailoo, *Drawing Blood*, 160; see also Tapper, *In the Blood*, 87. Subsequent research by the anthropologist Frank Livingstone offered that malaria was endemic to regions where slash-and-burn agriculture was used, changing the existing ecosystem such that humans became the most available host for the malaria parasite. See Frank B. Livingstone, "Anthropological Implications of Sickle Cell Gene Distribution in West Africa," *American Anthropologist* 60 (1958): 533–62.

75. *Black Panther*, December 4, 1971.

76. Testimony of Representative Dan Kuykendall, *Hearings before the Subcommittee*, 33; also quoted in Wailoo, *Dying in the City of Blues*, 188–89.

77. James B. Herrick, "Peculiar Elongated and Sickle-Shaped Red Blood Corpuscles in a Case of Severe Anemia," *Archives of Internal Medicine* 6 (1910): 517–21. An account of Herrick's contribution is also provided in Conley, "Sickle Cell Anemia." Although Herrick's intern, Ernest Irons, had previously alerted Herrick to the sickling of red blood cells in the patient, Herrick's publication is regarded as its "discovery" in the medical literature. See Todd L. Savitt and Morton F. Goldberg, "Herrick's 1910 Case Report of Sickle Cell Anemia: The Rest of the Story," *Journal of the American Medical Association* 261 (1989): 266–71. Sickle cell anemia disease was known in African oral history. Savitt writes, "Though Western medicine did not discover SCA until Herrick's report in 1910, the condition had actually existed for centuries: first in Africa and the southern Mediterranean area and later, transported by black slaves, in the West

Indies, South America, and the United States. African tribes in Ghana, Nigeria, and the Cameroons had known of the disease and had named it centuries earlier. Oral traditions had kept knowledge of SCA and its hereditary character alive for each succeeding generation" ("Invisible Malady," 739–40). Probable cases of the disease were described in eighteenth-century southern medical papers. See Savitt, *Medicine and Slavery*.

78. For example, in 1943, a southern physician, M. A. Ogden, wrote that "intermarriages between Negroes and white persons directly endanger the white race by transmission of the sickling trait. . . . Such intermarriages, therefore, should be prohibited by federal law" ("Sickle Cell Anemia in the White Race," *Archives of Internal Medicine* 71 [1943]: 164–82, quoted in Wailoo, *Drawing Blood*, 137. See also Tapper, *In the Blood*, 3.

79. Ogden, "Sickle Cell Anemia in the White Race," 164–82, quoted in Wailoo, *Drawing Blood*, 137.

80. Savitt, "Invisible Malady," 744.

81. On sickling and the privileging of patient's experience, see Wailoo, *Dying in the City of the Blues*, 167–68. An exemplary case study of how "experiential knowledge" can be mobilized by activists is presented in Epstein, *Impure Science*.

82. Following Wailoo, this perspective was also consistent with "African medicine's historical concern for pain and the patient's experience" (*Dying in the City of the Blues*, 167).

83. Arthur Kleinman, *The Illness Narratives: Suffering, Healing, and the Human Condition* (New York: Basic Books, 1988), 49.

84. A first-person account from a sickle cell sufferer was published more than a decade prior to the Party's illness narratives in the black issues magazine *Ebony*. In the article "'I'm Living on Borrowed Time,'" twenty-one-year-old college student, Marclan Walker, described the more than 250 blood transfusions that had been required to keep her alive and her struggle to finish school, despite the hurdle presented by her illness. See Marclan A. Walker, "'I'm Living on Borrowed Time,'" *Ebony*, January 1959, 41–46.

85. "America's Racist Negligence in Sickle Cell Research Exposed by Its Victims, *Black Panther*, June 19, 1971, 3–4.

86. Ibid.

87. There were other instances in which having the trait for sickle cell anemia or the disease itself was used to justify educational or workplace restrictions. For example, after four unrelated deaths of U.S. Army basic training recruits in high altitudes were associated with the sickle cell anemia trait, the U.S. Air Force banned those with the trait or disease from flight duty. This ban lasted for six years. See Duster, *Backdoor to Eugenics*, 24–28. Yet the Party argued that such exclusions could be highly subjective and politically motivated, as was alleged to be the case with Army Private James Powell. According to the Panthers' account, Powell, who was a carrier of sickle cell trait, was denied a medical discharge and thus exemption from military service in Vietnam (which required a

long, pain-inducing flight). Moreover, he was subsequently assigned to duty at a military base located at a high altitude in Colorado despite the fact that others in the armed forces were being excused from some duties based on their sickling carrier status. The state "discriminated against" Powell, the Party contended, by using the soldier as "cannon fodder for the U.S. Imperialists' genocidal military aggression against innocent Vietnamese people" rather than attending to his healthcare needs. For more on the risks of discrimination presented by genetic screening, see also Dorothy Nelkin and Laurence Tancredi, *Dangerous Diagnostics: The Social Power of Biological Information* (Chicago: University of Chicago Press, 1994).

88. The Panther leader's imperious presence also brought into relief a gender paradox both of the Party's vanguard philosophy of "serving the people body and soul" and of its valorization of popular wisdom; for this positioning of Seale (and by implication Party cadre) as the caretaker of these women had the subtle effect of undermining the very experiential knowledge it sought to celebrate, by perhaps rendering it subject to male authority.

89. In a discussion of Claudette Colvin and Rosa Parks, she writes insightfully about the role of the icon of the respectable woman in civil rights movement era politics.

90. "America's Racist Negligence," 4.

91. Ibid.

92. Ibid.

93. Ibid.

94. "Another Battle Lost in War on Black Genocide: Sickle Cell Anemia Claims Life of 11-Year Old," *Black Panther*, August 19, 1972.

95. "So, He Has Sickle Cell Anemia."

96. Kleinman, *Illness Narratives*, 3, 5.

97. Ibid., 6.

98. "BPP Trains Houstonians for Free Medical Testing Program"; "Legacy of the Black Panther Party," *It's About Time*, Fall–Winter 2001, 11.

99. Brody, "Panthers Map a People's Medical Plan," 9.

100. Anonymous, "Sickledex—a Rapid Sickle-Cell Screening Test," *Medical Letter on Drugs and Therapeutics*, July 25, 1969, 61; D. M. Canning and R. G. Huntsman, "An Assessment of Sickledex as an Alternative to the Sickling Test," *Journal of Clinical Pathology* 23 (November 1970): 736–37; James B. Powell and Douglas J. Beach, "A Modification of the 'Sickledex' Test for Hemoglobin S," *Clinical Chemistry* 17 (October 1970): 1055–56; and J. M. Ravi, "Detection of Hemoglobin S Utilizing Sickledex Solubility, Reduced Oxygen Tension, and Electrophoresis," *American Journal of Medical Technology* 38 (January 1972): 7–8. In 1953 H. A. Itano, a coauthor of Pauling's important work on the molecular attributes of hemoglobin S, reported that HbS was insoluble when placed in a phosphate buffer solution. Drawing from Itano's observation, a solubility test that used a dithionite-phosphate reagent to detect the presence of HbS in a blood sample was developed. See Israel Davidsohn, "The Blood," in

Todd-Sanford Clinical Diagnosis by Laboratory Methods, ed. Israel Davidsohn and John Bernard Henry, 13th ed. (Philadelphia: Saunders, 1974), 19.

101. Small, interview with author, February 26, 2006.

102. "Sickledex—a Rapid Sickle Cell Screening Test," 61. The pathologists Canning and Huntsman described the test similarly as "reliable in inexperienced hands"; see D. M. Canning and R. G. Huntsman, "An Assessment of Sickledex as an Alternative to Sickling Test," *Journal of Clinical Pathology* 23 (8): 736–37.

103. Brody, "Panthers Map a People's Medical Plan." Sickledex is the brand name of a differential solubility test. Slide elution tests were also used by the Party and had limitations similar to that of Sickledex as described below.

104. The research that would make Linus Pauling famous was his introduction of a technique typically used in chemistry—electrophoresis—a technology adapted from chemistry by Pauling and his colleagues to test the electrophoretic mobility of hemoglobin molecules.

105. "Sickledex," 61.

106. "Another Battle Lost," 6; "Interview with Dr. Tolbert Small by Lewis Cole."

107. "BPP Trains Houstonians for Free Medical Testing Program," 5; Edwin Black, "Racism in Red Blood Cells: The Chicago 45,000 and the Board of Health," *Chicago Guide*, September 1972, 5; "Black Panther Party to Provide Free Sickle Cell Anemia Test to Black," *Medium* (Seattle), December 17, 1970, 1. Although only these nine clinics carried out sickle cell testing, because much of the Party's health education outreach took place via forms of widely and readily disseminated media, to some extent the entire network of PFMCs might be said to have participated in the sickle cell anemia campaign.

108. Black, "Racism in Red Blood Cells," 5; Turner, "Free Health Clinics," 1350.

109. Zane and Jeffries, "Panther Sighting," 74.

110. Black, "Racism in Red Blood Cells," 5. This chapter subsequently administered Sickledex tests to students at additional elementary schools, a high school, and a junior college in the greater Chicago metropolitan area. See also "Will the Real Sickle Cell Program Please Come Forward," *Black Panther*, February 5, 1972; and Turner, "Free Health Clinics," 1348.

111. Black, "Racism in Red Blood Cells," 5. See also "Will the Real Sickle Cell Program Please Come Forward"; and Turner, "Free Health Clinics," 1348.

112. "The Black Panther Party's Anti-War, African Liberation, Voter Registration, Survival Conference," *Black Panther*, June 10, 1972.

113. On Portland, Davis, telephone interview. See also "Panthers Sweep Berkeley Elections!" *Black Panther*, June 10, 1972.

114. "Dr. Tolbert Small: Journey of a People's Doctor," 7. Electrophoretic analysis was also required in those instances in which the liquid's density was "borderline"; see "Sickledex," 61.

115. Susan Reverby, *Tuskegee's Truths: Rethinking the Tuskegee Syphilis Study* (Chapel Hill: University of North Carolina Press, 2000).

116. Small, interview.

117. Small, interview with author, October 18, 2005. See also "Dr. Tolbert Small: Journey of a People's Doctor."

118. Ibid.; "Interview of Dr. Tolbert Small by Lewis Cole"; Armour, interview.

119. Zane and Jeffries, "Panther Sighting," 73–74.

120. Black, "Racism in Red Blood Cells," 13.

121. "Fred Hampton Memorial Clinic Offers Free Health Services," *Chicago Guide*, April 29, 1970.

122. Davis, telephone interview.

123. Black, "Racism in Red Blood Cells," 5, 13.

124. Ibid., 43.

125. Ibid.

126. Ibid.

127. Duster, *Backdoor to Eugenics*, 47–48.

128. Roberts, *Killing the Black Body*, 257. Lack of knowledge about sickle cell anemia was widespread. Health activists and health organizations were not the only ones to commit the error of confusing sickle cell trait and disease. For example, a sickle cell law in Washington, D.C., "equated sickle cell anemia with a communicable disease." In the state of Massachusetts, a "sickle cell anemia law" confused the disease and the trait, referring to "the disease, known as sickle cell trait or sickle cell anemia" (all quotes from Robert Milton Schmidt, "Law, Medicine, and Public Policy: The Sickle Cell Anemia Control Act of 1972, A Case Study" [PhD diss., Emory University, 1982], 60, 67. Schmidt was program director of the Center for Disease Control National Sickle Cell Disease Laboratory from 1972 to 1978).

129. Roberts, *Killing the Black Body*, 257.

130. Markel, "Appendix 6," 163. See also Leslie Roberts, "One Worked; the Other Didn't (Genetic Screening Programs for Tay-Sachs and Sickle Cell Anemia)," *Science*, January 5, 1990, 18.

131. Markel, "Appendix 6," 163. See also Roberts, "One Worked," 18.

132. Hilliard and Cole, *This Side of Glory*, 339.

133. Bert Lubin, interview with author, October 7, 2007, Oakland, California.

134. Davis, telephone interview.

135. Keith Wailoo, "Detecting 'Negro Blood': Black and White Identities and the Reconstruction of Sickle Cell Anemia," in *Drawing Blood*, 154.

136. Ward Churchill and Jim Vander Wall, *Agents of Repression: The FBI's Secret War against the Black Panther Party and the American Indian Movement* (Boston: South End, 1988); Brian Glick, *War at Home: Covert Action against U.S. Activists and What We Can Do about It* (Boston: South End, 1989); Nelson Blackstock, *COINTELPRO: The FBI's Secret War on Political Freedom* (New York: Vintage, 1975); and Ward Churchill and Jim Vander Wall, *The COINTELPRO Papers: Documents from the FBI's Secret Wars against Domestic Dissent* (Boston: South End, 1990).

137. Churchill and Vander Wall, *Agents of Repression*, 37–99.

138. During the Watergate scandal, it was also revealed that Huey P. Newton

and the Black Panther Party had been identified by the Nixon administration in 1971 as an "enemy" of the White House. See Paul Houston, "White House Plan to Use IRS to Harass Foes Told in Memos," *Los Angeles Times,* June 28, 1973; and "White House List of Nixon 'Enemies,'" *Los Angeles Times,* June 28, 1973.

139. In Chicago the FBI used a media smear campaign to discredit the local Party chapter's Breakfast for Children program (Churchill and Vander Wall, *Agents of Repression,* 68).

140. Lincoln Webster Sheffield, "People's Medical Care Center," in Foner, *Black Panthers Speak,* 173.

141. Hilliard and Cole, *This Side of Glory,* 383; also Churchill and Vander Wall, *COINTELPRO Papers,* 146 and chap. 5; and J. F. Palmer Jr., "Out to Get the Panthers," *Nation,* July 28, 1969.

142. Brown, *Taste of Power,* 196; Churchill and Vander Wall, *COINTELPRO Papers,* 142–43; Churchill and Vander Wall, *Agents of Repression,* 68.

143. Churchill and Vander Wall, *Agents of Repression,* 68.

144. Churchill and Vander Wall, *COINTELPRO Papers,* 159, 161–64.

145. "Phoney Sickle Cell Group Conspires with Police."

146. From FBI file, p. 56, roll 58, slides 112–13.

147. Ibid.

148. Ibid., 57.

149. On the evolution of the Nixon's sickle cell initiative, see Schmidt, "Law, Medicine, and Public Policy," 82.

150. "President's Message to Congress," *Weekly Compilation of Presidential Documents* (Washington, D.C.: Government Printing Office, 1971), 253–54. The Party's sickle cell anemia campaign preceded Nixon's address.

151. Savitt argues that it was the twinned effects of Scott's 1970 *JAMA* article and the Nixon address that transformed sickle cell anemia from "an unknown disease" to "a recognizable badge of black identity and subject of explosive national importance" ("Invisible Malady," 745).

152. Schmidt, "Law, Medicine, and Public Policy," 19.

153. Wailoo, *Dying in the City of Blues,* 113.

154. In addition, the heavyweight boxer Joe Frazier, whose son Mark has sickle cell anemia, established the Yancy Durham Jr. Memorial Clinic for the treatment of sickle cell anemia in Philadelphia ("Frazier Joins Sickle Cell Fight," *Los Angeles Times,* November 5, 1973).

155. *Hearings before the Subcommittee,* 20. Scott's study was also invoked by Senator Ted Kennedy, a cosponsor of the bill, as well as senators Jacob Javits and Edward W. Brooke *(Hearings before the Subcommittee).*

156. This act, Public Law 92-294, which was unanimously approved by both the U.S. Senate and House of Representatives, was passed on May 16, 1972.

157. "Sickle Cell 'Game.'"

158. Brown, *Taste of Power,* 276–77.

159. "Sickle Cell 'Game.'"

160. Williams, "Combatting Genocide."

161. "Sickle Cell 'Game.'"

162. My use of *categorical* is drawn from the sociologist Steven Epstein's use of the same term. Epstein writes of "'categorical alignment'—the merging of social categories from the worlds of medicine, social movements, and state administration." The Party's response to the mainstreaming of sickle cell anemia eradication suggests that the categorical statement process may extract different types and degrees of concessions from distinct stakeholders, with activists potentially having the most to lose. The Black Panther example, in which varied black philanthropies and cultural groups vied to speak on behalf of African Americans' biological citizenship, also indicates that the agents who fill the "activist" function in the categorical alignment process may be moderates and reformers rather than health radicals. See Epstein, *Inclusion*, 13, 90–93.

163. Tapper, *In the Blood*, 113.

164. Although both organizations had been involved with black health issues for many years. See, for example, Gamble, *Making a Place for Ourselves*; *Hearings before the Subcommittee*, 21.

165. Spivak, "Boon or Bane for Blacks?" 22.

166. Ibid.

167. Elaine Brown, Flores Forbes, and some others who were actively involved with the Party in the early 1970s argue that the organization's change of course during this time did not reflect a shift to less radical politics. Rather, they contend that the group's engagements with health politics and electoral politics were facets of a reimagined (but never discarded) revolutionary strategy. With this new strategy, the Party aimed to incrementally take over the city of Oakland by assuming positions as political appointees and elected officials. I have no reason to doubt that this was the Party's intent. However, because members of the organization were aware of this strategy but members of the general public were not necessarily, the impression—and most importantly, the overall effect—was of a shift to a more reformist position. See Flores Forbes, *Will You Die with Me? My Life and the Black Panther Party* (New York: Atria Books, 2006); Brown, *Taste of Power*, chaps. 15, 16; Brown, interview.

168. Black Panther Party, "Sickle Cell Anemia Research Foundation," 23.

169. Ibid. In her autobiography, Brown recalled that Party members without medical training worked as "maintenance people, records clerks, drivers, and liaisons with medical professionals" (*Taste of Power*, 330).

170. "Community Health Fair Emphasized Preventative Medicine," *Black Panther*, July 28, 1975.

5. As American as Cherry Pie

1. For more on the Party's health-related programs, see Black Panther Party (guest editors), *CoEvolution Quarterly* 3 (Fall 1974). For information on the radical health movement that was contemporaneous with the Party's activism, see, for example, Ehrenreich and Ehrenreich, *American Health Empire*; Ann

Arbor Science for the People Collective, *Biology as a Social Weapon* (Minneapolis: Burgess, 1977); and Robert J. Bazell, "Health Radicals: Crusade to Shift Medical Power to the People," *Science*, August 6, 1971, 506–9. For a historical account of one aspect of the radical health movement, see Rogers, "'Caution.'" For women's health advocacy, see Boston Women's Health Book Collective, *Our Bodies, Our Selves: A Course by and for Women* (Boston: Boston Women's Health Course Collective and New England Free Press, 1971); and *Ruzek, Women's Health Movement*.

2. Herbert Weiner and Joe Yamamoto, "Obituary: Louis Jolyon West, M.D. (1924–1999)," *Archives of General Psychiatry* 56 (July 1999): 669.

3. For example, David Abrahamsen, "Comeback of Violence in America," *US News and World Report*, October 22, 1973, 45–49; Joseph Morgenstern, "New Violence," *Newsweek*, February 14, 1972, 66–69; Jesse L. Steinfeld, "TV Violence Is Harmful," *Readers Digest*, April 1973, 37–38; P. J. Weber, "Violence Stalks the Land," *America*, December 29, 1973, 501–3; and National Center for Health Statistics, "Death Rates for Assault (Homicide), according to Sex, Race, Hispanic Origin and Age: United States, Selected Years, 1950–99 (Table 46)" (Hyattsville, Md.: U.S. Department of Health and Human Services, Center for Disease Control and Prevention, 2001), 215.

4. A COPAP leader described the organization as a "Bay Area group" of "primarily social scientists, lawyers, and physicians" that came together "out of our joint work last year in questioning the propriety of the psychosurgery project that had been proposed through the CCCJ . . . for the University of California, San Francisco" (Edward M. Opton Jr., Ph.D., to Dr. Charles E. Young, Chancellor, University of California, February 14, 1973, 1, Chancellor Charles E. Young Papers, Department of Special Collections, University Archives, University of California, Los Angeles).

5. "H. Rap Brown on Violence," http://www.youtube.com/watch?v=scYQGiybjbY (accessed November 24, 2009).

6. Phil Brown, *Toxic Exposures: Contested Illness and the Environmental Health Movement* (New York: Columbia University Press, 2007).

7. Zola, "Medicine as an Institution of Social Control," in *The Cultural Crisis of Modern Medicine*, ed. J. Ehrenreich (New York: Monthly Review Press, 1978), 95.

8. David Shaw, "Bright, Young Lawyers Seek Social Change," *Los Angeles Times*, September 19, 1974.

9. Kline had worked as an attorney for the Party in the past (Brown, *Taste of Power*, 361–62).

10. Shaw, "Bright, Young Lawyers Seek Social Change," 14.

11. Fred J. Hiestand, "Of Panthers and Prisons: An Interview with Huey P. Newton," *National Lawyers Guild Practitioner* 29 (Summer 1972): 57–65.

12. Fred J. Hiestand, interview with author, June 1, 2006, Sacramento, California.

13. Fred J. Hiestand, telephone interview with author, May 20, 2002.

14. Newton, *War against the Panthers*, 32.

15. Hiestand, telephone interview; see also Shaw, "Bright, Young Lawyers Seek Social Change,"14.

16. Hiestand, interview; see also *Black Panther Party v. Granny Goose*, No. 429566, Alameda I Superior Ct. (1972).

17. See *Black Panther Party v. Kehoe* (1974) 42 C.A.3d.

18. Hiestand, interview. Members of Seniors Against a Fearful Environment were also taught to be peer health workers; working with Party medical cadre, they conducted hypertension testing at the Oakland Tower Senior Citizen Center. See Black Panther Party, "Seniors Against a Fearful Environment (S.A.F.E.)," *CoEvolution Quarterly* 3 (Fall 1974): 19–20; and Shaw, "Bright, Young Lawyers Seek Social Change," 14.

19. Hiestand, telephone interview; Testimony of Fred J. Hiestand before the Senate Health and Welfare Committee, May 9, 1973, Department of Special Collections, Stanford University; and Fred J. Hiestand to UCLA Chancellor Charles Young, August 17, 1973, box 41, Chancellor Charles E. Young Papers, Department of Special Collections, University Archives, University of California, Los Angeles. See also Committee Opposing Psychiatric Abuse of Prisoners to Dr. Charles E. Young, Chancellor, University of California, February 14, 1973, Department of Special Collections, University Archives, University of California, Los Angeles.

20. Brown discussed her working relationship with Anthony Kline of Public Advocates in *Taste of Power* (chaps. 17–18). She also briefly mentions Hiestand on page 407.

21. Jeffrey Ogbar, "Rainbow Radicalism: The Rise of Radical Ethnic Nationalism," in *The Black Power Movement: Rethinking the Civil Rights–Black Power Era*, ed. Peniel E. Joseph (New York: Routledge, 2006). On the Party and the Brown Berets, see Brown, *Taste of Power*, 155. On the Party and UFOC, see Brown, *Taste of Power*, 373–74. On the Party and the NWRO, see Guida West, *The National Welfare Rights Movement: The Social Protest of Poor Women* (New York: Praeger, 1981), 219.

22. "Chronological Sequence of Events—Center for the Study and Reduction of Violence, June 28, 1972 to July 27, 1973," box 41, series 594 (Administrative Files of Chancellor Charles E. Young), Department of Special Collections, University Archives, University of California, Los Angeles; and Stubblebine, Hearing on Proposed Center for the Study and Reduction of Violence at UCLA.

23. Loïc Waquant, "Deadly Symbiosis: When Ghetto and Prison Meet and Mesh," *Punishment and Society* 3 (2001): 95–134; and Ruthie Wilson Gilmore, *Golden Gulag: Prisons, Surplus, Crisis, and Opposition in Globalizing California* (Berkeley: University of California Press, 2007).

24. I will leave for other scholars to consider the place of the violence center in the politics of race and incarceration in the United States. Here I focus on the particular role of the Party in contesting the center, employing a strategy that drew

on its activities in prison politics and personal experiences therein and also in the broader context of its *health* politics and its challenge to medical discrimination.

25. One supporter of the violence center believed that it was the public support from Governor Reagan that undermined the center's success. See Ursula Vils, "UCLA's Strife-Torn Violence Center," *Los Angeles Times*, March 21, 1973. This mistrust of government extended to the federal level. West acknowledged in a *Los Angeles Times* article that "the Watergate revelations have provided 'an example of the power of people high in government to use science . . . for nefarious purposes." The Watergate scandal "raised the level of suspicion of the center's motives" (Harry Nelson, "Watergate Dims Hope for Center on Violence," *Los Angeles Times*, June 15, 1973).

26. William Endicott, "$850 Million Surplus in Taxes Told. Reagan Calls for Refunds," *Los Angeles Times*, January 12, 1973.

27. Ibid.

28. See Verne Orr, Director, California Department of Finance, to Honorable Willie L. Brown, et al., May 2, 1973, UCLA Library, Dr. Louis Jolyon West Papers, Department of Special Collections, University Archives, University of California, Los Angeles.

29. Louis Jolyon West, "Center for Prevention of Violence," Neuropsychiatric Institute, UCLA, September 1, 1972, box 41, series 594 (Administrative Files of Chancellor Charles E. Young), Department of Special Collections, University Archives, University of California, Los Angeles.

30. Ibid.

31. However, there were serious disagreements as to whether to lay the blame at the feet of the U.S. military and its domestic partner, local law enforcement agencies; popular culture; or "militant" activists like the Black Panther Party (William Gamson, "Violence and Political Power," *Psychology Today*, July 1974, 35–41; and Ernest Van Den Haag, "Political Violence and Civil Disobedience," *Commentary*, April 1973, 97–98; see also Abrahamsen, "Comeback of Violence in America"; Morgenstern, "New Violence"; Steinfeld, "TV Violence Is Harmful"; and Weber, "Violence Stalks the Land").

32. Louis Jolyon West, Center for Prevention of Violence proposal, Neuropsychiatric Institute, UCLA, September 1, 1972, Dr. Louis Jolyon West Papers, 1–2, UCLA Library, Department of Special Collections, University Archives, University of California, Los Angeles.

33. Louis Jolyon West, State of California Health and Welfare Agency, Center for the Reduction of Life Threatening Behavior grant proposal, 2, 5–6.

34. See Testimony of Fred J. Hiestand, 4.

35. Ibid.

36. Vernon H. Mark and Frank R. Ervin, *Violence and the Brain* (New York: Harper and Row, 1970), 3. *Violence and the Brain* received mixed reviews. A reviewer in *Psychosomatic Medicine* noted that "the high level of their previous scientific publications lends weight to the interpretations the authors give to their clinical research." Although this reviewer commented that the work was a

"small volume" that seems "hastily written" and that contains "a number of inaccuracies in the bibliography," he concluded that the "importance of the message vastly overshadows deficiencies in the volume." A review by the influential neuroscientist Bryan Jennett described the work as "a biologically oriented approach to the problem of violence." He suggested that the book was a marked departure for a "medical profession [that] has not been greatly involved in the polemics of violence." Jennett observed that the work's "canvas is broad" and concluded that it was "an interesting and unusual little book." See Russell R. Monroe, "Review of *Violence and the Brain*," *Psychosomatic Medicine* 34, no. 3 (1972): 286; and Bryan Jennett, "Review of *Violence and the Brain*," *Journal of Neurology, Neurosurgery, and Psychiatry* 35 (1972): 420.

37. Mark and Ervin, *Violence and the Brain*, 7.

38. Ibid., xi.

39. Ibid., 5.

40. Ibid., 70. A comprehensive history of psychosurgery is provided by Elliot Valenstein in *Great and Desperate Cures: The Rise and Decline of Psychosurgery and Other Radical Treatments for Mental Illness* (New York: Basic Books, 1986).

41. Valenstein, *Great and Desperate Cures*, 30–31.

42. "Letter to the Editor: The Role of Brain Disease in Riots and Urban Violence," *JAMA*, September 11, 1967, 895. A similar thesis was expressed in chapters 11 and 12 of *Violence and the Brain*.

43. Mark report, cited in Gerald Horne, *Fire This Time: The Watts Uprising and the 1960s* (Charlottesville: University Press of Virginia, 1995), 39, 376, 377n.

44. Peter Conrad and Joseph W. Schneider, *Deviance and Medicalization: From Badness to Sickness* (Philadelphia: Temple University Press, 1992).

45. Ibid. Conrad and Schneider maintain that medicalization occurs in five stages: definition of a behavior as deviant; prospecting for medical discovery; competing claim-making by medical and lay communities; legitimacy by authorities (usually the state), and finally, institutionalization, in which a condition or behavior becomes accepted as medicalized by medical profession and in other domains including the legal system.

46. Louis Jolyon West, "Center for Prevention of Violence," Neuropsychiatric Institute, UCLA, September 1, 1972, box 41, series 594 (Administrative Files of Chancellor Charles E. Young), Department of Special Collections, University Archives, University of California, Los Angeles.

47. Louis Jolyon West, Center for the Prevention of Violence proposal, Neuropsychiatric Institute, UCLA, 5, Dr. Louis Jolyon West Papers, Department of Special Collections, University Archives, University of California, Los Angeles.

48. Erving Goffman, *Asylums* (New York: Anchor, 1961). See also Samuel Wallace, "On the Totality of Institutions," in *Total Institutions*, ed. S. E. Wallace (New Brunswick, N.J.: Transaction, 1971), 1–7.

49. See, for example, Arthur R. Jensen, "How Much Can We Boost I.Q. and Scholastic Achievement?" *Harvard Educational Review* 33 (1969): 1–123; and Jensen, *Genetics and Education* (New York: Harper and Row, 1972).

50. Jensen, *Genetics and Education.*

51. "Black Panther Party Challenges Racist to Intellectual Duel," *Black Panther,* September 8, 1973. Courtesy of Billy X. Jennings, Its About Time Black Panther Party Archive, Sacramento, California.

52. On race and psychiatry in the 1960s and 1970s, see Metzl, *Protest Psychosis.* On the persistence on racial science between the end of World War II and the genomic turn, see Jenny Reardon, *Race to the Finish: Identity and Governance in an Age of Genomics* (Princeton, N.J.: Princeton University Press, 2005), 17–44.

53. W. E. B. Du Bois, "The Conservation of Races," American Negro Academy Occasional Papers, no. 2 (1897), in *W.E.B. Du Bois Speaks: Speeches and Addresses, 1890–1919,* ed. Philip Foner (Atlanta: Pathfinder, 1971), 75.

54. "Black Panther Party Challenges Racist to Intellectual Duel."

55. Ibid.

56. Ibid.

57. Epstein, *Impure Science,* 17.

58. On biomedical knowledge and credibility struggles, see Epstein, *Impure Science,* 14–19. Stepan and Gilman identify "scientific counterdiscourses" as a tactic employed by opponents of scientific racism ("Appropriating the Idioms of Science," 183).

59. "Black Panther Party Challenges Racist to Intellectual Duel."

60. Ibid.

61. Richard C. Lewontin, "The Apportionment of Human Diversity," *Evolutionary Biology* 6 (1972): 391–98.

62. "Black Panther Party Challenges Racist to Intellectual Duel."

63. Ibid.

64. Ibid.

65. Ibid.

66. Jessica Mitford, "Experiments behind Bars: Doctors, Drug Companies, and Prisoners," *Atlantic Monthly,* January 1973, 66–73. Mitford was a Party supporter; she raised money and spoke in support of the Panthers' activities. Thus there was likely some mutual influence between the Party's campaign against the medicalization of violence at UCLA and her reporting on research on prisoners at Vacaville. On Mitford's support of the Black Panthers, see Kate Coleman with Paul Avery, "The Party's Over," *New Times,* July 10, 1978, 28.

67. Leroy Aarons, "Brain Surgery Is Tested on 3 California Convicts," *Washington Post,* February 25, 1972.

68. Eldridge Cleaver, *Soul on Ice* (1968; repr. New York: Dell, 1991).

69. George Jackson, *Soledad Brother: The Prison Letters of George Jackson* (New York: Bantam, 1970).

70. See, for example, "Political Prisoners Southern California," *People's News Service* (Southern California chapter), July 13, 1972; and Sharon Williams, "Sharon on Prisons," *Black Panther Community New Service* (Southern California chapter), January 19, 1970.

71. Fred J. Hiestand, telephone interview with author, May 20, 2002.

72. Mitford, "Experiments behind Bars," 72.

73. Hiestand, telephone interview.

74. B. J. Mason, "New Threat to Blacks: Brain Surgery to Control Behavior—Controversial Operations Are Coming Back as Violence Curbs," *Ebony*, February 1973, 62–64, 66, 68, 72.

75. See J. B. Barber, "Psychosurgery: Viewpoint of a Black Neurosurgeon, *Urban Health* 4 (October 1975): 22–23, 48; V. Cohn, "Psychosurgery Makes Gain—Two Black Doctors Urge Limited Use of Operation," *Washington Post*, January 8, 1976; "Minority Speakers Criticize Researchers," *JAMA* 235 (February 1976): 462; and "On the Issue: Psychosurgery—Murder of the Mind (Congressional Black Caucus)," *Essence* 7 (September 1976): 6.

76. Mason, "New Threat to Blacks," 64.

77. Ibid., 63. In an essay on the evolution of psychosurgery, Elliot Valenstein, the foremost historian of brain surgery, explained that evaluations of psychiatric surgical procedures judged success by how manageable the patient became after treatment. He writes, "A number of studies that emphasized the positive results of psychosurgery gave too much weight to the elimination of behavior that was most troublesome to the hospital staff and family and placed less emphasis on the present quality of the life of the lobotomized patients. There is a recurrent and disquieting theme throughout the older psychosurgical literature suggesting that problems of management played too large a role, both in the selection of patients and in the evaluation of the results. . . . Although these descriptions of the consequences of psychosurgery were written by strong advocates of this operation, they contain much that could be used by those opposed to this practice." See Elliot Valenstein, "Historical Perspective," in *The Psychosurgery Debate: Scientific, Legal, and Ethical Perspectives,* ed. Elliot Valenstein (San Francisco: Freeman, 1980), 35, 38.

78. One such pamphlet was the SDS-authored "A UCLA Center for Psychosurgery?" n.d., UCLA Special Collections, Students for a Democratic Society folder. See also "Violence Center Foes at Work," *UCLA Daily Bruin,* January 11, 1974; Byron H. Atkinson, UCLA Oral History Project, 206. On rallies, see Coalition Against Psychosurgery at UCLA and Students for a Democratic Society, "Forum on Psychosurgery and the 'Violence Center'" (announcement flyer), (Administrative Files of Chancellor Charles E. Young), Department of Special Collections, University Archives, University of California, Los Angeles; and Coalition Against Psychosurgery and Human Experimentation and SDS, "Stop Psychosurgery and the UCLA 'Violence Center,'" July 19, 1973 (Administrative Files of Chancellor Charles E. Young), Department of Special Collections, University Archives, University of California, Los Angeles.

79. See "The Psyche and the Surgeon," *New York Times,* September 1973.

80. Louis Jolyon West to Dr. J. M. Stubblebine, director of health, California State Office of Health Planning, January 1973. See also Alan Gilbert, "Shooting Down the Violence Center," *UCLA Daily Bruin,* January 31, 1974; and Ken

Peterson, "Plans for Acquiring Missile Base by Violence Center Fail," *UCLA Daily Bruin*, January 25, 1974. Stubblebine's agency had had jurisdiction over the Neuropsychiatric Institute until it was turned over to the control of UCLA in July 1973. The letters were circulated by the office of state Senator Henry Waxman who had requested correspondence dealing with the violence center (Peterson, "Plans for Acquiring Missile Base by Violence Center Fail").

81. See "Psyche and the Surgeon."

82. Al Hick to Charles V. Keeran, associate director, Administration, Neuro-psychiatric Institute (internal UCLA memo), April 11, 1974, Department of Special Collections, University Archives, University of California, Los Angeles; and Jim Stebinger, "Three Demonstrators Arrested in NPI Office," *UCLA Daily Bruin*, April 12, 1974.

83. See Louis Jolyon West, M.D. to Mr. Tommy Curtis and Mr. Bill Walton, February 12, 1974, box 41, series 594 (Administrative Files of Chancellor Charles E. Young), Department of Special Collections, University Archives, University of California, Los Angeles. A more influential local celebrity, the actor Charlton Heston, was a supporter of the violence center. See Charlton Heston to The Honorable Ronald Reagan, Governor of California, May 15, 1973 (Administrative Files of Chancellor Charles E. Young), Department of Special Collections, University Archives, University of California, Los Angeles.

84. Isidore Ziferstein, "Critic of Violence Center Speaks Out," *Los Angeles Times*, April 11, 1974. For more about Ziferstein's stance on the violence center, see Ursula Vils, "UCLA's Strife-Torn Violence Center," *Los Angeles Times*, March 21, 1973.

85. Hiestand, telephone interview.

86. Report of Budget and Program, Center for the Study and Reduction of Violent Behavior, Phase One (to June 30, 1973), UCLA University Archives, Department of Special Collections, box 42, series 594 (Administrative Files of Chancellor Charles E. Young), Department of Special Collections, University Archives, University of California, Los Angeles; and Verne Orr, Director, California State Department of Finance to Honorable Willie L. Brown, et al., May 2, 1973, box 42, series 594 (Administrative Files of Chancellor Charles E. Young), Department of Special Collections, University Archives, University of California, Los Angeles. For press coverage of these planned allocations of state funds, see David Perlman, "Violence Control—Senators' Doubts," *San Francisco Chronicle*, April 4, 1973; and "State Center for Study of Violence," *Daily Commercial News* (San Francisco), April 11, 1973. Monies allocated in section 28 of the state budget were technically apportioned to the California Department of Health and Welfare, which would then pass these monies on to the violence center.

87. West to Beilenson, June 11, 1973, Dr. Louis Jolyon West Papers, Special Collections, University of California, Los Angeles; and Stubblebine, Hearing on Proposed Center for the Study and Reduction of Violence at UCLA.

88. West expressed this sentiment in a letter to Health and Welfare Committee chair Senator Anthony Beilenson; West to Beilenson, June 11, 1973.

89. Peter Breggin, "The Return of Psychosurgery and Lobotomy," *Congressional Record*, February 24, 1972, 5567. Breggin expressed similar views in *Congressional Record*, March 30, 1973, 11396.

90. *New York Times Magazine*, September 30, 1973. See also Valenstein, *Great and Desperate Cures*.

91. In September 1973 Congress passed the National Research Act. Part of the act placed a two-year moratorium on psychosurgery in facilities or research programs funded by the federal government, until a presidential body, the National Commission for the Protection of Human Subjects of Biomedical and Behavioral Research, could track the extent of the use of surgeries and evaluate whether they were ever necessary or appropriate (The National Commission for the Protection of Human Subjects of Biomedical and Behavioral Research, *Psychosurgery: Reports and Recommendations*, March 14 (Washington, D.C.: U.S. Government Printing Office, 1977).

92. Perlman, "Violence Control—Senators' Doubts."

93. Ibid. For an illuminating discussion of the role of metaphor in social and cultural conceptions of medicine, see Susan Sontag, "Illness as Metaphor," in *Illness as Metaphor and AIDS and Its Metaphors* (New York: Doubleday, 1990).

94. Senator Anthony Beilenson, State of California Health and Welfare Committee, Hearing on Proposed Center for the Study and Reduction of Violence at UCLA, May 9, 1973, boxes 66, 68, series 590, CSRV file, Department of Special Collections, University Archives, University of California, Los Angeles; Senator Anthony Beilenson, State of California Senate Health and Welfare Committee, in the Matter of The Proposed "UCLA" Center for the Study and Reduction of Violence (Reporter's Transcript of Proceedings), April 11, 1973, 1; and Perlman, "Violence Control—Senators' Doubts."

95. Terry Kupers, "Violence Center: Psychotechnology for Repression," *Science for the People*, May 1974, 17–21. See also Kupers, telephone interview with author, October 16, 2007.

96. Fred J. Hiestand, State of California Health and Welfare Committee, Hearing on Proposed Center for the Study and Reduction of Violence at UCLA, May 9, 1973, box 66, 6, series 590, CSRV file, Department of Special Collections, University Archives, University of California, Los Angeles.

97. Ibid.

98. *Black Panther Party et al. v. Center for the Study and Reduction of Violence et al.*, Administrative Complaint, filed Before the California Council on Criminal Justice, July 26, 1973, 1-2, Dr. Huey P. Newton Papers, Department of Special Collections, University Archives, Stanford University Library.

99. *Black Panther Party et al. v. Center for the Study and Reduction of Violence et al.*, Administrative Complaint, filed Before the California Council on

Criminal Justice, July 26, 1973, 7, Dr. Huey P. Newton Papers, Department of Special Collections, University Archives, Stanford University Library.

100. This phrasing appeared in the violence center proposal submitted to the CCCJ on May 1, 1973, and which was initially approved for $750,000.

101. *Black Panther Party et al. v. Center for the Study and Reduction of Violence et al.*, Administrative Complaint, filed Before the California Council on Criminal Justice, July 26, 1973, 7, Dr. Huey P. Newton Papers, Department of Special Collections, University Archives, Stanford University Library.

102. Fred J. Hiestand, State of California Health and Welfare Committee, Hearing on Proposed Center for the Study and Reduction of Violence at UCLA, May 9, 1973, box 66, 20, 22, series 590, CSRV file, Department of Special Collections, University Archives, University of California, Los Angeles. Hiestand claimed that the proposals had been sanitized in response to the fact that there was little evidence that the center's research intentions had truly changed. See *Black Panther Party et al. v. Center for the Study and Reduction of Violence et al.*, Administrative Complaint, filed Before the California Council on Criminal Justice, July 26, 1973, 11, Dr. Huey P. Newton Papers, Department of Special Collections, University Archives, Stanford University Library. Ziferstein characterized the many revisions to the violence center proposal as "'launderings in response to criticism and protests,'" while West described them as being written specifically for the funding audience to whom they were submitted. See Ziferstein, "Critic of Violence Center Speaks Out."

103. Correspondence from Anthony C. Beilenson to Robert H. Lawson, Executive Director, California Council on Criminal Justice, May 21, 1973, CSRV file, Department of Special Collections, University Archives, University of California, Los Angeles.

104. Ibid.

105. 1973 Budget Act (Stats. 1973, Ch. 129, Section 28.8, A.B. 110), 167.

106. Fred J. Hiestand, State of California Health and Welfare Committee, Hearing on Proposed Center for the Study and Reduction of Violence at UCLA, May 9, 1973, box 66, 20, 13, series 590, CSRV file, Department of Special Collections, University Archives, University of California, Los Angeles.

107. "Chronological Sequence of Events," Center for the Study and Reduction of Violence, box 41, series 594 (Administrative Files of Chancellor Charles E. Young), Department of Special Collections, University Archives, University of California, Los Angeles.

108. U.S. Department of Justice, Law Enforcement Assistance Administration Guideline, "Use of LEAA Funds for Psychosurgery and Medical Research," February 14, 1974, Dr. Jolyon West Papers, Department of Special Collections, University Archives, University of California, Los Angeles. In July 1973 the CCCJ, the state agency in charge of allocating federal LEAA funds, had agreed to provide $750,000 in funding to the violence center. These monies were to be matched by state funds. At this time, a CCCJ report said that it believed that no experimentation on prisoners was planned and hoped that the studies at the

center would help curtail violence at California Youth Authority facilities ("The State," *Los Angeles Times*, July 26, 1973, pt. 2; and "$750,000 Grant Approved for Center on Violence Research," *Los Angeles Times*, July 28, 1973, pt. 1). But the LEAA's reversal of this decision six months later effectively meant that previous promises of funding for the center from the CCCJ were withdrawn.

109. Robert A. Jones, "Mind Control Studies Will Lose Funding," *Los Angeles Times*, pt. 1. See also Lesley Ceisner, "United States Bans Crime Fund Use on Behavioral Modification," *New York Times*, February 15, 1974.

110. LEAA guidelines defined medical research as "those medical or surgical procedures on human beings involving: observation, systematic changes in conditions, accompanied by observation before, during, and after these changes are made, and involving some degree of risk, however slight, and which is experimentally applied to the individual subject, not so much in his own interest as in the interest of humanity through the advance of medical science" (Santarelli, "Use of LEAA Funds for Psychosurgery and Medical Research," 1–2; see also Ceisner, "United States Bans Crime Fund Use on Behavioral Modification"; and Jones, "Mind Control Studies Will Lose Funding").

111. Louis Jolyon West, M.D. to Anthony L. Palumbo, Director, Office of Criminal Justice Planning, April 2, 1974, and Anthony L. Palumbo to Louis Jolyon West, M.D., April 10, 1974, Chancellor Charles E. Young Papers, Department of Special Collections, University Archives, University of California, Los Angeles.

112. Memo to Albert A. Barber, et al. from Louis Jolyon West, April 15, 1974, Chancellor Charles E. Young Papers, Department of Special Collections, University Archives, University of California, Los Angeles.

113. Ken Peterson, "Violence Center Draft Receives Major Revision," *UCLA Daily Bruin*, February 8, 1974; and Edwin S. Shneidman, "The Case for Violence Research," *UCLA Daily Bruin*, February 8, 1974. West contended that the change stemmed from the fact that new centers are usually developed for new research endeavors. According to West, the center was not a new research initiative "involving activities unlike anything going on before"; rather, the "Center was mainly a device to get funding for faculty already working in these areas who were not able to develop their work for lack of funds." Later West said that through the CCCJ the LEAA would give away more than $50 million in research money, mostly to the police. "If there are any finds that can be gotten freely, as the law permits, then I say get them. Some of that [CCCJ] money can be used for research if it can be connected with the prevention of crime. We stretched that point and said acts of violence by mentally, emotionally unstable people qualify . . . as I see it: it is a better use of the money to study certain kinds of violence behavior in a medical setting than to buy computers or weapons for the police" (Memo to Albert A. Barber, 16).

114. Shneidman, "Case for Violence Research."

115. Brown, *Taste of Power*, 395–96.

116. Ibid.

117. Armour, interview, March 19, 2009.

118. The violence center controversy might be understood as marking a moment of transition between biologization and medicalization, or bio-medicalization. I use the hyphenated "bio-medicalization" to mark this moment of flux. For Clarke et al., "biomedicalization" refers to the emergence, professionalization, and institutionalization of "scientific medicine," characterized by (1) a *bios*-centered political economy of medicine, illness, and life itself, (2) a focus on "health" very broadly conceived, including enhancement and optimization; (3) intervention of technoscience into biomedicine; (4) a computer- and information-mediated production of biomedical knowledge; and (5) the constitution of "technoscientific identities." Some of these currents are present or just emerging at the time of the Black Panthers' health politics. The Party's initiatives reflected the use of or response to the expansion technological developments including Sickledex and psychosurgery, but did not include the structural technoscientific shifts that Clarke and colleagues describe; its mobilization of sickle cell anemia relied on the framing of the trait and disease as a collective identity, but the identity as an oppressed class, as slave descendants and poor people was more salient. On the other hand, its social health perspective *did* attend to health and well-being in the widest terms in addition to both healing bodies and protecting them from harm. See this important article: Adele E. Clarke, Jennifer Fishman, Jennifer Fosket, Laura Mamo, and Janet Shim, "Biomedicalization: Technoscientific Transformations of Health, Illness, and U.S. Biomedicine," *American Sociological Review* 68 (April): 161–94; and the elaboration of these themes in *Biomedicalization: Technoscience, Health, and Illness in the U.S.*, ed. Adele E. Clarke, Janet Shim, Laura Mamo, Jennifer Fosket, and Jennifer Fishman (Durham, N.C.: Duke University Press, 2010).

119. Conrad and Schneider, *Deviance and Medicalization*, 224–26.

Conclusion

1. Arthur Harris, interview with author, July 15, 2007, Seattle, Washington.

2. Silvers, interview with author; Boston Women's Health Book Collective, ed., *Our Bodies, Ourselves: A Book by and for Women* (New York: Simon and Schuster, 1973).

3. Small named the clinic in honor of Tubman, who in addition to being a leading abolitionist "also performed as a medic in the Union Army." See Wiley Henry, "'Dr. Tubman, We Presume,'" *Tri-State Defender,* June 12–16, 2004.

4. "Dr. Tolbert Small: Journey of a People's Doctor"; "Black Panther Party Members on Way to China," *Los Angeles Times,* March 6, 1972. Eighteen Party members and affiliates were on this trip, including Small, Los Angeles minister of justice Masai Hewitt, Oakland minister of culture Henry Douglas Jr., and Allan Brotsky, an attorney.

5. The Coalition of Concerned Medical Professionals is a voluntary organization that advocates for universal, free preventative health care. Similar to

the Party's health politics coalitions, membership in the organization is open to medical professionals and laypeople, who are provided with training.

6. Interview with author, March 19, 2009.

7. On the history of the New Orleans Party chapter, see Orissa Arend and Judson L. Jeffries, "The Big Easy Was Anything but for the Panthers," in Jeffries, *On the Ground,* 224–72.

8. Ibid., 24.

9. Malik Rahim, UNC Oral History Project, 31. My thanks to Josh Guild for bringing this narrative to my attention. See also Orissa Arend, "Birth of the Common Ground Clinic," *New Orleans Tribune,* October–November 2007, 20–21.

10. Not only did Rahim bring past experience to bear on the formation of Common Ground, he also reactivated activist alliances: "I knew that after seeing that this city was without healthcare, that it was something that had to be developed. . . . it wasn't nothing for me to make a call for healthcare professionals. . . . I knew a doctor that had been in the Party. . . . I made a call out to her; she called other health professionals" (UNC Oral History Project, 24).

11. Ibid., 29–30.

12. Judith Blake, "Panthers' Progress," *Seattle Times,* October 24, 1986.

13. Ibid.

14. Nikolas Rose, "The Politics of Life Itself," *Theory, Culture, and Society* 18 (2001): 1-30; in biopolitical citizenship, see Epstein, *Inclusion,* 21. See also Clark et al., *Biomedicalization,* chap. 1.

15. Petryna, *Life Exposed.*

16. "Civil Rights and Medical Leaders Call for Social Justice in Health Care," National Minority Quality Forum, press release, September 26, 2007, http://www.nmqf.org/press%5CPress%20Release_9-26-07_final-2.pdf.

17. Ibid.

18. Ibid.

19. See http://www.bidil.com/pnt/questions.php#1.

20. "Civil Rights and Medical Leaders Call for Social Justice in Health Care."

21. Anthony Appiah, *In My Father's House: Africa in the Philosophy of Culture* (New York: Oxford University Press, 1992), 46.

INDEX

Aarons, Leroy, 250n67
Abrahamsen, David, 246n3
Abrams, Fred, 170
Abron, JoNina M., 97, 142, 199n14, 205n62, 217n33
access to healthcare services, 8, 10, 14–15, 20, 181; "inclusion-and-difference" paradigm in 1970s, 21, 186; Party's amended ten-point platform and, 73; spatial segregation and psychic distance as hurdle to, 78. *See also* institution building; People's Free Medical Clinics; trusted experts
acupuncture, 71, 182
Affordable Care Act (2010), ix
African American health-focused activism (pre-1966), 23–48; institution building, 24–36; integrationism, 25, 36–42; long-standing tradition of, 8–9, 15–17; politics of knowledge, 25–26, 42–47, 153. *See also* Black Panther Party health politics

African Americans: citizenship contradiction for, 10–11, 184
African culture: collective political memories of, 215n17; cultural nationalism and, 50–55, 72
African Legion, 32
African origins: framing of sickle cell anemia in relation to, 134–35, 238n70
Afro-American Association, 53
Afrocentricity, 239n72
Alameda County Lung Association, 152
Algeria: Fanon's analysis of medical oppression in colonial, 65, 67–69
Allison, Anthony C., 134, 239n71
Alprentice Bunchy Carter People's Free Medical Clinic (Los Angeles), 62, 90, 99–100, 102, 103–9, 113, 226n65
ambulance service, 6, 110, 111, 201n15, 232n178
American Cancer Society, 152

Benford, Robert D., 203n40
Berkeley Free Clinic, 83, 84
Berkeley PFMC. *See* George Jackson
People's Free Medical Clinic
Bernstein, Adam, 235n36
BiDil: differential efficacy by race of,
185, 186, 187
biocultural broker: Party as, 84,
225n39
biological citizenship, 120, 148,
184–85, 234n10, 245n162
biological determinist model of social
aggression, 162, 164
biologically essentialist theories,
Jensen's, 165
biologization of violence, contesting,
xii, 20, 153–80; coalition for,
154, 157–59; hearings before
California Senate Committee on
Health and Welfare and, 171–77;
preventing medicalization of
violence, 155; specific troubling
research projects and, 162–64,
173–75
bio-medicalization: transition
between medicalization and,
256n118; of violence, 179
biomedical racialization, 21, 187; politics of knowledge and disruption
of, 25–26
biomedicine: history of racial formation in, 212n105; medical apartheid in, xi; politics of knowledge
and, 42–48; potential abuse
from exposure to biomedical
power, 20, 69; shift from medicine to, 59
Biondi, Martha, 201n18
biopower, 133, 238n63
Bird, Joan, 228n94
Bischoff Medical, 102
Black, Edwin, 144, 242n107
black communities: gendering of
caretaking in, 207n13; institu-

tion building and, 27, 28; sickle
cell anemia activism and Party
legitimacy in, 116, 119–20
Black Community Survival Conference at De Fremery Park (1972),
1–4, 115, 233n1–2
Black Cross Nurses (BCN), 31–33,
209n49–50; mission of, 32–33
black cultural nationalism. *See* cultural nationalism
"Black Genocide: Sickle Cell Anemia" *(Black Panther)*, 126–27,
134, 238n70
black hate groups: COINTELPRO
against, 146
black hospital movement, 8
Black Panther (weekly newspaper),
xiii, 14; "America's Racist Negligence in Sickle Cell Research
Exposed by Its Victims," 136–37;
on Black Community Survival
Conference attendance, 115;
"Black Genocide: Sickle Cell
Anemia," 126–27, 134, 238n70;
Cleaver's view of community
programs in, 63; editors, 132,
198n14; expanded slate of
community service programs
announced in, 63–64; on failure
of mainstream medicine, 75–76;
as FBI target, 147–48; "Medicine and Fascism," 121; "The
People's Fight against Sickle Cell
Anemia Begins," 125; sickle cell
anemia issue and, 19, 120, 121,
125, 149–50, 238n62; solicitation
of donations for sickle cell anemia, 122, 123–24, 234n23–24,
235n28; on teaching and public
hospitals, 60; on Tuskegee
syphilis study, 16
Black Panther Party: collective oral
histories at fortieth-anniversary
gathering, xiv; community

service orientation, forging of, 17; deradicalization, 1972 as year marking, 2; establishment of, 5–6, 50–51, 55–56, 60, 72; as extension of civil rights era, 9; FBI's efforts to discredit, 124, 146–48, 244n139; formal end in 1980, 22; health problems among activists in, 93–95; iconography, 22; interaction with federal antipoverty programs, 55–57, 60, 72; in international context, 219n85; membership decimated by repressive police power, 17; mission, trajectory, and impact, 6–7; name, inspiration of, 216n24; recruitment for, 56; ten-point platform, 4, 11, 55, 56, 57, 64, 72, 184, 216n25; ten-point platform revision (1972), 49, 73; UCLA campus support for, 171

Black Panther Party et al. v. Center for the Study and Reduction of Violence et al., 253n99, 254n101–102

Black Panther Party for Self-Defense, 55

Black Panther Party health activism: crafting critique of medicine, 64–66; Maoist health politics, 69–71, 73; origins of, 49–74; political theorists influencing, 17, 51, 64–71, 73, 154, 164, 219n80, 219n85, 220n87, 221n96, 222n112, 222n116–117; rethinking Fanon's *The Wretched of the Earth*, 67–69; from self-defense to self-determination, 61–64, 72–73, 217n33; serving the people as response to cultural nationalism, 50–55, 72; serving the people as response to the War on Poverty, 50, 55–60,

72. *See also* African American health-focused activism

Black Panther Party health politics, xii–xvi; clinics/facilities remaining from, xiv–xv; collaborators in, xiv; healthcare crisis and, 12–15; health defined, 11; health rights demanded, 9–12, 21–22; lasting effect of participation on Party members, 181–83; legacy of African American health politics tradition in, 8–9, 15–17; Party members' visit to China, 70–71, 223n123, 256n4; from practical issues to ideational concerns, xii–xiii; scope and ambition of, xvi, 4; sensitivity to black body as representative of broader treatment of blacks, 187; signpost of, 2–4, 8; social-structural transformations and, xv–xvi; sources for researching, xiii–xv; two interrelated emphases of, 20; wide range of responses, 183–84. *See also* biologization of violence, contesting; People's Free Medical Clinics; sickle cell anemia, politics of; social health perspective

Black Panther Party v. Granny Goose, 158

Black Panther Party v. Kehoe, 158

black power movement, 201n18

Black Power: The Politics of Liberation in America (Carmichael and Hamilton), 217, 221n110

black radicalism: ideological differences within, 215n20. *See also* Black Panther Party; cultural nationalism

Black Skin, White Masks (Fanon), 68

Blackstock, Nelson, 243n136

black studies, 53–54

Blake, Judith, 257n12

139–41; of medical practice and biomedical knowledge, 18, 82, 170–71

demystification of medical power, 79, 87–90

dental care, 93, 106, 111–12

Depo-Provera, 199n15

deprofessionalization of medicine in China, 70–71

desegregation of healthcare system and medical profession, 25, 36–42, 211n86. *See also* integrationism

DeVaughn, Gerald, 185

Dingell, John, 38

disease: among Black Panther Party members, 94–95; concept of, 138; racial hierarchization and, 43. *See also* sickle cell anemia, politics of

distrust of medical system, xi, 15, 84, 87, 145, 198n11, 204n52, 205n55, 221n105

Dittmer, John, 82, 201n14, 201n18, 205n64

division of labor, gendered, 27. *See also* women

Dixon, Elmer, 183

donations: *Black Panther* solicitation of, for sickle cell anemia campaign, 122, 123–24, 234n23–24, 235n28; to PFMCs, 102–6; to PSCARF, 122. *See also* fundraising efforts

Douglas, Emory, 22

Douglas, Henry, Jr., 70, 257n4

Douglas, Mike, 129, 130, 131, 237n54

Downs, Carolyn, xv, 109

Drew, Charles, 204n52

drugs in black communities: unchecked proliferation of, 132

Drummond, William J., 229n111

Du Bois, David, 199n14

Du Bois, W. E. B., 25, 165, 187,

213n116–120, 238n65, 250n53; critique of Hoffman's study, 44–45; on race and brain size, 46, 207n12; writings on health of Negro, 44–47, 213n118–120

Dudziak, Mary, 201n18

Duster, Troy, xii, 145, 198n12, 212n105

DuVal, Merlin, 148

Dying Colonialism, A (Fanon), 68

Eaton, Hubert, 211n88

Eaton et al. v. James Walker Memorial Hospital, 211n88

Ebony magazine, 169; illness narratives in, 240; on psychosurgery, 176

economic citizenship: demand for full, 56

economic inequality: interlocking oppressions of racism and, 202n20

Economic Opportunity Act (1964), 49, 55; Title II of, 57. *See also* War on Poverty

Edelstein, Stuart J., 235n31

education: medical, 59–60, 137; political, 12, 80, 87, 127–39. *See also* health education

educational restrictions: sickle cell anemia and, 136–37, 240n87

Education Opportunities Service Corporation, 179

Ehrenreich, Barbara, 203n39

Ehrenreich, John, 203n39

elderly: initiatives involving the, 158–59

electoral politics: Party involvement in, 2, 200n4, 216n32, 245n167

electrophoresis analysis: hemoglobin, 86, 122, 139, 140, 141, 143, 235n31, 242n104, 242n114

Embree, Edwin R., 207n9

emergency medical services, 110

Endicott, William, 248n26

epidemics: black experience of, 24–25; poverty and, 47

Epstein, Steven, 21, 186, 205n58, 205n61, 206n69, 245n162

equal protection mandates of U.S. Constitution, 39

Ervin, Frank R., 162–64, 169, 170, 176, 180, 249n36

Esch, Betsy, 70, 71, 222n114

ethnopsychiatry: Fanon's critique of, 67–68

Evans-Young, Gloria, 153

experiential knowledge, 241n88; expertise based on, 88; valorization of, 99–100, 112; valorization of, in sickling discourse, 136–39, 240n81

expertise: authentic, 129, 237n55; lay, ideal of, xiv, 88–90; overturning bourgeois notions of, 71; trusted experts, 6, 79, 80, 84–87, 96–99, 112, 129

faculty protest against UCLA violence center, 170–71

Fanon, Frantz, 80, 87, 220n87, 221n100, 225n44; foundational influence on Party, 17, 51, 73, 154, 165, 187; ideological indoctrination of trusted experts using, 80, 87; influence on Cleaver, 221n96; on medical oppression in colonial Algeria, 65, 67–69

Farmer, Paul, 212n104

Fayer, Steve, 216n23

federal antipoverty programs. See War on Poverty

Federal Bureau of Investigation (FBI), 51, 112, 113, 123; counterintelligence program, or COINTELPRO, 62, 146, 215n20; stoking of ideological differences among black radicals, 215n20;

work to discredit the Party, 124, 146–48, 244n139

federal community clinic program, 13, 83, 224n26

federal programs: association with, 58, 217n43

feminist health radicals: medical patriarchy as concern of, 88–89; self-health among, 89

Fenderson, Lewis H., 207n22

Fett, Sharla, 203n38

Fine, Richard, 229n111

First International Conference of the Negro Peoples of the World, 31

Fishman, Jennifer, 256n118

Foner, Philip, 199n14

Food and Drug Administration, 185

Forbes, Flores, 245n167

Ford, Kent, 64, 98, 106, 111, 123, 144

Ford Foundation, 157

Foreman, James, 35

Fosket, Jennifer, 256n118

Foucault, Michel, 133, 238n63

framing: concept of, 203n40. See also social health perspective

Franklin Lynch PFMC (Boston), 81, 93

Frazier, Joe, 244n154

Fred Hampton Memorial PFMC (Portland), 63, 93, 98, 100, 107, 110, 226n65

Free Breakfast for Children Program, 90, 112

"free clinic" movement, 82, 83–84, 224n26

Freedom Summer (1964), 9; influence on Panthers' PFMCs, 13, 71, 82–83, 224n26; parents of summer project volunteers, 210n61; SNCC and MCHR clinics and, 33–36, 82–83, 98, 224n26

Freeman, Ronald, 69

freeze list to prevent spread of STDs, 95

Guerrilla Warfare (Guevara), 65, 66
Guevara, Ernesto "Che," 17, 51,
    65–66, 73, 165, 220n85,
    220n90–92
Guild, Joshua, 257n9
Guild Practitioner (National Lawyers
    Guild), 158
Guyton, Donald (now Malik Rahim),
    182, 257n9–10

Haag, Ernest Van Den, 248n31
Haight-Ashbury Free Clinic, 83
Haley, Alex, 210n60
Hall, Jacqueline Dowd, 7, 201n17
Hallgren, Dick, 199n1, 233n1
Hamer, Fannie Lou, 7–8, 97, 202n22
Hamilton, Charles, 217n33, 221n110
Hammonds, Evelynn, xii, 198n12
Hampton, Fred, 58, 236n45
Hampton, Henry, 216n23
Hampton Institute, 29; Du Bois's
    studies of students at, 46
Harding, Elizabeth H., 225n40
Harding, Sandra, xii
Harlan, Louis R., 207n24, 208n33
Harriet Tubman Medical Clinic
    (West Oakland, California),
    xiv–xv
Harriet Tubman Medical Office, 181
Harrington, Charlene, 225n40
Harris, Arthur, xiv, 181, 256n1
Haven, Sheba, 95
*Hawkins v. North Carolina Dental
    Society*, 211n88
Head Start, 55
health: good society embodied in,
    ix–x; link between individual
    and collective, Guevara on,
    66; as politics by other means,
    ix–xvi; racial health disparities
    in U.S., xi; social inclusion in
    United States and, x; WHO defi-
    nition as universal right, 11
health advocacy, African American,

xii, 20, 25, 42, 49, 51, 121; patient
    advocacy, 6, 19, 56, 79, 109, 181,
    184, 232n172; tradition of black
    political culture, 15. *See also*
    knowledge, politics of
*Health and Physique of the Negro
    American, The* (Du Bois), 45–47,
    213n117–118
healthcare: commodification of, 12, 14
healthcare access. *See* access to
    healthcare services
healthcare crisis in late 1960s and
    1970s, 12–15
healthcare neglect and disparate
    biomedical inclusion: paradox
    of, xii–xiii
"Health Care Priority and Sickle Cell
    Anemia" (Scott), 121–22
healthcare reform, ix–x, 13, 14
healthcare services from PFMCs, 79,
    106–14
health clinics, SNCC and MCHR,
    9, 33–36. *See also* People's Free
    Medical Clinics
health education: accusations of
    state-sponsored genocide,
    132–34; black suffering, theme
    of history of, 134–38; experien-
    tial knowledge, valorization of,
    99–100, 112, 136–39, 240n81;
    institution building dissemi-
    nating, 26–27; media used in,
    126–32; resilience, theme of,
    135–36; on sickle cell anemia,
    116, 118–19, 126–39
health inequality, xiii; forms of, 15,
    183; Jim Crow, 183; legacy of
    tactical responses to racialized,
    17; Panthers' challenge to, 18;
    persistence of, 9–10
Health Maintenance Organization
    Act of 1973, 13–14
Health Policy Advisory Center
    (Health/PAC), 14, 18, 81, 98

Huggins, Erika, 57, 94, 96, 198n14, 217n43
Huggins, John, 62, 215n20
Hughes, William Hardin, 208n29
human experimental research: black subjects, historical use of, x–xi, 59, 137, 185, 204n48; controversy over, in U.S. Senate, 172
human genetic variation: research on, 166–67
Hunter, Tera, 208n35
Huntsman, R. G., 241n99, 242n102
Hutton, Robert (Li'l Bobby), 56, 62, 233n1
hygiene: Washington's passion for, 28–29
hysterectomies, 60

iconography, 22
ideological indoctrination of trusted experts, 80, 87
illness: concept of, 138
illness narratives, 136–39, 240n84
Imhotep (physician), 211n83
Imhotep movement, 211n86
Imhotep National Conference on Hospital Integration, 38
"I'm Living on Borrowed Time" (Walker), 240n84
incarceration: use of prisoners for experiments and, 167–69
incarceration policy, 159–60
inclusion-and-difference paradigm, 21, 186
inequality. See health inequality
infant mortality, 47
institutional racism, 221n110
institution building, 24–36; black communities/laypeople and, 27, 28; by Black Panthers, 48; Garvey and Black Cross Nurses of UNIA, 30–33; meaning of, 24–25; model clinics, 33–36;

PFMCs as reflection of tradition of African American, 78; Progressive Era, 27–30
insurance industry: racism of, 44, 212n113
"Integration Battlefront, The" (Cobb's column), 37
integrationism, 25, 36–42; NAACP–NMA collaboration, 36–38; Simkins v. Cone and, 23–24, 39–42, 206n4
Intercommunal Youth Institute, 96, 178–79
intermarriage: sickle cell anemia and, 240n78
International Genetic Foundation, 165
Irons, Ernest, 239n77
Isaac, Larry, 201n17
Itano, H. A., 235n31, 241n99

Jackson, George, 77, 99, 168, 250n69
Jackson, Jesse, 185
JAMA. See Journal of the American Medical Association
Javits, Jacob, 38, 40, 244n155
Jeffries, Judson L., 231n138, 257n7
Jennett, Bryan, 249n36
Jennings, Billy X., xiv, 250n51
Jensen, Arthur R., 165, 166–67, 249n49
Jim Crow: battle against, 8; health inequality under, 183; legal defeat of, xv; limits of legal defeat of, 183; medical, 23; teaching hospitals during, 59–60
Job Corps, 55
Johns Hopkins Hospital, 59
Johnson, Lyndon B., xv, 12, 38, 50; administration under, 55, 58, 72; community clinic program under, 13; Kerner Commission, 163–64; Medicare and Medicaid

203n38, 207n10, 212n105, 212n108
McClanahan, David, 98, 229n109
MCCR. *See* Medical Committee for Civil Rights
McCulloch, Jock, 67, 69, 221n99
McDonald's: in-kind donations for sickle cell initiative, 122
MCHR. *See* Medical Committee for Human Rights
McKnight, Gerald D., 202n21
McMillan, Leigh Somerville, 232n183
Mealy, Rosemary, 96
media: bias toward Black Panther Party, xiii, 198n13; coverage of civil rights struggles of 1950s and 1960s, 200n11; sickle cell anemia outreach and education via range of, 126–32
medical apartheid, xi
medical civil rights movement, xiv, 36–42, 202n24, 211n88; long, 5–9; NAACP–NMA collaboration, 36–38; NAACP suit in opposition to "separate but equal" medical facilities, 23; *Simkins v. Cone* and, 23–24, 39–42, 206n4. *See also* African American health-focused activism
Medical Committee for Civil Rights (MCCR), 34, 41. *See also* Medical Committee for Human Rights
Medical Committee for Human Rights (MCHR), 5, 9, 14, 62, 81, 159, 205n64, 224n21; agenda, 210n73; clinics and medical services, 33, 34–36; expansion of, 35; first national convention (1965), 35; Freedom Summer and, 33–36, 82–83, 98, 224n26; integration of AMA and, 41; as medical arm of New Left, 83; national health activist platform, 35–36; Panthers' health activ-

ism and, 80; position paper on national healthcare (1971), 89; SHO and, 225n33; specialized care through, 107; transformation of medical volunteers during Freedom Summer, 34–35; trusted experts affiliated with, 98
medical discrimination, xi; African American confrontation with, case of, xi–xii. *See also* African American health-focused activism; Black Panther Party health politics; sickle cell anemia, politics of
medical education: shortcomings of, 137; teaching hospitals and, 59–60
medical–industrial complex, 48; critique of, 12, 67, 69, 76, 79, 203n39; neglect as power exercised by, 187; proliferation of, under Nixon, 14
medicalization: defined, 164; negative, 179; stages of, 249n45; transition between biomedicalization and, 256n118; of violence, 155, 164, 179, 180, 250n66. *See also* biologization of violence, contesting
medical patriarchy, 88–89
medical profession: desegregation of, 25
medical school students: at teaching hospitals, 59–60; volunteer, 34, 97, 100, 107, 229n106, 232n163; Williams, 122, 127, 129, 130, 131, 135, 150, 229n106, 237n56
Medicare and Medicaid, xv, 13, 14, 55
medicine: in China, deprofessionalization of, 70–71; colonial, 65, 67–69, 239n71; construction of race in, 17; crafting critique of, 64–66; culture of, medical civil

use of, 158–59; on contradiction between Panthers' and governmental social programs, 79; Fanon's influence on, 65, 67; on federal antipoverty programs, 57; founding of the Party, 5–6, 50–51, 55–56, 60, 72; goals of, 214n5; incarceration of, 51, 61, 62, 168; inspiration from revolutionary struggles in Africa, 218n59, 221n98; legal defense, 218n66; meeting of Hiestand, 158; release from prison (1970), 157; on required survival programs, 219n81; revision of ten-point platform, 49; on service programs as organizing tools toward revolution, 200n5; shift in Panthers' efforts to health politics, 62, 63, 157, 158

New York City, 21, 228n94; labor and leadership of Panther women, 96

New York Times, 170; Hoover's denunciation of Black Panthers Party, 146; Tuskegee syphilis experiment exposé, 15, 144, 169, 205n55, 221n105

New York Times Magazine, 172, 214n5

Nike missile base in Santa Monica Mountains: West's proposal for, 170

Nixon, Richard M., and Nixon administration, xv, 113, 119, 148, 202n21; appropriation of black power as black capitalism, 135; national health strategy, 13–14; Newton and Black Panther Party identified as "enemy" by, 244n138; sickle cell crisis and, 119, 120, 146, 148–49, 150, 151, 244n149–151

NMA. *See* National Medical Association

Northington Gamble, Vanessa, 202n24

North Oakland Neighborhood Anti-Poverty Center, 53, 55–56, 58

NOW, 154, 159, 175

nursing: Black Cross Nurses, 31–33, 209n49–50; black nurses during World War I, 30, 209n50, 209n54; Bolton Bill and federal funding for training nurses, 42; exclusion of black nurses from American Red Cross, 209n50, 209n54; integration of American Nursing Association, 40, 41–42; programs for black women, 27–28; shortage of nurses of color in 1970s, 225n47

NWRO, 247n21

Oakland, California: Black Community Survival Conference at De Fremery Park (1972), 1–4, 115, 233n1–2; Brown's candidacy for city council seat, 2, 200n4, 200n6; deindustrialization and white migration from, 52–53; Seale's candidacy for mayor of, 2, 199n4, 200n6

Oakland Children's Hospital: volunteers from, 100

Oakland Community School, 94, 228n84

Obama, Barack, ix–x

Office of Economic Opportunity, 56, 83, 148, 214n3, 217n36, 224n31; community clinic program funded by, 13, 59–60; Summer Health Projects (SHPs) funded by, 225n33

Office of Negro Health Work, 30, 208n40

Ofili, Elizabeth, 185

Ogbar, Jeffrey, 247n21

Ogden, A. G., 136

sickle cell anemia campaign, 151–52

professionals, health. *See* nursing; trusted experts

Progressive Era: black health activism in, 8, 27–30, 202n24

Progressive Labor Party, 169

Provident Hospital and Nurse's Training School (Chicago), 27, 28

Prudential Insurance Company, 44

PSCARF (People's Sickle Cell Anemia Research Foundation), 116, 122–24

Psychosomatic Medicine, 249n36

psychosurgery, 169, 246n4, 249n40; controversy over, in U.S. Senate, 172; *Ebony* article on, 176; inconsistencies in UCLA violence center's plans involving, 176–77; making violence biological and medical and, 161, 162–63, 164; record of support for, 180; success of, evaluating, 251n77; two-year moratorium on, 253n91; use of, on prisoners, 168

Public Advocates, Inc, 157–58

public health: exposing failings of system of, 126; institution building disseminating health education, 26–27; National Negro Health Week and, 28; Provident Hospital and, 28

public health agencies: repression and regulatory hounding of PFMCs by, 112–13; sickle cell anemia and, 120, 121, 144, 145

public interest lawsuits, 158–59

Quotations from Chairman Mao Tse-Tung, 69–70, 222n112, 222n117

race: brain mass and, 46, 207n12; construction of, in medicine, 17;

health and, in post–civil rights era, 181–87; political economy of cities and, 52–53, 215n11; politics of health and, 20–21; racial categories, arbitrariness of American, 45–46; racial hierarchization, 43

race-biased or race-based medicine, 185–86

"race-specific" drug, 185, 186, 187

Race Traits and Tendencies in the American Negro (Hoffman), 44–45

racialism, sociomedical, 17, 43, 165, 212n105; recontextualization as response to, 43–47, 48, 153, 186

racialization, biomedical: politics of knowledge and disruption of, 25–26; Du Bois's critique of, 45–46

racism: as form of social disease, 202n23; institutional, 221n110; insurance, 44, 212n113; interlocking oppressions of economic inequality and, 202n20; of mainstream medicine, 88–89; racist geneticists, Party's challenge to, 165–67; state-sponsored genocide, accusations of, 132–34, 138, 187, 238n62, 238n65

radical health movement, 114, 245n1; clinic culture and, 80–90; democratization of medical practice and biomedical knowledge in, 82; goal of overturning health inequality, 112; inspiration for, 82–84; mission of, 18, 81–82; multifaceted community collaborating in, 18, 81

Rahim, Malik (formerly Donald Guyton), 182, 257n9–10

rainbow coalition, 159, 205n64, 225n48

Sharpton, Al, 185
Shaw, David, 246n8
Shaw, Richard A., 227n65, 230n131
Sheffield, Lincoln Webster, 205n64,
    244n140
shigella, 94
Shim, Janet, 256n118
Shneidman, Edwin S., 178, 255n113
SHO. *See* Student Health
    Organization
Showell, Catherine, 96
sickle cell anemia, 12, 48; "dis-
    courses" on, 130–32; error
    of confusing sickle cell trait
    and disease, 243n128; framed
    as simultaneous biological,
    historical, and sociopolitical
    phenomenon, 126; genetic
    transmission of, 237n52; known
    in African oral history, 239n77;
    molecular basis of, Pauling's
    establishment of, 122–23; preva-
    lence of, 238n70
sickle cell anemia, politics of, 115–52,
    212n105; bringing "invisible
    malady" into relief, 119, 120–25;
    campaign to raise awareness, 19,
    21, 86, 125–46; genetic screen-
    ing for, 4, 19, 90, 115, 116–17,
    139–46, 233n3, 241n87, 241n99,
    242n102–103, 242n107,
    242n110; illness narratives,
    136–39, 240n84; inclusion in
    national healthcare agenda, 116,
    119–20; massive educational
    campaign, 116, 118–19, 126–39;
    neutralizing of Party's larger po-
    litical critique, 148–52; politico-
    etiological account, 118–19,
    134–36, 238n70; professional-
    ization of Panthers' campaign,
    151–52; reversal of pejorative
    associations between blackness
    and sickling, 135–36; Scott's

article in *JAMA*, 119, 121–22,
    124–25, 132, 149, 244n151; sickle
    cell "crisis," 119–20, 146–52,
    233n5–6
Sickle Cell Detection and Informa-
    tion Center, 123
Sickle Cell Disease Association of
    America, 123
Sickledex kit: limitations of, 142–43
    use of, 116, 139–45, 241n99,
    242n102–103, 242n110
sickness: concept of, 138–39
Sidney Miller PFMC (Seattle), 101,
    102, 104–5, 107–9, 226n65
Silvers, Cleo, xiv, 56, 221n98,
    224n18; lasting effect of Party
    membership on, 181; on political
    reeducation of expert collabora-
    tors, 80, 87
Simkins, George, 39
*Simkins v. Moses H. Cone Memorial
    Hospital*, 23–24, 39–42, 206n4
Singer, S., 235n31
Singh, Nikhil Pal, 201n17
Skloot, Rebecca, x, xi, 20, 204n48
slavery: link between contempo-
    rary suffering from sickle cell
    anemia and, 134–35, 238n70;
    tradition of African American
    health politics developed dur-
    ing, 8
Small, Tolbert S., xiv, xv, 71, 80,
    222n119, 231n139, 235n25,
    235n38, 236n45, 238n69; back-
    ground of, 97; at Berkeley clinic,
    92, 100; donations sought by,
    102, 104; on government neglect
    of sickle cell anemia, 125; lasting
    effect of Party involvement on,
    181–82; as personal physician to
    Newton and other members, 99;
    PSCARF and, 122; sickle cell
    screening and, 141, 143; on staff-
    ing arrangements for PFMCs,

trusted experts, 6, 96–99, 112; ideological indoctrination of, 80, 87; importance to Party's health initiatives, 129; role in PFMCs, 79, 84–87

Tsuchida, Elichi, 97, 229n100

tuberculosis among blacks, 44, 46–47

Tubman, Harriet, 256n3

Tunney, John, 124, 149

Turner, Irene R., 224n17

Turner, Wallace, 214n5, 218n62

Tuskegee Hospital and Nurse's Training School, 28, 29

Tuskegee Institute, 28, 29, 30

Tuskegee syphilis experiment, x, xv, 16, 129, 198n9; *New York Times* exposé on, 15, 144, 169, 205n55, 221n105

"Two Common Diseases of Blacks: Origin of Sickle Cell Anemia and G6PD Deficiency" (brochure), 129

Tyson, Timothy B., 201n18, 202n18

UCLA. *See* University of California at Los Angeles

UNIA, 31–33, 71

United Farm Workers Organizing Committee (UFOC), 154, 159, 175

United Nations Convention on the Prevention and Punishment of Crime of Genocide, 133, 238n65

United Nations Universal Declaration of Rights, 11

universal healthcare, 13–14, 73

Universal Negro Improvement Association (UNIA), 31–33, 71

University Muslim Medical Association clinic (Los Angeles), 182

University of California at Los Angeles: Faculty Committee against Racism, 170; "High Potential Program," 215n20; Neuropsychiatric Institute, 153, 170, 178, 252n80. *See also* Center for the Study and Reduction of Violence

urbanization: structural process of, 52

Urban League, 151

urban unrest, 161, 164

U.S. Air Force: restriction of sickle cell carriers in, 240n87

U.S. Constitution: equal protection mandates of, 39

U.S. Court of Appeals, 24

U.S. Department of Defense, 170

U.S. healthcare polity: sickle cell anemia care and incorporation of blacks into, 120

U.S. National Institutes of Health, 119, 124, 148

US Organization, 54, 62, 113, 215n20, 227n66

U.S. Public Health Service (USPHS), 30

U.S. Supreme Court: *Brown v. Board of Education of Topeka, Kansas,* 23, 39, 40; *Simkins v. Cone* and, 24, 39, 40, 206n4

Vacaville: California Medical Facility, 98–99, 167–68, 250n66

Valenstein, Elliot, 249n40, 251n77

Vietnam War, 12, 161; veterans, 100

Villarosa, Linda, 198n11

Vils, Ursula, 248n25

violence: medicalization of, 155, 164, 179, 180, 250n66; shift from self-defense to self-determination, 61–64, 72–73; social etiology of, 154–55; social health perspective on, 20, 155. *See also* biologization of violence, contesting

Violence and the Brain (Ervin and Mark), 162–64, 249n36

"Violence and the Brain" (research project), 162
violence center. *See* Center for the Study and Reduction of Violence
Virchow, Rudolph, 203n38
Virginia, Negro Organization Society of, 29
volunteer medical professionals, 79, 80, 84–87, 96–99, 129
volunteers at PFMCs, community, 79, 99–100
Volunteers in Service to America (VISTA), 55, 56
voter registration drive, 2
Voting Rights Act (1965), xv, 9, 49–50
vulnerable communities: in New Orleans in aftermath of Katrina, 183; UCLA violence center and, 154, 164, 167–69

Waddell, Joseph, 110
Wailoo, Keith, xii, 146, 149, 198n12, 243n135
Walker, Marclan A., 234n13, 240n84
Wall, Jim Vander, 227n67, 243n136
Wallace, Samuel, 249n48
Wall Street Journal, 133
Walton, Bill, 170, 252n83
Waquant, Loic, 247n23
War on Poverty, xv, 12, 13, 17, 24, 34, 47, 118, 127, 133; as depicted by the Party, 50; maximum feasible participation, debates over, 57–60, 72; serving the people as response to, 50, 55–60, 72
Washington, Booker T., 28–30, 36, 204n48, 208n30
Washington, D.C.: labor and leadership of Panther women, 96
Washington, Harriet, xi, 20, 197n7, 211n95
Watergate scandal, 244n138, 248n25
Watts Happening Coffee House, 56

Watts Health Foundation, 182
Watts uprising (1965), 164
Waxman, Henry, 252n80
Waxman, Julia, 207n9
Weber, P. J., 246n3
We Charge Genocide (Patterson report), 133, 238n65
Weeks, Lewis E., 206n2
Weiner, Herbert, 246n2
Weiss, Gregory L., 224n26
welfare state: survival programs as stopgap solution to shrinking, 1
well-being: relative definition of, 17
Wells, Aaron O., 210n62
Wells, I., 235n31
West, Guida, 247n21
West, Louis Jolyon, 248n25, 248n29, 248n32–33, 249n46–47, 252n80, 252n83, 253n88, 255n111–112; on funding for violence center, 255n113; Hiestand's administrative complaints criticizing violence center plans of, 173–77; professional history, 153–54; proposal for UCLA violence center, 159–61, 164, 167, 170; student protests against, 170; testimony before California Senate Committee on Health and Welfare, 172
West Oakland Model Cities, 57
WGBH (PBS affiliate): show on sickle cell anemia (1971), 236n51
White, E. Frances, 215n17
white coat of medical science, 84, 85
white flight: violence center and alternative to, 161
whites-only professional associations: integrating, 40–42
Whitten, Charles, 123
Whittier, Nancy, 206n70
Whole Earth Catalog, 132; *CoEvolution Quarterly* supplement to, 132, 152, 204n47, 219n81, 236n51

WILD radio station (Boston), 150
Wilkerson, Isabel, 214n8
Wilkins, Michael, 98, 102, 229n108,
229n110, 230n132
Wilkins, Roy, 219n81
Williams, Daniel Hale, 27–28,
207n21
Williams, Donald, 122, 135, 150,
229n106; on *Mike Douglas
Show*, 127, 129, 130, 131, 237n56
Williams, Juan, 204n42
Williams, Robert F., 201n18
Williams, Sharon, 250n70
Williams, Yohuru, 201n18
Willis, Daniel Joseph, 226n65
Willowbrook State School, 98,
229n108
Wilson, William Julius, 215n12
Winston-Salem emergency medical
services, 110, 111
Witt, Andrew, 227n72
Wolinsky, Sidney M., 157
women: black, in Party health cadre,
96; Black Cross Nurses, 31–33,
209n49–50; black woman
laborer as source of contagion,
208n35; centrality to health
initiatives, 229n99; citizenship contradiction for, 10; in
civil rights movement, 207n18,
241n89; of color, treatment
at teaching hospitals, 60;
forced sterilization of African
American, xv, 8, 60, 132–33, 145,
199n15; gendering of caretaking
in black community, 207n13;
health centers for, 89; in health
social movements, 207n19;
institution building and, 27, 28;
integration of ANA, 40, 41–42;
medical patriarchy and, 88–89;

nursing programs for black,
27–28; in Party leadership, 96,
228n99; reproductive healthcare, 76, 89
women's health movement, 205n64,
224n21
Wood, Anton, 217n32
Woodard, Komozi, 52, 200n10,
201n18, 214n5
Woods, Sylvia, 88, 89
Work, Monroe, 208n38
workplace restrictions: sickle cell
anemia and, 240n87
World Health Organization: constitution, 11, 203n33
World War I: black nurses during, 30,
209n50, 209n54
World War II: integration of nursing
corps, 42
Wretched of the Earth, The (Fanon),
65, 220n87, 221n96; rethinking,
67–69

XYY chromosome syndrome, 161

Yamamoto, Joe, 246n2
Yancy Durham Jr. Memorial Clinic,
244n54
Young, Charles E., 246n4
Young, Quentin, 36, 112–13
Young Lords Party, 81, 83, 84, 89,
159
Young Patriots, 159
youth programs, 179

Zane, Jeffrey, 231n138
Zavestoski, Stephen, 205n63
Ziferstein, Isidore, 170–71, 252n84,
254n102
Zola, Irving, 155
Zolacoffer, Charles, 96

ALONDRA NELSON is associate professor of sociology at Columbia University, where she also holds an appointment in the Institute for Research on Women and Gender. She is coeditor of *Technicolor: Race, Technology, and Everyday Life* and *Genetics and the Unsettled Past: The Collision of DNA, Race, and History.*